ACHIEVING COMPETENCE IN SOCIAL WORK
THROUGH FIELD EDUCATION

Field education is considered by social work students and graduates to be the most crucial component in their preparation for professional practice. It is in the field practicum that students learn to apply theoretical concepts, empirically derived knowledge, and social work values, principles, and skills. Students engage in field learning by serving individual clients, communities, and organizations under the guidance of an experienced social worker appointed as a field instructor. Schools of social work use a range of pedagogical approaches to assist students to link knowledge presented in the classroom with practice issues confronted in the field.

Changes to the organizational context of field education, to university expectations for faculty members teaching in social work programs, and to the nature of the student body have stimulated new thinking and empirical studies on field learning. In this book, Marion Bogo, an international leader in social work field work education, synthesizes current and emerging knowledge about field education including relevant concepts from higher education and professional education theories, from practice wisdom about field instruction in social work, and from findings in the empirical literature. The volume is divided into three sections: frameworks for understanding field education; educating for professional practice including principles, methods, and formats for facilitating learning in the field; and evaluation of competence. The text is followed by a series of practical evaluation tools designed for use by instructors. With new emphasis on field education as the signature pedagogy of social work and the importance of using a competency framework in education, the book offers frameworks, approaches, and principles for field education in an in-depth yet accessible manner.

MARION BOGO is a professor in the Factor-Inwentash Faculty of Social Work at the University of Toronto.

MARION BOGO

Achieving Competence in Social Work through Field Education

UNIVERSITY OF TORONTO PRESS
Toronto Buffalo London

© University of Toronto Press Incorporated 2010
Toronto Buffalo London
www.utppublishing.com
Printed in Canada

ISBN 978-0-8020-9280-4 (cloth)
ISBN 978-0-8020-9534-3 (paper)

∞

Printed on acid-free, 100% post-consumer recycled paper with vegetable-based inks

---

Library and Archives Canada Cataloguing in Publication

Bogo, Marion
Achieving competence in social work through field education / Marion Bogo.

Includes bibliographical references and index.
ISBN 978-0-8020-9780-4 (bound). ISBN 978-0-8020-9534-3 (pbk.)

1. Social service – Fieldwork.   2. Social work education.   I. Title.

HV11.B63 2010   361.3071'55   C2010-903921-1

This book has been published with the help of a grant from the Canadian Federation for the Humanities and Social Sciences, through the Aid to Scholarly Publications Program, using funds provided by the Social Sciences and Humanities Research Council of Canada.

University of Toronto Press acknowledges the financial assistance to its publishing program of the Canada Council for the Arts and the Ontario Arts Council.

 Canada Council   Conseil des Arts
for the Arts   du Canada

 ONTARIO ARTS COUNCIL
CONSEIL DES ARTS DE L'ONTARIO

University of Toronto Press acknowledges the financial support for its publishing activities of the Government of Canada through the Canada Book Fund.

This book is dedicated to
Norman, Geoffrey, Jonathan, Shona, Lauren, and Dylan

Contents

Preface and Acknowledgments   ix

Introduction   3

PART ONE: FRAMEWORKS FOR SOCIAL WORK FIELD EDUCATION

1 The Context of Field Education   11

2 The Nature of Professional Social Work Practice   35

3 Competence   55

4 Perspectives on Student Learning   76

PART TWO: FIELD EDUCATION FOR PROFESSIONAL PRACTICE

5 Facilitating Student Learning   101

6 Principles and Methods for Field Instruction   124

7 Approaches and Formats for Field Instruction   149

PART THREE: EVALUATION AND BEYOND

8 Evaluation of Competence in Field Education   175

9 Towards Multiple Approaches to Evaluation of Competence   199

Appendix A: Competency-Based Evaluation (CBE) Tool   211

Appendix B: Vignette Matching Evaluation (VME) Tool   216

Appendix C: Practice-Based Evaluation (PBE) Tool   236

References   245

Index   267

Preface and Acknowledgments

Field education is a highly valued component of social work education, and its development has been fuelled over decades by social work practitioners and faculty members in schools of social work. I have been fortunate to be part of this community – as a social work student, a field instructor, field coordinator-director, and faculty member at the Factor-Inwentash Faculty of Social Work at the University of Toronto. The basis for the material presented in this text comes from my experiences in these various roles as well as from many sources. The longstanding body of literature on social work field education provides the foundation for this work. As field coordinator-director at the University of Toronto I had the opportunity to develop a program of scholarship and research on field education, which has led to the theory development and related practices presented in this book. My early work in field education occurred in partnership with Elaine Vayda as we developed the Integration of Theory and Practice (ITP) Loop Model and wrote our original text, *The Practice of Field Instruction in Social Work: Theory and Process* (Bogo & Vayda, 1998).

I subsequently embarked on a program of research on field education which led to numerous empirical studies funded by grants from the Social Sciences and Humanities Research Council of Canada, from 1998 to 2001, 2002 to 2005, and 2007 to the present. Some studies were supported during my term as the Sandra Rotman Chair in Social Work at the Factor-Inwentash Faculty of Social Work, University of Toronto. More recently I have engaged with colleagues involved in education research for health professions at the Wilson Centre of the Faculty of Medicine, University of Toronto. These interprofessional collaborations on topics of mutual interest have provided access to relevant literature and stimulated new ways of thinking about education for all professional practices.

In the fall of 2004 the editors of *The Clinical Supervision Journal* invited me to join a group of colleagues from a range of human service professions to review and present the state of the art of research published in peer-reviewed journals in our respective fields during the period from 1999 to 2004. While literature on field education and staff supervision in social work originally developed from the same foundation of theory and practice, in recent decades separate and distinct bodies of research have emerged, and hence two reviews were conducted (Bogo, 2005; Bogo & McKnight, 2005). Eighty-three peer-reviewed journal articles on field instruction in social work were located, 40 of which reported on empirical studies. The review of this material stimulated me to examine field education knowledge historically and in relation to contemporary trends. It also provided the impetus to embark on a larger project this text, which would synthesize concepts, processes, and techniques for field education and examine trends and themes in relation to higher education and professional education theories and approaches.

I appreciate greatly the support of two deans at the Factor-Inwentash Faculty of Social Work, Jim Barber and Cheryl Regehr, and that of Virgil Duff, executive editor at the University of Toronto Press, all of whom encouraged me to undertake this endeavour.

I owe a great debt of gratitude to the many students and field instructors who voluntarily participated in numerous studies on field education, and contributed their time and perspectives to advancing knowledge. I was fortunate to benefit from the many stimulating discussions with colleagues in the field practicum department at the University of Toronto, Roxanne Power, Andrea Litvack, and Eileen McKee; my co-investigators on the grants, Judith Globerman, Cheryl Regehr, Glenn Regehr, Peter Newman, and Faye Mishna; the research coordinator at the Faculty of Social Work, Joanne Daciuk; and the many doctoral students who participated as research assistants, Tamara Sussman, Judy Hughes, Michael Woodford, Andrea Daley, Carmen Logie, Ellen Katz, and Lea Tufford. In recent years I have been blessed by a lively collaboration with two outstanding scholars in field education, Miriam Raskin of George Mason University and Julianne Wayne of the University of Connecticut. In the final stage of preparing and reviewing the manuscript I was fortunate to have the assistance of Patricia Thorvaldson, whose expertise as an editor I greatly value. The text is improved as a result of her careful work.

ACHIEVING COMPETENCE IN SOCIAL WORK
THROUGH FIELD EDUCATION

Introduction

Without question, field education has always been a central feature of the preparation of social work practitioners. The importance of learning in settings where social work services are delivered is recognized in North America and internationally. This is so regardless of level of intervention: in direct practice with individuals, groups, and families; in community practice; in administration; in social policy development; and in research and evaluation. As a result, all systems of accreditation of schools of social work include standards for the field practicum component. The designation of field education as the 'signature pedagogy' for social work education in the *Educational Policy and Accreditation Standards* of the Council on Social Work Education, United States (EPAS, 2008, p. 8) signals the importance of this domain for teaching and learning.

Over time, a rich and diverse set of theoretical concepts and educational practices have developed to inform the design, implementation, and evaluation of field programs. Originally these ideas arose from the experiences of countless social workers in agency settings and faculty members in the schools, who were able to articulate and disseminate their impressions about effective ingredients in providing a quality field opportunity for students. Concepts and practices understandably reflected, to some degree, prevailing social work practice values, theoretical perspectives, models, and techniques. Over time, research on various components of field education was conducted, yielding data to begin to construct an evidence base for best practices or guidelines for field programs and field learning and teaching. As a result, currently there is a substantial body of knowledge about many aspects of field education.

Social work educators will find kinship with educators in related health and human service professions. A growing cadre of education researchers is also interested in the dynamics of teaching and learning which contribute to the most effective ways to prepare students for ethical and competent professional roles in contemporary society. The Carnegie Foundation for the Advancement of Teaching has provided invaluable leadership in the development and dissemination of knowledge about distinctive and universal aspects of professional preparation through its Preparation for the Professions Program (PPP). The foundation has sponsored studies of the art and science of education in medicine, law, nursing, engineering, and the clergy. Information, approaches, and insights from this work can inform social work education in general, and, due to the emphasis on professional practice, contributes to advances in social work field education.

The aim of this book is to synthesize current knowledge about field education, including relevant concepts from higher education and professional education theories, from practice wisdom, and from findings from the empirical literature. The goal is to provide frameworks and related practices that will be useful to the many participants in the field endeavour. Reflecting on my own knowledge needs as a new field instructor, and then as a new field practicum coordinator-director, I have attempted to produce a book that offers an overview of key topics with extensive references for more in-depth reading in particular areas. For experienced field instructors, faculty field liaisons, field coordinators and directors, and faculty members, the information and analysis of issues in this book will hopefully stimulate thoughts about field learning and teaching, and encourage discussion, experimentation, and innovation. The book is also designed for use in doctoral courses on the theory and practice of teaching in social work. It is hoped that this text will contribute to encouraging the next generation of teachers to engage in scholarship and research in field education.

The development of social work field education depends on the commitment and efforts of a number of participants and constituencies. Of crucial importance are the many social workers in agencies who willingly and voluntarily devote time and energy to teaching social work students. It is also dependent on enlightened agency and institutional directors. Despite competing and never-ending demands for scarce resources, such leaders recognize that nurturing and renewing the workforce is reliant on high-quality field education experiences in real-world settings. Naturally, field directors and those in field liaison roles will champion the importance of well-resourced field programs. It is crucial that they are supported by teaching faculty and deans and directors who acknowledge that quality field education is a primary pathway to preparing students as competent social work practitioners. Enthusiastic, energetic, and motivated students enrich the teaching and learning milieu, bring fresh perspectives, curiosity, and their desire to contribute to human well-being and social justice. This book is designed to provide knowledge for all of these participants.

This book will present frameworks, approaches, and principles for field education. The aim is to offer useful ways of thinking about and carrying out field teaching and learning in social work in a manner that is accessible for faculty members, field instructors, and student learners. The text is divided into three sections: (1) frameworks for understanding field education; (2) educating for professional practice, including educational principles, methods, and formats for facilitating learning in the field; and (3) evaluation and beyond, which includes evaluation of student learning, innovative and tested approaches, and future possibilities, with appendices of evaluation tools (see Appendices A, B, and C).

Part 1 is entitled 'Frameworks for Social Work Field Education,' and in chapter 1 the key contextual factors that impinge on field education are examined.

The nature of professional social work practice is the focus of chapter 2, and attends to various epistemologies of professional work, drawing on the seminal work of Donald Schon on reflective practice as well as the current emphasis on evidence-based practice in the helping professions. These theories about professional practice have an important influence on the way in which we think about and construct learning and teaching experiences.

Chapter 3 aims to illuminate the concept of competence and to introduce social work educators to current formulations and critiques of competence in related professional fields. Since there is a renewed interest in defining competence as educational outcomes for social work, the lessons learned in other professions and from social work educators internationally can contribute to current deliberations and avoid the expenditure of limited resources in reinventing models that already exist. Social work educators can benefit from the successes and failures of other professions.

Continuing the theme of frameworks for understanding field education, chapter 4 focuses on the student and introduces a number of perspectives and themes related to the learner. Themes include the importance of self-awareness and the way in which personal and professional issues interact when learning social work practice. Contributions from adult learning theory and social identity theory inform this discussion and set the stage for understanding the needs of a range of students and ultimately for developing relevant and helpful educational strategies.

Part 2, 'Field Education for Professional Practice,' includes chapters on facilitating student learning. The ideas presented in Part 1 are integrated throughout these chapters, and used to identify principles, methods, and approaches for field education. Chapter 5 is a close companion to the previous chapter, as it draws on concepts for understanding the dynamics of learning to identify approaches to assisting students in their efforts to become competent social workers. These efforts focus on facilitating cognitive, affective, and behavioural gains. The context of the field instructor and student relationship is fully examined, including its strengths and potential pitfalls.

A set of principles and an extensive array of methods of field instruction have arisen over time, and are reviewed in chapter 6. Direct and explicit teaching methods include observation and review of practice, observing others, role play preparation, coaching, direct supervision, and review of written recordings and reports. Also discussed are methods which are implicit. This refers to role modelling on the part of the field instructor and the parallel process that may exist when students learn from their experience in the student and field instructor relationship and transfer aspects of that experience to the relationship between student and client or service consumer.

Chapter 7 presents a review of the approaches or formats for field education, including not only the predominant individual dyadic tutorial model but also group approaches and use of task instruction. Models that vary in their structure, such as rotational models, are discussed, as well as models that vary in timing, such as delayed-entry, concurrent, and block arrangements.

Part 3 of the text, 'Evaluation and Beyond,' covers conceptual and measurement information relevant to conducting reliable, valid, and useful evaluations of student learning and practice competence. An ongoing multi-phase program of research on conceptualizing and measuring student competence conducted by a team of researchers at the University of Toronto (Bogo, Regehr, Power, & Regehr, 2007; Regehr, Bogo, Regehr, & Power, 2007) is reported in chapter 8, and three of the tools developed and tested are made available in the appendices. The final chapter considers additional approaches to evaluation of competence drawing from experiences of related health professions' education. A concluding section in this chapter summarizes key themes throughout the book, with thoughts about future steps.

While it is anticipated that this book will be of interest to all those involved in field education, specific sections may be of greater interest to various groups. Part 1 presents frameworks for social work field education, and may be of greatest interest to field coordinators/directors, faculty members, and education researchers. Field instructors may also find these chapters of interest. Part 2 offers important information about the conduct of field instruction and should be useful to field instructors and students as well as to field liaisons and field coordinators/directors. Part 3 focuses on evaluation of competence, and, while useful for field instructors, field liaisons, and field coordinators/directors, it is also likely of interest to faculty members concerned with developing effective assessment methods and evaluation programs for their schools.

PART ONE

Frameworks for Social Work Field
Education

1 The Context of Field Education

Field education is considered by students and alumnae to be the most crucial component in their preparation for social work practice. This finding has been supported both in formal studies and through informal anecdotal reports (Kadushin, 1991; Lager & Robbins, 2004; Raskin, 1989; Tolson & Kopp, 1988). It is understandable that this should be so. Students generally enter social work educational programs to prepare for their chosen career of social work. They expect to become practising social workers, and as a result are highly motivated to learn to become competent, effective practitioners. While course work, projects, and informal learning in the university provide necessary foundation knowledge, ways of thinking, and many admirable role models, it is in the field practicum that students learn to practice.

Field education provides many learning opportunities. Students learn to apply theories to real-world situations and to examine these situations through the lens of a variety of conceptual frameworks. They learn to apply empirically supported models and to modify those models based on the contingencies of unique situations. They learn procedural knowledge and skills specific to working with a population or carrying out the mandate of a particular setting, and the practice wisdom and 'know-how' accumulated by experienced workers. Students learn to use social work values in general and when faced with ethical dilemmas. Importantly, students learn to think as practising social workers do, and to bring reflection and judgment to assessment, planning, and intervention. And they learn to engage clients and communities in helping and change processes, skilfully and effectively.

Employers also highly value the field practicum for the preparation for practice which it provides. Frequently students find their first employment in settings where they have completed their practicum, as agencies appreciate that these new workers are already oriented to agency policy and practices, are socialized to the organization culture, and can fairly quickly offer service based on this foundation of knowledge and skill. In this way agencies value the reciprocal benefits of providing learning opportunities for social work students, recognizing the way in which it prepares their future workforce (Globerman & Bogo, 2003).

While field learning has been a part of social work education since its inception, it is only recently that the Council on Social Work Education in the United States has identified its premier importance and designated it the signature pedagogy of social work, placing it on par with the university-based courses in the program (EPAS, 2008). In countries where social and human services are more exclusively government-funded, policy-makers recognize the link between the nature and quality of education and the outcomes of programs staffed by qualified professionals. For example, in the United Kingdom social work educators, in conjunction with government policy-makers concerned with social care (social work) and health services, acknowledge the importance of what is referred to as 'practice or workplace learning' with qualified 'practice teachers or assessors' (a term similar to 'field instructors') (Slater, 2007). In Australia, Cooper (2007) challenges the higher status accorded university-based courses over field learning as outdated, given that government's policy expectations for quality teaching and learning in universities that prepare for workplace productivity. With reinvigorated interest in field education from government and accreditation bodies, the next decade may witness increased scholarship, research, and innovation in teaching and learning models.

Towards a Definition and Framework for Field Education

Throughout this text the various components of field education will be presented and discussed in great detail. Key dimensions will be examined drawing on the empirical literature, traditional and contemporary theoretical approaches and models, and practice wisdom. The aim is to extract useful ways of thinking about and carrying out field teaching and learning in social work. To set the stage, however, elements in a definition of field practicum education are warranted at this point.

Bogo (2005) has described the essence of field education as learning through delivering a social work service in a practice setting under the tutelage of an experienced social worker. Student assignments cover a range of practice with individuals, families, small groups, communities, and organizations. The service setting ranges from formal, large, complex interprofessional settings, to small social service agencies, to grassroots organizations, and community-based pilot projects. Regardless of setting, students' practice is examined and discussed with a field instructor, and, at times, with other social workers and members of interdisciplinary teams in the organization. The review of students' practice is aimed at helping students integrate and apply theory to practice, to critique and test knowledge, values, and principles studied in classroom courses. Based on the preferred intervention models and programs of specific settings, students will learn both generic and specific techniques and models, and learn to skilfully adapt practice to the unique conditions presented in their practice. Practice settings develop their own approaches to meet the challenges presented by their clients. These approaches may include adapting known models to work with specific populations, applying innovative ways of implementing a policy or program, and experimenting and creating new approaches. Students in such settings are fortunate, as their learning will also include these practices. Field education is also the place where students learn to handle the tensions between social work ethics and values and the realities of societal injustice and discrimination based on a range of diverse cultural factors, and to examine the way the profession responds to inequity (Lager & Robbins, 2004). Field education includes implicit and explicit socialization to the profession, and through this experience each student finds a way to develop a sense of self as a professional.

Schools of social work use a range of pedagogical approaches to assist students in linking knowledge presented in the classroom with practice issues confronted in the field. For example, evaluation methods in many classroom courses require students to examine their practicum assignments through the lens of particular theories, practice models or principles, or policies. This approach can facilitate critical thinking as students examine their assessments and interventions through the lens of approaches that are useful and identify those that do not fit well with situations found in the field setting.

Integrative seminars may be offered as a vehicle to assist with theory-practice linkages, although accreditation standards have not required this particular pedagogical approach (Wayne, Bogo, & Raskin, 2006). In a survey of undergraduate programs, Poe and Hunter (2009) found almost 96 per cent of responding field coordinators (almost half of the population responded) reported the presence of a seminar, although only half of respondents indicated linking theory and practice as the most emphasized aspect. The researchers also found wide variation in concept, purpose, and structure of the seminars, as well as similarities, especially in student assignments. There are no studies of integrative seminars in graduate social work programs, while anecdotally it seems as if the use of this educational approach is less pervasive. The prevalence, process, and educational outcome of such vehicles for facilitating learning to practice are clearly worthy of further study.

All programs appoint a faculty-based individual as liaison or advisor to link the student, field instructor, and the school. The occupant of this role may be a full-time tenure stream faculty member or adjunct faculty hired specifically for this role. Poe and Hunter (2009) observe that when adjunct faculty lead field seminars and serve as field liaisons, it may be difficult for meaningful integration of class and field if these teachers do not have an integral role in curriculum development and implementation.

The role of faculty field liaison varies, as schools differ in the extent to which they use a model with prescribed visits or a trouble-shooting model. In the former, the liaison role consists of three roles: facilitator, monitor, and evaluator. Two influential papers by Rosenblum and Raphael (Raphael & Rosenblum, 1987; Rosenblum & Raphael, 1983) recommended four visits per academic year to examine student learning goals and performance and the relationship with the instructor. The focus is on linking class and field, monitoring the student's learning and the practicum process, participating in the evaluation of student learning, and consulting and managing problems in learning. Fortune and colleagues (1995) compared the four-visit model with an approach they termed the trouble-shooting model. Trouble-shooting involves providing field instructors with supports they perceive they need, when requested. Their study found field instructors in both models ranked ready access to the liaison when problems arise as the most important factor. Since both integrative seminars and field liaison absorb considerable resources, it is unfortunate that so little research is available that illuminates effective pedagogical processes in these two domains, and that links these educational activities with student learning outcomes. These topics are worthy of further serious study to provide important evidence-based knowledge for the signature pedagogy of social work.

As noted earlier, students engage in field learning through providing a service to clients, communities, and organizations. The paradox of all learning in clinical or practice settings is that students must intervene while they are still learning to become competent. This is true of medical students and interns, of students learning to be elementary and high school teachers, and so on. Hence, students' practice must be guided by an experienced professional; in social work, a field instructor who is a staff member in the setting is appointed to provide education, support, assistance, and oversight. In conjunction with schools of social work, service organizations appoint an experienced social worker as field instructor to function as the primary educator for the student. The roles of the field instructor are many. They serve as educator, coordinator of student experience in the setting, and evaluator of student learning. They liaise with the university to ensure that learning objectives and competency expectations of student performance are met. They also have administrative accountability and responsibility in the agency to ensure that administrative and practice standards are met; hence, some use the term 'supervision' to refer to their work with the student. While there is an aspect of administrative oversight on the part of the experienced practitioner, the intention of the field experience is student education, rather than 'work.'

Field Learning as Preparation for a Profession

To understand the importance and challenges of field education it is useful to place it within a broad context and consider relevant societal, organizational, and professional issues. The fundamental significance of practice or field-based education in human service and health professions is that it teaches *how to practice* the profession. Professional practitioners are needed in society to provide a range of specialized services. Professions are characterized by a considerable knowledge base, usually acquired by students through a lengthy period of study, a well-developed set of skills and procedures to apply that knowledge to situations brought to the practitioners, and a set of values and ethical principles since professionals are expected to act with integrity (Shulman, 2005a). Given the importance of professionals' specialized knowledge and expertise it is understandable that their educational preparation is of concern to members of a particular profession, but also to society in general. There is an intricate relationship between the quality of education and the quality of professional services. This is especially true of clinical internships in health professions, the field practicum for social work and psychology students, or classroom practice teaching for pre-qualification primary and secondary school teachers. It is in these types of service delivery or clinical systems where students in professions develop the professional competence which forms the foundation and basis for their future practice and contribution to societal goals.

Prior to the last century, preparation for the professions was largely informal and taught through apprenticeship (Cheetham & Chivers, 2005). Training was provided to young individuals in exchange for contributing to the employer's business, arrangements organized by the guild to which the master teacher/employer belonged (Eraut, 2003). The master coached, facilitated learning in the workplace, and supervised the novice. Apprenticeship-based training has been replaced, for professions, by formal academic-based learning in university programs. While workplace learning is still valued and offered in internships and in the field practicum, Cheetham and Chivers (2005) observe that specialist knowledge and theory, taught in university courses, may have come to be seen as more important than practice skills. In Donald Schon's (1983, 1987) seminal and influential work on professions he argues persuasively for the importance of knowledge derived from the real-world activities of professional practice, characterizing practice as complex, indeterminate, and not easily framed and addressed through formulaic models. Schon (1987) proposed the reflective practicum as the place where students could engage with experienced practitioners in an environment where they tackle real-life problems and learn how to think, reflect, and know-in-action. He argued that learning and practising in close contact with experienced practitioners provides students with insight into the process of constructing, deconstructing, experimenting, reflecting, and deciding on future interventions. Schon's work was based on observations of a range of professions as they inculcated new students into their ranks. He wrote extensively about the design studio model where expert and novice work and learn together. His writing predates Shulman's (2005a) discussion of professional education although both authors' concepts share similarities. Shulman, an education scholar and former president of the Carnegie Foundation, studied a variety of professions examining the distinctive ways in which they teach and socialize students. For example, Shulman describes the way the medical profession uses teaching rounds to prepare students in that profession's fundamental ways of thinking, performing, and acting with integrity. In rounds, medical students participate with senior residents and physicians and review patients' symptoms, engage in diagnostic thinking, and bring clinical judgment to bear on determining the course of treatment. Shulman describes the way students learn: through observing and participating in complex performances of observation and analysis, question and answer, conjecture and refutation, problem and hypothesis generation, individual invention, and collective deliberation. He argues that rounds are part of the 'signature pedagogy' (p. 52) of medicine: unique and distinctive educational methods designed by a profession to transform knowledge attained to knowledge for use, and to create the basis for new kinds of understanding that can only be realized experientially and reflectively.

Social work educators have, from the earliest days of educating for the profession, recognized the importance of providing learning experiences in field settings, and over time have increasingly highlighted its importance. For a historical analysis of the development of field standards see Raskin, Wayne, and Bogo (2008), who trace the structure and related accreditation standards for what was originally termed 'fieldwork.' Historical research notes that in 1981, the Commission on Accreditation of the Council on Social Work Education defined the structure for the practicum as 'clearly designed as an educational experience incorporating standards for agency selection and criteria for selecting field instructors and for evaluating student learning in the practicum' (p.176). Recently the Council on Social Work Education designated field education as the signature pedagogy of social work (EPAS, 2008), recognizing its central importance for learning and socialization. 'The intent of field education is to connect the theoretical and conceptual contribution of the classroom with the practical world of the practice setting. It is a basic precept of social work education that the two interrelated components of curriculum – classroom and field – are of equal importance within the curriculum, and each contributes to the development of the requisite competencies of professional practice. Field education is systematically designed, supervised, coordinated, and evaluated based on criteria by which students demonstrate the achievement of program competencies' (p. 8). This is a strong and compelling value statement, which, for champions of field learning, underscores its importance and elevates its status. Such a statement promises to stimulate scholarship, research, and innovation in pedagogy and models for field-based learning. In an era where educational programs are held accountable for the quality of their graduates, this policy resonates with contemporary societal expectations for well-prepared competent professionals.

If the 2008 policy succeeds in generating more attention on field education on the part of social work educators in the United States, they will confront many challenges. The primary challenge relates to the way social work education is structured: specifically, that it divides the sites, focus, and teachers into either classroom or field setting. Permanent social work faculty members appointed to the tenure stream are typically located in the university, where they teach courses and develop and test new knowledge through scholarship and research. While research projects are usually conducted in conjunction with social service agencies, communities, or organizations, studies emanate from the individual faculty member's program of research and scholarship. When full-time faculty members teach courses they strive to make the links with their own practice experiences, although many faculty members have not carried a practice role in many years. Part-time instructors who teach at the university level are more likely to be employed simultaneously at an agency and have current experience in practice and in the community. In contrast are those social workers who provide field instruction and whose primary location is the community agency. They may be more or less familiar with the school's program, based on their own education, practice interests, and continuing professional development. The knowledge and skill base they use in their practice in field teaching is likely to reflect the nature of the population, the program, and their own preferences for models and approaches. Given the location, preparation, and aims of these various types of instructors, the degree of congruence between the material taught in the academic courses and in the field setting is likely to vary considerably. There may be great similarity and high compatibility (for example, a social work program with course instructors committed to teaching evidence-based practice, and an agency and social work field instructors who are using empirically supported treatments and best practice guidelines). Or there may be little similarity and divergence of opinion about what matters for practice (for example, a social work program with course instructors committed to generalist practice and an agency and field instructors who use a limited number of highly specialized intervention models). Students are then in the position where they must navigate between these two domains of education and make sense of the divide between course material and field experiences.

Schools are certainly sensitive to practice realities in their community, and strive to provide relevant curricula. They are also expected, however, to teach generic knowledge for social work as well as emerging knowledge. Students often struggle to implement ideas learned in school in their practicum assignments; they struggle as well to conceptualize practice phenomena in relation to some explanatory framework (that may or may not offer specific guidance for intervention) taught in the school's program. They may experience a disconnect between the knowledge and models taught in the school and the knowledge and practices they perceive they need to practice in their field setting. In earlier eras efforts were made in social work education to articulate and coordinate class and field learning (Sheafor & Jenkins, 1982). Given the enormous diversity of practice settings, and the specialized knowledge needed and available to effectively respond to specific populations and problems currently, coordination of content may be unrealistic.

An excellent example of an innovative approach to bridging university and community agencies is the initiative of the Hartford Practicum Partnership Project. The goal of this project is to increase social work's capacity to serve a growing elderly population through increasing students' knowledge of aging programs, improve their ability to practice with elderly clients, and increase the capacity of schools and settings to prepare graduate students to work with the elderly (Scharlach, Damron-Rodriguez, Robinson, & Feldman, 2000; Scharlach & Robinson, 2005). Program components of each site vary; however, there are essential elements, as follows. Partnerships are developed between university social work programs and a range of community agencies serving the elderly in the health and social services sector. Competencies for practice with the elderly were developed through an iterative process with expert practitioners and scholars (described in chapter 3, on competence), which served as the framework for designing field experiences. A novel element was the use of rotations to provide integrated field experiences where students moved through a range of programs and services for older adults. Seminars and mentorship programs were designed to facilitate integration. Agency staff were involved in expanded educational roles, as field instructors for all or part of the rotation, coordinating learning across settings, and developing integrative seminars to include policy and clinical content; and were consulted on curriculum for course modules and educational resources so that gerontological content was infused into university-based courses. Students were recruited to study social work with the elderly, and were offered incentives such as stipends, conference attendance, and networking and career counselling opportunities. Positive results are reported for all aspects of these partnerships, with training sites benefiting and reporting a 'new or renewed organizational emphasis on training students and hiring master's-level social workers' (Scharlach & Robinson, 2005, p. 434). In other sites in Hartford-sponsored partnerships, positive results, challenges, and lessons learned are well described (see, for example, Lager & Robbins, 2004; Zendell, Fortune, Mertz, & Koelewyn, 2007). It is clear from these innovations that university and community agency social workers can produce creative and more effective educational models when supported to do so. Such efforts can contribute to the knowledge base of field education as alternate approaches are developed and tested.

New ways of thinking about the goals of field education can also offer bridging and collaborative experiences. For example, in an extended program of research, Bogo and colleagues worked with field instructors to articulate the implicit or tacit ways in which they construct the concept of competence (Bogo, Regehr et al., 2004; Bogo, Regehr, Woodford et al., 2006). Through a series of studies, these researchers engaged field instructors in describing qualities, characteristics, and practice behaviours of students at various levels of performance. The resulting evaluation tools and approaches defined competence at a level of abstraction broad enough to encompass a variety of practice approaches, and that may offer a unifying framework for educators in both class and field.

Small structural changes in schools' course offerings may facilitate learning in the field and integrate theoretical material with the reality of practice. An example is offered by Teigiser (2009), who argues that as a result of organization changes, such as those reviewed earlier in this chapter, the University of Chicago created collective learning experiences in seminars based on specific geographical locations where students attended a practicum designed to teach students generalist social work. Students were in similar geographical areas; in the same section of direct practice, programs, and policies courses; and in a special seminar taught by a master practitioner instructor, who worked in the area with a faculty member. The intention of this structural arrangement was to increase the integration of theory and practice. Small positive effects on students' perceptions of what they learned are reported.

Curriculum Content and Field Education

In the earlier discussion of the definition of field education the focus was largely on the structure and process of field education. Structure refers to the various locations within which field learning takes place, the service settings, and the organizational arrangements with the university program. Process refers to the pedagogy of field education, the art and science of teaching students in the field and supporting their learning through classroom courses and assignments. A central theme in the discussion in this chapter is that field education aims to teach students to think and act as a social worker would in professional practice. Analytic and intellectual habits are developed with respect to teaching students to engage with the practice situations they confront, to assess, to plan, and to intervene in a collaborative manner with clients, consumers, and members of the interprofessional team and the organization. This inventory describes some of the general content of field education.

Each program of social work will work within the policy framework of the accrediting body to define its mission and goals, informed by the profession's values and purpose and the program's 'historical, political, economic, social, cultural, demographic, and global contexts, and by the ways they elect to engage these factors' (EPAS, 2008, p. 2). This policy statement does not prescribe content or curriculum. Consistent with the use of a competency-based framework, curriculum planning shifts the focus from input to output (Epstein & Hundert, 2002). Previously, curriculum discussion focused on input: which bodies of knowledge students are expected to master and how this information would be organized and presented in courses. An outcomes-oriented approach focuses on output: what competencies students should be able to master and demonstrate in practice behaviours. Such an approach certainly acknowledges the importance of knowledge acquisition as knowledge underpins understanding phenomena and offering effective interventions. It recognizes, however, that mastery of knowledge is simply not sufficient for effective professional practice. Rather, it is how that knowledge is used which is the ultimate important outcome.

To return to the question of content, or what to teach, each program will work within the competency outcomes provided, and others that they define, to identify the knowledge, values, and skills they believe are required to enact and demonstrate those competencies. A curriculum design for both classroom and field will be constructed to offer the learning opportunities to achieve the program outcomes. As a result, field education programs will share many commonalities with respect to content expected and outcomes to be achieved, and may also vary from school to school to reflect local focus and context.

The issue of curriculum content both for the classroom and for the field has often been identified as problematic by field instructors who question the inclusion of certain topics and the omission of others. The importance practitioners give to content that is crucial is likely affected by the population, setting, and models they work with. All practice is to some extent highly specialized and related to the context in which it is enacted. Practical knowledge, the way general concepts are applied in specific circumstances, is highly situated in the particular agency, program, and team. Eraut (2003) draws on Wenger's (1998) concept of situated knowledge, and observes that knowledge is 'created, shared and used by groups of people working together, networking or socially interacting with each other' (p. 118). Knowledge may differ in different parts of an organization, and is given meaning and interpreted differently by various individuals. The novice is confronted with the need to learn about this situated knowledge, that which is shared within the organization and that which is unique to her or his immediate instructor. The challenge for the novice is that this type of knowledge can operate at a tacit level, is not easy to communicate in explicit terms, and is not easy to interpret (Eraut, 2003). It is 'the way things are understood, the way things are done here' (p.120).

The tension between specific knowledge (what is used in the setting) and general knowledge (overarching concepts for the profession) will always exist at both macro and micro levels. At a macro level, schools are expected to educate for the profession in general and must cover a broader range of content knowledge and skill. As the curriculum becomes packed with ever-increasing new knowledge, the depth of study of any particular subject may be compromised. At a micro level, each learner is faced with the matter of transfer: how to use knowledge acquired in one context, such as in a formal course, in a very different context, such as the field. In the field, knowledge must be transformed into application to unique situations. Learners must know the content of the material to be transferred; as well, they must develop considerable understanding of situations in the new context and be able to select and transform this general content knowledge for use in the particular situation (Eraut, 2002).

Based on the field instructor's own educational program and perception of knowledge needs in the setting, she may find the knowledge base the student is learning either lacking in important material or offering new and very helpful information. Again, the structural divide in social work education presents a challenge, which at this time can be addressed in part through communication between faculty members and field instructors. Efforts to share with field instructors the rationale for the substantive content students are learning provide some clarity. It is also important for faculty to hear from field instructors what they perceive students need to learn in order to support student achievement of competencies. Through mutual interchange, curricula can evolve and better coordination between class and field can result.

Bogo and Vayda (1998) observed that the curriculum of any school of social work is an expression of the view of its faculty members and key stakeholders at a particular point in time: their perception about what social work should look like; what knowledge base is important; their ideologies, values, preferred methodologies, and skills. Debates about the key components of the knowledge base are the subject of conferences, meetings, and scholarly papers. Reamer (1994) proposed that the debate about what students should be taught, about 'the merits and demerits of particular schools of thought and practice, ranging from theories of human behaviour and intervention techniques to the political aims and agenda of the profession' (p. ix), is essential to the growth of any vibrant and socially relevant profession. Years later, Reamer's comments are still valid and attest to the energetic intellectual climate of social work practice and education.

Shaping and changing the curriculum frequently involves the contributions of stakeholders such as teaching faculty, students, field instructors, agency employers, and, in the United Kingdom, service users and consumers. Since the academic program is located within a university, the mission of that institution will also affect the emphasis. Other influences may come from the nature and needs of the geographical community, the scholarly and practice interests of the faculty members, the contemporary job market, and funding opportunities for new areas of practice or research. As a result, curriculum planning involves accommodation and negotiation between these key constituencies and groups. Change occurs over time as a result of many factors: new realities arise, host universities change their expectations of professional schools, and national accreditation bodies change their policies and standards.

The Organizational Context of Field Education

Field education rests on the collaboration between university-based programs of social work and the practice community, especially a wide range of social, health, and human service organizations. Field education programs could not exist without their commitment and willingness to offer learning experiences for students and the largely voluntary participation of social workers who serve as field instructors, usually without any evident reduction in their service load. Decades ago, Frumkin (1980) cautioned that schools of social work could not expect agencies to offer field learning simply because of their commitment to the profession, and argued for the study of school-agency relationships. Few scholars took up this challenge until changes in agencies' ability to continue to offer quality field placements, and in enough numbers, began to be recognized as a threat to the continuity of field learning. Based on a review of the literature on inter-organization models for field education, Bogo and Globerman (1995, 1999) developed and tested a conceptual framework for analysis of arrangements and their comparative effectiveness. The framework consists of four key components: commitment to education, organizational resources and supports, effective interpersonal relationships between the organization and the university, and collaboration and reciprocity. In their analysis of agencies along these dimensions they identified three 'types' of settings along a continuum. At one end of the continuum are those settings with a formal relationship to the university and the inclusion of education in the mission statement. In these settings, which the researchers called 'Teaching Centres,' there is the expectation that significant numbers of students will be received and that this agreement need not be negotiated annually. At the other end of the continuum are settings that have an informal relationship with the university, where one social worker independently agrees to provide field education for one year. The setting may be 'here today and gone tomorrow,' and requires annual negotiation based on the interest and availability of the individual staff member. The researchers character-

ized this type of setting as a 'Lone Ranger.' In the middle of the continuum were organizations that made a semi-formal relationship with
the university and aimed to offer more than one social work
practicum. While there was an agency representative with whom the
school could interact, annual availability of placement opportunities
was variable. The researchers named this type of setting 'Key Contact.'

In a mixed method study the researchers examined each type of
setting along the four dimensions identified to study inter-organizational relationships (Bogo & Globerman, 1999). Commitment to education refers to the degree to which an organization recognizes education as part of its mission statement and goal. For example, in agencies
designated as Teaching Centres, usually university-affiliated teaching
hospitals, part of their mission statement and goal is to educate students in health professions. This goal is especially strong with respect
to medical students and nursing students, and may be more or less
robust for other members of the interprofessional team, including
social workers. In a related study these researchers found that the
elimination of central social work departments in hospitals had profound effects on the viability of student programs (Globerman & Bogo,
2002). Social workers were now assigned to specific programs and had
to negotiate individually with their teams if they wished to use part of
their time for student field instruction. While the rhetoric of the teaching hospital was to educate students for health profession careers, the
reality was that in the absence of a senior advocate for social work, the
number of practicums – decreased. As these hospitals evolved in their
program management structures, the head of academic professional
health programs at the university, such as in occupational, physical,
and speech therapy, joined together to work with the senior managers
of the hospitals to advocate for education for all health disciplines.

In contrast to these complex, multi-function organizations are the
many small, community-based social service settings that philosophi-
cally may be committed to education but do not have the time, space,
or resources to make more than an annual agreement to have one
student. In some instances, taking a student is motivated by the need
for 'another pair of hands' rather than to contribute to the social work
education enterprise.

The second component refers to the nature of the organizational
support and resources devoted to student education. As noted above
in the Teaching Centre model, organizations enter into long-term relationships with schools of social work and identify education as one of

their institutional goals. A structured and complex educational program is designed that includes, but is not limited to, assignments to individual field instructors. These Teaching Centres design seminars and observation activities that present social work's knowledge and expertise with the particular population; the way in which theory, research, and practice are integrated and provide additional venues for student learning. A senior social worker is appointed as educational coordinator and given an adjunct teaching appointment. This coordinator has responsibility for orientation to the setting; recruiting field instructors, and assisting in student matching; developing a field manual for the setting; and identifying social workers able to contribute in seminars or in limited task assignments. Such settings view field instructor training at the university or on-site as continuing professional development activities for their staff. In many such centres, regular field instructor education and support group meetings are held (Bogo & Globerman, 1999).

In contrast are settings where the administration perceives that they do not have enough personnel to meet their service needs and are reluctant to use precious and limited staff time for any activity other than service delivery. While such settings may be willing to take on one or even more students, there may not be protected time for observation of student practice or regular field instruction sessions. In the study, which compared this type of setting with Teaching Centres, Bogo and Globerman (1999) found that in all settings students are encouraged to participate in the life of the agency; to become involved in cases, groups, and projects with other social workers and other professionals; and are invited to staff meetings and educational events. It appears that despite the lack of formal commitment and assignment of resources to student education, once students are present, social work field instructors, regardless of agency commitment, try to find educational resources to provide as much opportunity for learning as is possible. The limitations of the study findings are that only 62 respondents in one program were surveyed. The positive findings with respect to interest and engagement with students is in contrast to qualitative studies of small samples of students, where there are reports of negative experiences with field instructors who were pressured by their agency to take a student, despite not wishing to do so; and of students being ignored or receiving little structured or systematic field instruction (Litvack, Bogo, & Mishna, 2010). Similarly, a national random sample of social workers asked them to recall critical incidents with their former field instructors, and found some respondents reported a lack of supervision, including lack of structure, direction, and feedback (Giddings, Vodde, & Cleveland, 2003).

The third component in the inter-organizational relationships framework is effective interpersonal relationships between personnel in the organization and in the university. In the Teaching Centre model an educational coordinator is appointed with responsibility for coordination with the university and the faculty field liaison for students in the centre. In this role, these practice leaders can influence the school's practicum policy and procedures, are frequently consulted for their advice on practicum matters, and are members of practicum advisory committees where these exist. Through the intensive processes of field instructor recruitment, student matching, and overseeing the educational program on-site, they develop expertise about student field education and are seen as invaluable by the university field practicum faculty and staff. In contrast are those individual field instructors who may interact infrequently with the university, and perhaps only through the field liaison. It has been estimated that approximately half the individual instructors turn over each year. Hence, the relationship between the setting's representative and the university personnel is not likely to be continuous or of great familiarity. In contrast is the educational coordinator, an experienced practitioner who chooses to invest some portion of her or his career as an educator, and views interaction with the educational programs as a valued activity.

The fourth component in the framework is collaboration and reciprocity, which entails joint educational and research activities that contribute to social work knowledge for practice. For example, such endeavours may include advocacy work together on relevant social issues, sponsorship of lectures or conferences for the professional community, sharing audiovisual library collections, social workers in settings lecturing in university courses, and faculty sharing their expertise and research in agency meetings, as well as members from each organization serving on committees in the other organization. The comparison of types of agencies found that representatives of Teaching Centres were more likely to serve on university committees and in planning activities and have agency involvement in research. However, social workers from all types of agencies provided lectures in the university program and attended educational events.

Reviewing the findings from the study leads to the conclusion that organizations with more formal agreements with the university are more involved with the university, and in a more continuous manner (Bogo & Globerman, 1999). Relationships are built and maintained through participating in field seminars, and social workers learn about the program and faculty research and are in a better position to become involved in collaborative activities and to make requests of the university for assistance with continuing education or research. These findings support authors who have called for expanding the vision of field education to shape both social work education and social work practice, and for rethinking the community-agency relationship (Lager & Robbins, 2004; Reisch & Jarman-Rohde, 2000).

An additional finding of this study was the high degree of commitment provided in the other two types of settings to provide the best possible field education experiences for students. Despite the lack of a formal relationship with the university, the field instructors offered a range of quality educational experiences for students despite little reciprocity from the university. This finding stimulated the researchers to further investigate the motivations of the social workers in these settings. In a qualitative exploratory study of 20 social workers, randomly selected, the researchers found that these practising social workers value the field practicum and their role as field educators for generative, professional development and for the personal stimulation it provides (Globerman & Bogo, 2003). Furthermore, these social workers' motivation was highly related to perceiving their organization as one that values learning for its entire staff, and perceives student education as part of that commitment. In such organizations social workers recognize that they have unique and specialized knowledge, 'something special to offer to students and the university' (p. 68). When organizations value and take pride in the collective expertise of their staff, high motivation to find the time and resources to provide field education was evident. Social workers also talked about the new knowledge and perspectives students offer to their field instructors, team members, and the organization in general. Hearing about new approaches provided a sense of keeping up to date, and were also experienced as challenges to typical frameworks and ways of practising. Students brought enthusiasm, optimism, and vitality, and practitioners felt 'rejuvenated and refreshed' (p. 69).

Positive findings about field education benefits and costs were reported by Barton and colleagues (Barton, Bell, & Bowles, 2005) in a qualitative study of 43 field instructors in Australia. Field instructors reported benefits for all involved: themselves, their agency, clients or service users, the university programs, and students. Learning outcomes are achieved by students and through professional development of the instructors, who gain new knowledge and find that teaching stimulates their own reflection on their practice. Agencies benefited from the work performed by students, and for those students who were subsequently hired, they were already well-oriented to the agency practice. Stronger agency and university relationships also developed.

In earlier literature on field education, personal and intrinsic motivators for social workers to provide instruction to students were reported (Bogo & Power, 1992; Lacerte, Ray, & Irwin, 1989). It appears that in the context of unsettled and changing agency contexts such as financial constraints, managed care, hospital restructuring, and increased demands for public accountability, individuals' motivations are highly related to their organizations' capacity to continue to value continuing education for staff and students. Of particular interest was the interlinked nature of organizational factors such as the environment, how an organization reacts to financial crises, whether it values continuing education for staff, and perceives that it has unique knowledge to contribute to future social workers.

Globerman and Bogo (2003) further reflect on various ways in which organizations respond to changing realities, from maintaining almost exclusive focus on service delivery to searching for innovative ways to keep going in order to offer service, education of students, and continuous learning for staff. The later organizations valued field education, as they recognized the positive impact of students' energy and that new perspectives rejuvenated staff. While caution must be exercised in generalizing these findings, the authors propose that field education is no longer simply about individual social workers' motivation and choice to provide the student practicum. It is about organizations' climate, values, and attitudes about the contemporary work environment, and whether it is beneficial to include field education when they are already burdened with multiple demands and too few resources. Leadership is needed at institutional levels, from both universities and agencies, to recognize their mutual interests. Agencies need university programs to ensure the renewal and preparation of the professional workforce. Universities cannot effectively prepare students for competent practice without cooperation from field agencies. It has been demonstrated that the key component in field education is the field instructor (Alperin, 1998; Fortune & Abramson, 1993; Raskin, 1989).

These recent studies, however, clearly demonstrate the central role played by organizations, as field instructors' decisions about offering student placements are highly dependent on their organizations.

Field Instructor Preparation

As noted throughout this chapter, social workers willingly and largely voluntarily offer to educate students despite the subtle and largely invisible addition to their workload. Field directors are cognizant of these workload issues and reluctant to institute mandatory training programs. However, there is a substantial knowledge base about field instruction which is important for new instructors to master.

A variety of formats for training new field instructors exist, including regular seminars to workshop or modular sessions. Regular seminars are usually offered in a bimonthly format that field instructors attend concurrently as they provide their first student practicum. Provided in a group format, participants engage in mutual aid, gain support from peers and the faculty leader, and are able to integrate field instruction knowledge with teaching tasks as they occur in beginning, middle, and ending stages. The knowledge base for these seminars is presented in-depth in the text by Hendricks, Finch, and Franks (2005). A seven-session modular training program is provided by Detlaff (2003), with related handouts and materials which could be used in such seminars or in workshops. Bogo and Vayda (1998) present a training curriculum of eight modules, with cases and exercises based on their approach to field instruction.

An exploratory study of Bogo and Vayda's program, offered in a regular bimonthly group format, examined instructors' perceptions and satisfaction and found instructors most satisfied with educational activities which addressed their immediate learning needs, especially the current tasks they were engaged in with their students, such as orientation, contracting, reviewing learning assignments, and conducting mid-term evaluations. All instructors valued structured teaching, a positive and helpful group climate, and experienced and knowledgeable group leadership. Instructors in direct practice settings valued discussion of common concerns or a specific instructor's concern. In contrast, instructors in community and organization practice preferred sessions with clear goals and a clear agenda and focus (Bogo & Power, 1994).

A thorough review of content for field instructor training is found in Detlaff and Dietz (2004). Using adult learning theory, these researchers then asked field instructors to discuss their training needs in two focus groups, one consisting of new field instructors and one consisting of experienced instructors. Participants identified as important, knowing about the mission of field education and the school's field program including expectations for students. They recommend that instructors receive training in understanding their role and developing a vision for teaching. Participants in this study also identified their needs for learning skills for field instruction consisting of methods of teaching that emphasize teachable moments and integrate theory and practice. Similar to the findings of Bogo and Power (1994), these instructors found small-group activities and discussion the most helpful teaching methods.

The wish for mentoring relationships with more experienced field instructors is an important finding from the Detlaff and Dietz (2004) study. Field education literature has not attended to the rich resource of knowledge and wisdom that experienced instructors' posses. Rather, faculty members and field liaisons have generally led new instructor programs. Barlow, Rogers, and Coleman (2003) describe a successful peer support model which used groups of experienced instructors to provide advanced and in-depth learning opportunities.

As time for training poses challenges for attending seminars and workshops, there are increasing anecdotal reports of online training opportunities for new field instructors. Such arrangements are also practical in schools that use practicum settings at a great distance from their campus. Research on the effectiveness of such methods is likely to develop as more programs develop and evaluate these experiences.

Challenges: Service Organizations, Universities, Students

These are interesting times for field education. On the one hand, there is renewed support for its primacy and importance; on the other, a number of challenges to quality field education have been recently documented in the literature. These challenges are beyond the individual student and field instructor dyad, and are related to contextual factors. They are briefly presented in this chapter, and new approaches that potentially can address some of these issues and offer alternatives are reviewed further in the text, in chapter 7, on approaches and formats for field instruction.

As noted in the studies reviewed above, there have been changes in organizations which have made it increasingly difficult to rely on agencies' ability to provide a high-quality field practicum for students. The changes relate to financial constraints, downsizing, and, in health settings, the elimination of central social work departments and the assignment of social workers to program management structures. Managed care has also impacted the availability of an appropriate field practicum. A number of researchers have documented how funding based on managed care has resulted in increased productivity demands and heavier caseloads for staff, with low priority for non-reimbursed field instruction (Bocage, Homonoff, & Riley, 1995; Donner, 1996; Raskin & Bloome, 1998). As well, many settings do not provide students with the range of social work practice learning experiences required for generalist education at baccalaureate or master's levels; rather, the focus is on direct service to specific populations (Poulin, Silver, & Kauffman, 2006). In the United Kingdom, educators express concerns about heightened expectations for universities to be accountable for competent graduates without allocating additional resources or management commitment to practice teaching (field education) (Furness & Gilligan, 2004; Parker, 2007). Arguments are made for the need for learning organizations and stronger academic and community agency partnerships that focus on both education of students and continuing professional education of staff (Skinner & Whyte, 2004).

Exacerbating the lack of field opportunities is the expansion of social work programs. In various locales, agencies receive requests from a number of programs for the limited number of places they do have available. Recently, 33 representatives from 27 baccalaureate and master's programs in the northeastern United States met for an all-day meeting to identify and address common concerns in their efforts to continue to offer high-quality practicums (Wayne et al., 2006). They identified diminishing resources due to such factors, and to the resulting competition created between schools as they encounter additional pressures in their attempts to secure field education sites.

Changes in the universities with respect to the roles and productivity of faculty members has had a significant impact on field education. Originally, through some form of faculty field liaison, it was envisaged that the two sites of education, the agency and university, would be connected, and some faculty advisement or teaching related to student learning in both domains would occur (Raskin et al., 2008). It appears that over time a variety of appointments at the staff and faculty levels are used as liaison. Changing expectations for faculty members has been proposed as the reason for diminished involvement in field education (Kilpatrick, Turner, & Holland, 1994). As university appointments, especially in research-intensive institutions, require increased levels of research and publication for tenure-stream faculty members, they have moved away from field-related roles (Peebles-Wilkins & Shank, 2003; Wheeler & Gibbons, 1992).

Field liaison functions in some programs are now largely carried by part-time staff, who may or may not have influence in designing the curriculum or extensive engagement with the program's mission. For example, in a survey of 69 schools of social work, Burke, Condon, and Wickell (1999) found that 62 per cent of schools did not assign a full-time faculty member to the liaison role. A separate field education department was more likely to exist in large programs, and special adjunct staff hired for liaison and field management. Hiring non-tenure stream staff to administer and implement the field program may be a pragmatic and effective means of ensuring the time and resources needed to provide a quality field program. If such arrangements become typical, thought must be given to ensuring an environment where these field educators are recognized and valued for their expertise, contribute to curriculum decisions, and can collaborate on field education research and scholarship.

The student body includes individuals who are progressing directly through their educational programs, as well as individuals who are already employed in social or health services and those who are embarking on a second or third career. Many students have family roles and responsibilities, and need sources of income beyond bursaries and loans. For some time now, educators have acknowledged that students require financial aid and flexibility in classroom and field schedules to accommodate part-time employment (Jarman-Rohde, McFall, Kolar, & Strom, 1997). Part-time programs, intensive weekend-long or compressed course offerings, and online courses are some flexible ways of meeting student needs. Since practicum learning is based on engagement in continuous learning in a practice setting over a substantial period of time, it is less amenable to experimentation. One accommodation is the employment-based practicum where students' field education assignment is in their home agency, with assignments and a field instructor different from their usual work role. Students do not lose their usual employment income and are still able to meet field requirements. There is little empirical evidence to evaluate the success of these arrangements, although one study found that students in such settings reported a positive learning experience when doing their practicum in a unit different from their usual assignment (Hopkins, Bloom, & Deal, 2005). On the other hand, anecdotally, there are reports of tensions when students report that their employing agencies did not give priority to their learning needs over service delivery and yet student-employees are in a powerless position and reluctant to report this (Raskin et al., 2008). In summary, changes in organizations, in the university, and in the student body affect traditional field education models. These changes also stimulate development of innovative approaches which maintain the best practices of field education while creating methods more responsive to current realities.

This chapter reviewed many significant contextual features and changes at a macro level which affect educational policy, programs, and ultimately field education as well. Continuous change may be the nature of contemporary society and even as new approaches are developed to respond to identified trends, new circumstances and factors may be emerging that will require further innovation. Therefore an important stance for social work educators is to be open to fresh ideas and willing to consider their promise. At the same time there is a significant body of practice wisdom about field education which has served the profession well over time. Where possible, this wisdom should be tested to determine whether there is evidence for beliefs about 'what works' and the willingness to discard traditions which do not stand up to rigorous examination.

2 The Nature of Professional Social Work Practice

Social Work as a Profession

Modern-day society is highly dependent on professional practitioners in all walks of life. The complexity of contemporary problems in economic, political, environmental, health, and social realms require ever-increasing specialized and interdisciplinary responses. As rapid changes and advances in knowledge creation and technology occur, individuals are needed who are not only knowledgeable, skilled, and creative, but also committed to using new discoveries and approaches in their fields.

Professions are distinguished by a number of features, and, while definitions of professions vary, there is general agreement about the following characteristics. Professional practice is based on a foundation of theoretical and procedural knowledge which is complex and requires specialized study and training. The purpose of such training is to learn how to 'apply skilled service or advice to others' (Cheetham & Chivers, 2005, p. 13). Professionals are informed by an ethical code, are client focused, and are self-regulating (Downie, 1990). Professionals are organized into associations, and in many jurisdictions there is some form of legislation which defines the scope of practice of each profession.

Professionals often practice in formal organizations or agencies, and this is especially true for the majority of social workers. Organizations significantly impact the role of social workers and the nature of their practice. As a result of economic and political shifts, there has been continuous reorganization of health and social services to the extent that downsizing and restructuring have become characteristic of work life.

Commercialization of traditionally non-profit social and health services has also limited the services which are funded. In publicly funded organizations there is concern that regulation-dominated practices, or bureaucratization, override clinical judgments. These organizational changes and their impact on education were discussed in greater depth in the previous chapter on organizational contexts for field education. At this point it is important to note that organizational factors exert a profound influence on the nature of professional practice.

Understandings of Professional Practice

Before considering concepts and practices for teaching students it is important to develop an understanding of what professional practice consists of, or the epistemology of practice. Epistemology refers to concepts about 'how professionals operate, how they "know what they know," how they "do what they do," and how they solve problems in their day to day professional lives' (Cheetham & Chivers, 2005, p. 130). There exists debate about the epistemologies of professional practice contrasting what has been called a technical-rational view of practice with the principle of reflective practice (Schon, 1983, 1987). Both perspectives offer useful insights about professional practice and have significant implications for education. Rather than polarizing these positions, more can be gained through extracting the strengths of each so that a multi-dimensional view may emerge.

The Technical-Rational Approach

The traditional view of professional practice is that it entails application of rigorous specialized knowledge to problems confronted by practitioners. The assumption is that knowledge is developed and empirically tested and leads to principles, procedures, and techniques that can be used to address the real-world situations brought to the professional. Explanatory knowledge can be used to understand the nature of human and social functioning, to analyse function and dysfunction, and to determine what needs to change to improve the situation or problem. In this perspective, procedural or technical knowledge is available which describes how to intervene to bring about change leading to positive outcomes. Consistent with this view, evidence-based practice has been widely adopted in health science professions. In the past two decades there have been champions of evidence-based practice who advocate that social work incorporate this view into education and practice (Gambrill, 1999; Gibbs, 2002; Thyer & Myers, 1998), as well as critics (Witkin, 1998). The approach rests on the development of empirically validated interventions which demonstrate the effectiveness of a specific approach under controlled and rigorous conditions. The practitioner then learns how to search appropriate databases to extract information about what is known about what works, with a particular problem situation presented by a client. Databases consist not only of original empirical studies, but also of meta-analyses, syntheses, and systematic reviews that evaluate and collate the available evidence. Where there is enough strong data, practice guidelines for particular problems may exist that provide practitioners with direction about the steps and interventions to bring about change.

When practitioners search the literature it is with the intention of addressing the particular practice problem or situation posed by their client. Therefore, practitioners must be able to assess the applicability of the findings to the unique circumstances of each client. Moreover, proponents of evidence-based practice have expanded the perspective to include attention to the client's values, expectations, and preferences. The appropriateness of the intervention for the client as well as potential barriers to its use, including cultural issues, is also examined. The practitioner's expertise involves integrating the clinical state and circumstances, client preferences and actions, and the best empirical evidence (Gibbs, 2002; Haynes, Devereaux, & Guyatt, 2002).

To provide sound and effective services is an ethically and intellectually appealing proposition and expectation of professionals. Practitioners' confidence about the impact of our services would be greatly improved if we knew that what we offer actually works; hence the attraction and importance of evidence-based practice. However, this approach has been controversial, and there are a number of challenges regarding practitioners' training and ability to carry out this method. It is reasonable to ask whether social workers have the expertise, time, and resources to critically evaluate the literature. Is this an unrealistic expectation in current organizational climates? Is it more likely that practitioners may, at best, be interested in knowing which interventions have empirical support and then learning how to use those interventions effectively (Mullen, Shlonsky, Bledsoe, & Bellamy, 2005)? Simply knowing the evidence about the best interventions does not lead to competence in using those interventions. Learning opportunities in the agency or through continuing education must be available to develop enough skill to produce positive outcomes (Adams, LeCroy, & Matto, 2009). Similarly for social work students, opportunities to learn how to competently use specialized intervention models must be available in courses, field settings, or both.

Other critiques of evidence-based practice involve the nature of the evidence; are only results from rigorous randomized controlled trials considered evidence, and what about results from qualitative studies, and workers' past experiences or practice wisdom (Adams, LeCroy, & Matto, 2009)? Studies are generally conducted only on approaches that can be clearly specified in treatment manuals. This requires definition of procedures in operational terms. In the mental health field, behavioural models have been documented in this way, and studied. Approaches that are more humanistic and relationship-based can be more difficult to define and hence to measure using prevailing positivistic research methods. As a result, empiricism is privileged over other sources of knowledge such as information derived from qualitative research, practice wisdom, consumer perspectives, cultural considerations, and situational context (Adams, LeCroy, & Matto, 2009).

Another problematic issue relates to the samples used in empirical studies. Where there are sound enough methodologies to receive positive peer review for publication, samples often are not representative of the population that social workers see in their day-to-day work. In order to achieve control over variables that would confound the research, inclusion and exclusion criteria must be used. Such criteria often remove clients with multiple problems and issues – the very group that social workers confront.

The potential reservoir of studies from which social workers could draw guidelines for practice has slowly increased over time, although significant limitations still exist in this knowledge base. For example, in a review and assessment of research capable of informing practice interventions published in a sample of leading social work journals in 1999, fewer than one in six reports of studies were found (Rosen, Proctor, & Staudt, 1999). Furthermore, of these studies, only 7 per cent were about practice interventions. Thirty-six per cent of the studies contributed descriptive knowledge and 49 per cent explanatory knowledge. The authors conclude that the state of social work research at that time did not address the needs of practitioners for information about what practices work and with what types of clients. More recently Reid and Fortune (2003) conducted a systematic review and analysis of empirically tested social work intervention programs in direct practice. Included in this review were programs whose goal was change or alleviation of problems in clients' circumstances. All studies met rigorous research methodology criteria. The authors reviewed 107 studies and found the majority of programs were group programs comprising 59 per cent, individual interventions accounted for 20 per cent of programs, family interventions for 9 per cent and mixed methods for the remaining 12 per cent. Two distinct types of programs were identified. One type involved structured cognitive-behavioural group interventions and used skills training, education, and group processes. The other type of programs involved individual intervention, similar to case management, and provided concrete services in the context of a helping relationship. Reid and Fortune concluded that a body of research now exists which could contribute to developing practice guidelines. They note, however, that these studies do not reflect 'the world of everyday practice [where] one finds considerable attention to any number of approaches that one finds little of in these tested programs – for example, generalist, ecological, solution-focused, and psychodynamic' (p. 70). Also, while the majority of studies investigated group interventions, in practice the majority of interventions are offered in an individual format.

The final consideration regarding the usefulness of evidence-based practice relates to social work's attention to context and diversity. Dominant professional frameworks such as the ecosystemic approach take into account the vast number of variables that affect individual's lives, the way problems are framed and understood, and the possible ways in which help could be sought and received. These variables are present at individual, family, community, and neighborhood levels, as well as within organizations providing service; local, regional, and national government programs; and the attitudes about social and personal issues found in the society. As a result, practice applications of these assumptions are that individuals must be understood within their own context, and that attempted change initiatives in one part of a system affect other parts of the system. These factors must be taken into account when applying findings from studies conducted in contexts different from the one represented by the current practice situation.

Social work has also recognized individual and group diversity by virtue of a range of social identity characteristics, including gender, age, race, ethnicity, class, religion, ability, sexual orientation, and so on. These diversities have a profound impact on values, world views, meanings attributed to events, needs, and problems. Social workers who use an ecosystemic framework and understand diversity can appreciate the need for unique and individual assessment and intervention plans. Information derived from studies can still be helpful; however, it requires critical thinking and judgment. Evidence can be used in a flexible way, as potentially offering concepts and practices to understand and assist clients and communities. Practitioners need to be mindful of the contingencies of each situation when they engage in evidence-based practice.

Significant implications for education of students flow from viewing practice as the application of theory and evidence and have influenced university programs throughout the twentieth century. The assumption was that in educational programs students learn specialist knowledge, theory, and technical information, and critical intellectual skills to analyse, critique, and evaluate this knowledge base. The practice of the profession, the application of theory to practice, will be learned in the field practicum, work study programs, or post-program internships. In social work, educators have traditionally recognized the challenge of linking theory and practice, and many university-based courses include some practice component, particularly using theoretical concepts to analyse cases. Courses primarily devoted to skill development, usually interviewing and communication skills are also present in many undergraduate and some graduate programs. The major emphasis in these programs, however, is on knowledge acquisition and analysis.

Clearly the advocates of evidence-based practice believe that this approach can add tremendously to social work practice, and they have creatively provided a model that is more consistent with social work values and principles. The model recognizes practitioner expertise and clients' contributions to determining which services and interventions are appropriate, and takes context and culture into account (see, for example, Mullen et al., 2005). Increasingly, social work educational programs have been defining and teaching ways to influence the links between research and the practice of social work. In the past, educators embraced and taught students empirically based practice, encouraged the scientist-practitioner model, and the use of single-subject research methods. As Mullen and colleagues astutely observe, while students learned these approaches in school, there is no evidence that these methods were then used in practice in any significant way. Hence, until agencies are committed to this approach and have the infrastructure to facilitate its use, new graduates may not find the support they need to transfer evidence-based practice into their everyday life as employees. A recent study found that field instructors viewed it as a useful development, but reported lack of time as a barrier to adopting the approach in their own work and hence in teaching students how to use evidence in the practicum (Edmond, Megivern, Williams, Rochman, & Howar, 2006)

The Reflective Practitioner Approach

The technical-rational approach described above pays little explicit attention to the ways in which practitioners' own perceptions, values, and personal attributes affect the way in which problems are defined and framed, the interventions chosen, and the ways in which they are provided. It is as if the practitioner is neutral, even-handed, or not an active player in construction and making meaning of the problem situation. In his seminal text, *The Reflective Practitioner*, Schon (1983) challenged the prevailing paradigm of professional practice as application of knowledge, and argued that the proposed links between basic science, applied science, and professional practice did not totally account for the way professionals understood, framed, and intervened to address the problems they confronted. He viewed professional practice as highly complex, with many unique features in individual cases which do not readily fit into explanatory categories or respond to technical, rational, or predictable processes. He argued that situations are often messy, indeterminate, and involve ethical or value dilemmas not easily answered. Schon studied a range of professions and observed professionals as they worked with unexpected and puzzling situations which did not fit theoretical propositions or respond to standard procedures. He proposed the reflective practice paradigm to capture these aspects of professional work that are beyond the application of knowledge and known principles. In this view the practitioner is important, and her tacit knowledge, or *knowing-in-action*, is considered significant. Reflection is key for practice, for education of students to become professionals, and for lifelong professional development.

Schon (1983) noted that, as in everyday life, part of professional practice involves a type of *knowing-in-action*, where our know-how is evident in our behaviour or performance, carried out in an almost automatic way, without thinking about it. Individuals draw on a tacit form of knowledge that has become a part of them. Tacit knowledge refers to the intuitive know-how of practitioners, which is drawn from a reservoir of informal knowledge built up over time and from past experiences with similar situations, creative use of formal knowledge, wisdom, and judgment. As a result, when practitioners engage with individual situations they can be seen to act and engage in corrective actions in a flexible and agile manner.

According to Schon (1987), when practitioners are confronted with situations that contain an element of surprise or do not respond to usual procedures, another process may come into play. For some practitioners, novelty and complexity may simply be ignored as they continue with their usual approach. Others, however, engage in 'thinking [which] serves to reshape what we are doing while we are doing it. I shall say, in cases like this, that we *reflect-in-action*' (p. 26). Schon describes this reflection as considering the phenomena confronted, using critical thinking, and questioning our assumptions. Ideally, this type of reflection leads to reconsidering the way the situation was framed or understood, and in turn arriving at new strategies for action. Since this reflection occurs while one is in the practice situation, it provides the chance for self-correction and experimentation with new actions. These actions may produce intended results or may stimulate the need for further reflection and subsequent new actions. Reflection-in-action is non-linear, likely not deliberative, but happens in the process. Experience, wisdom, and insight operate in a way that allows for flexibility in framing and re-framing the problem and using creativity and improvisation in trying new responses. This view is a constructionist view of practice where practitioners engage in new forms of meaning-making, which yield expanded opportunities for intervention. In a similar vein, England (1986) identified the integration of theory and practice as a unique and intuitive process in which social workers do not directly apply theory to practice; rather, they use their theoretical knowledge to construct coherence about the complex situations they encounter.

For Schon (1983), another feature of professional practice is *reflection-on-action*, where the professional looks back on her practice and critically reviews it. The aim is to re-examine the situation and the professional's experience of the event, thoughts about it including some evaluation of what transpired, and what actions were or were not successful. Ideally, through reflection the professional can learn from the experience so that in future interactions with the case interventions can be improved. However, as noted above, this is a constructionist

view; the practitioner's recall, including her perceptions, are a mani-
festation of her own view of the reality as she experienced it. Schon
(1987) comments that when practitioners try to report on what they
know and why they did what they did, they have difficulty. Others
have noted that practitioners' accounts of the rationale for particular
actions and judgments, or practice wisdom, has eluded concrete definition and explication and is difficult to study (Bogo, Regehr et al.,
2004; Eraut, 2002).

Reflection for the purpose of learning from experience had been previously described by Dewey (1933) in educational theory, and popu-
larized by Kolb (1984) in adult education and management education.
Schon's (1983, 1987) work reintroduced the notion of reflection as both
in the moment of practice and after the practice event. These are two
very different types of reflection, and the links between the two are not
always clearly specified in the original formulations or in the many
writings of scholars and educators. Indeed, there is abundant literature
on reflection and methods to foster reflection; however, these are
largely related to reflection-on-practice (Rogers, 2001). There appears
to be agreement about the importance of preparing reflective practitioners, and an implicit assumption that teaching students to reflect
after they have practised will ultimately enhance their ability to be
reflective *in* their practice. This assumption is untested. Nevertheless,
the reflective practice paradigm has attracted wide interest in a range
of professions such as teaching and nursing. Social work theorists and
educators in the United Kingdom also use this paradigm, although
there is scant social work literature in North America on the topic (for
exceptions see Bogo & Vayda (1998); Papell & Skolnik (1992); Vayda &
Bogo (1991).

Since there is an extensive literature from these various professions
and with somewhat different emphases, the following section aims to
define and explore the essence of the concepts associated with reflective practice. Since the great majority of the literature focuses on reflection-on-action, this section will begin with this concept. Reflection-on-
action involves returning to a situation after it has been completed,
and purposefully and systematically reviewing one's work and the
factors that affected the outcome. The aim is to draw out insights that
could inform future practice with this situation and with practice in
general in positive ways. The parameters for reflection vary. Some formulations draw on categories of knowledge as the framework for
reflection. Rolfe (2001), writing about nursing, identifies at least three

distinct kinds of knowledge practitioners can use when thinking back about a professional experience. One category includes the theoretical, empirical, or procedural knowledge of the profession, examining what concepts were used to understand and intervene and the way in which this information was useful or not. Concepts not previously used can be drawn in to provide alternative perspectives for re-evaluating the practice. A second category is experiential knowledge derived from the practitioner recalling her own practice in similar situations and looking for similarities, articulating specific principles, and learning which might apply in the present. The third category is self-awareness or personal knowledge gained from relationships with past clients. This type of knowledge is about ourselves and our needs, and can assist us in understanding the current client.

Johns (2005), also writing about nursing, defines reflection as subjective and particular to a practice event and context. The aim is to confront and understand 'why things are as they are ... gain new insights into self and be empowered to respond more congruently in future situations within a reflexive spiral towards developing practical wisdom and realizing one's vision as a lived reality' (p. 2). Viewing reflection as a fusion of sensing, perceiving, intuiting, and thinking, its purpose is to develop insight into self so that more knowledge for better practice results. Rolfe (2001) wisely notes that reflection is essentially subjective and hence cannot be easily defined; it is intuitive and holistic. Despite this caveat, Johns' (2005) model for structured reflection provides a number of questions to guide nurses through describing an experience and the significant issues which caught their attention. These questions can be easily adapted and applied to social work. Feelings of self and others and reasons for these feelings are examined. Attention is given to what the nurse was trying to achieve and whether her behaviour was effective. Consequences for the patient, the nurse, and others are considered. The nurse identifies factors which influenced feeling, thinking, or responding; knowledge used; and how congruent the action was with her own values. A series of reflective questions are provided to guide examination of how this situation connects with previous experiences, how the nurse might have responded more effectively if she could be involved in this situation again, potential consequences of alternative actions, and how she feels about this practice experience after these reflections. Consideration is given to whether the reflections have led to more support for self and others, more ability to realize desirable practice, and more use of alternative frameworks for understanding.

Writing about reflective practice in social work, Ruch (2002) refers to Rolfe (2001) and notes three types of knowledge useful for practitioners: (1) theoretical knowledge from formal theories and derived from empirical study, (2) practice wisdom or experiential or personal theory derived from integrating formal theory with one's own personal experiences, and (3) tacit knowledge, that which has been assimilated over time but is not necessarily easily articulated or made explicit. Drawing on van Manen (1977), four levels of reflection are proposed. The first is the level of technical reflection and involves examining practice through the lens of formal theory, models, and procedures to determine whether and why the practitioner did or did not achieve desired outcomes. The second level is practical reflection and includes the first level of formal knowledge along with tacit, personal, intuitive ways of understanding. The two ways of knowing influence each other, and through analysis both personal and professional assumptions underpinning practice are identified, with insights gleaned from both. The third level is critical reflection, which examines the practice phenomena through the lens of structural and systemic factors such as social, political, and economic conditions beyond the individual which maintain power and privilege and oppression and marginalization. This level is an important one for social work, with its commitment to social justice and its anti-oppressive stance. The fourth level involves reflecting on, thinking about, feeling, and acting on process dynamics. Through the use of psychodynamic concepts about unconscious and conscious, and relational and inter-subjective dynamics, social workers can develop understanding about their reactions to clients and their use of self.

Although the writings of Ruch (2002) drew on social work in the United Kingdom, and Bogo and Vayda (1987; 1998) wrote from a North American perspective, their models are very similar. Bogo and Vayda articulated a model to integrate theory and practice for use in field instruction. A systematic four-phase process was proposed as a loop (similar to the United Kingdom writers' use of a spiral). The loop metaphor was used to depict the cumulative and ongoing nature of reflection and action. This involves repeated activities of thinking, feeling, and doing, or taking some action again and again in a practice situation. Each phase of the loop affects the next in an iterative fashion. The phases include (1) retrieval and recall of the salient facts of a situation, (2) reflection on the practitioner's personal subjective associations and reactions to all or aspects of the situation, (3) linkage of both the facts and reactions to various concepts derived from the profession's knowledge base, and (4) professional response, which involves a reconsideration of the situation based on the previous steps, and planning for action in the next encounter with the situation.

With respect to the third phase of linkage, theoretical concepts are drawn from social work and relevant related disciplines. An articulated body of knowledge constitutes the underpinnings of professional practice and includes underlying explanatory theory, specialized practice approaches, empirically supported models, and generic social work principles. The term 'theory' in contemporary social work can be confusing, as it is used in various ways in the literature and in professional conversations.

The term will be used in two ways in this text. First, there are explanatory theories which represent a way of understanding the human condition, social functioning, and dysfunction. The concepts provided in such theories allow practitioners to answer the question, 'Why does this problem exist in this situation?' and to make sense of the situation. Theories provide a framework, with concepts and relationships between these concepts, so that practitioners know what data to gather and which factors to include or exclude in gaining information about the issues presented. Hence, social work's dominant or preferred theories reflect the professions' view of what is important in the way situations are understood.

The second type of theory is referred to as practice theory or practice models, and provides the vehicle to use to apply knowledge. Practice models incorporate selected explanatory theory and a theory of change. These models use these basic concepts to answer the questions, 'Why is there a problem?' and 'What is needed to bring about change?' Principles, staged processes, and techniques provide structure for workers to assess, plan, and intervene. Models vary regarding their specificity – from highly structured manualized approaches to general principles. They also vary with respect to the degree to which they have been rigorously tested and empirically supported, or are based on charismatic proponents and compelling anecdotal reports.

In each phase of the loop, attention is directed towards factors which are consistent with social work's ecological-systemic framework, incorporate notions of power and structural oppression, and encompass the individual, the social context, and the transactions between these various domains. In order to reflect in a way that links these various levels of attention taught in schools of social work with the particular features of individual clients, field instructors and students are encouraged to examine four factors. These include (1) psychosocial factors specific to the particular client system, (2) interactive factors related to the system created between the worker and client, (3) organizational factors consisting of agency policies, programs, and practices that affect the practice of the social worker with the client, and (4) contextual-societal factors such as attitudes, values, and beliefs which also impact social policy and practice. While all four factors or levels cannot be systematically examined in depth for each client, this template provides a framework for examining both personal subjective associations and cognitive theoretical associations. The assumption is that over time, as field instructor and student together examine numerous practice situations, students will come to reflect on their practice through a social work perspective, using a lens that integrates micro and macro levels.

Reflective practice is not without controversy, and has been critiqued for offering a 'rather scant template' for development of professional competence (Cheetham & Chivers, 2005, p. 57), relying on reflection as the key concept despite the lack of evidence that it results in learning or improves practice (Eraut, 1994; Ruth-Sahd, 2003). Other critiques include unsubstantiated hypotheses and inconsistencies in the work; for example, the lack of a coherent view of reflection, but rather a set of overlapping attributes which may have contributed to different ways of interpreting the concept and hence adding to conceptual confusion (Eraut, 1994; Rogers, 2001). Scholars and researchers have defined reflective practice in their own terms, leading to confusion. For example, in nursing, related concepts such as critical social theory or praxis are found (Ruth-Sahd, 2003); and in social work, reflective practice, critical self-reflectivity, and critical reflection have been used interchangeably without attention to the different intellectual traditions of these terms (Fook, 2004). Eraut notes that in the literature most reflection is described as a 'solitary affair' (Eraut, 2004, p. 50), and would likely benefit from working practices that encourage team, collegial, and group reflective activities. Following Brookfield's (1998) observation that individuals use their 'own interpretive filters to become aware of [their] own interpretive filters' (p. 200), reflection in clinical supervision or in peer groups may be more useful to fully promote new learning.

Thus far the discussion of reflective practice has focused primarily on reflection-*on*-action. To develop greater understanding of the concept of reflection-*in*-action, the contributions of scholars and practitioners interested in mindfulness for clinical practitioners provides an informative approach to what has appeared as somewhat elusive and not well defined. Recall that the concept of reflection-*in*-action entails being fully engaged and interacting in the present in a professional role, while at the same time maintaining a level of awareness that serves to provide information to guide further actions. The literature on reflection can be usefully supplemented by the concept of mindfulness, as reflection requires focused and heightened attention and awareness in the moment.

Kabat-Zinn (1990) introduced mindfulness-based stress reduction (MBSR) in behavioural medicine over 25 years ago, for various populations with chronic pain and stress-related difficulties, as a complement to traditional medical treatment. Empirical support exists for the effectiveness of MBSR in reducing conditions such as chronic pain, anxiety, and stress, and in promoting recovery from treatment (Kabat-Zinn, 2003). Mindfulness has been successfully incorporated in treatment models for specific mental health problems such as mindfulness-based cognitive therapy for relapse prevention in depression (Segal, Williams, & Teasdale, 2002), and for dialectic behavioural therapy for individuals diagnosed with borderline personality disorder (Linehan, 1993). Programs informed by mindfulness have been developed for a wide range of settings, such as schools, workplaces, and prisons (Kabat-Zinn, 2003). Recently, Mishna and Bogo (2007) have applied the concepts of reflective practice and mindfulness for social work educators in complex contemporary classrooms, where students' engagement with concepts about culture, power, privilege, and oppression can produce highly charged environments. Recognizing that education is a practice, they critically analyse the specialized social work educational literature on this topic and highlight its limitations – specifically, that it does not provide the type of thoughtful and creative thinking processes needed by course instructors at the moment: processes described in the reflective practice literature, reviewed above, and in the literature on mindfulness.

Drawing on the work of Kabat-Zinn (1990), mindfulness can be seen as attending to the moment-to-moment flow of experience with a receptive and non-judging awareness. It entails 'cultivating and refining our innate capacity for paying attention and for a deep, penetrative seeing/sensing of the interconnectedness of apparently separate aspects of experience, many of which tend to hover beneath our ordinary level of awareness regarding both inner and outer experience' (p. 15). Recognizing the ubiquitous and automatic nature of reactivity, mindfulness helps to disengage the linkages between perceptions, interpretations, and responses. This then allows an individual to respond through choice rather than to respond in a habitual and 'mindless' manner. Thus, mindfulness enables individuals to respond creatively and skilfully to the particular moment, situation, interaction, or relationship (Alper, 2005). Following from Mishna and Bogo's (2007) analysis of practice as educators, social work practitioners may find that mindfulness supports reflective practice and a stance that enables them to face rather than avoid challenges, to acknowledge rather than suppress discomfort, and to reflect in practice rather than react in a habitual way.

In medicine and other health professions' practice, Epstein, Siegel, and Silberman (2008) have applied mindfulness to self-monitoring and self-assessment both in and after practice. The analysis offered is part of an effort to provide a scientific understanding of the clinical act. These authors focus on neuro-cognitive and psychological aspects of practice as they relate to self-monitoring. They conceptualize self-monitoring in a manner similar to reflective practice, and, similar to the critique above, note that Schon's (1983) concept of reflection-in-action does not provide specific direction about 'how to achieve a state of active self-observation during everyday tasks' (p. 7). Attentiveness is proposed to address this gap, developing an observing self within the often chaotic environments in which health professions work and learn. Through conscious and intentional attentiveness to the present situation, practitioners can achieve a mindful practice, highly attuned to 'the raw sensations, thoughts, and emotions as well as the interpretations, judgments, and heuristics that one applies to a particular situation' (p. 9). Qualities associated with mindful self-monitoring are provided. First is the interest in accessing not only data about the client, but also practitioners' and learners' internal experience, feelings, thoughts, and reactions. Related to this is the developing awareness of what the stimuli for one's reactivity are, and lowering that reactivity so that internal and external responses are aligned for better client-centered care. These qualities are similar to the concept of self-awareness in social work with its attunement to the ways in which practitioners' inner experiences affect their practice. Mindfulness, however, adds other qualities. For example, curiosity, even in the face of receiving feedback about oneself that is negative or disconfirming one's self-image. Curiosity, open-mindedness to various possibilities, and flexibility – readiness to adopt more than one perspective – are offered as qualities which allow individuals to be more open to new information, information which can lead to taking new or different perspectives and actions. Epstein and colleagues (2008) also address self-monitoring and self-assessment after practice events, and note that such reflection can raise awareness of issues which later, when in the actual practice situation, the practitioner should attend to. Importantly, they caution that the affect of such post-hoc reflection on self-monitoring during practice needs to be tested rather than assumed. Put another way, there is an absence of empirical evidence that reflection-on-action improves practice.

Contemplative practices offer many ways, such as meditation, to train the mind for focused attention in practice. Though emanating from Eastern and Buddhist philosophy and meditative practices, MBSR interventions separate mindfulness meditation from these religious, cultural, and ideological origins. Kabat-Zinn (2003) maintains, however, that practitioners who use mindfulness must themselves have a certain level of understanding and commitment to its fundamental dimensions and to practicing meditation in their own lives. As the contributions of mindfulness are being adopted in human and health services, educators are beginning to incorporate contemplative practices in curricula (see, for example, Bruce & Davies, 2005; Shapiro, Schwartz, & Bonner, 1998).

In summary, it appears that the reflective practice paradigm involves two dimensions: (1) drawing on multiple explicit and implicit sources of knowledge to creatively and somewhat spontaneously attend and respond to complexities of practice in the moment; and (2) learning from the experience of the recent practice situation through reflecting on it, so that greater awareness of influences on practice become evident and new knowledge is generated for future practice in general, and for actions within the specific situation. The paradigm of reflective practice has the capacity to incorporate attention to a wide range of intellectual and affectively based knowledge components of practice. The models of reflective practice reviewed have all included attention to theoretical, empirical, and procedural knowledge. As well, these models recognize the importance of tacit knowledge built up from practitioners' similar past work experiences, as well as the profound influence of the self of the practitioner. Self-awareness is a recognized source of knowledge about our clients' and our own dynamics. In this respect the emotional impact of a practice event on an individual practitioner is recognized and seen as a potential stimulus and source for greater understanding and new learning. Social work models include understanding how structural and societal factors play out in both individuals' lives and in professional encounters.

The reflective practice paradigm, following Schon (1983, 1987), recognizes that when tested empirical knowledge is applied to practice situations it is not done in neutral and mechanistic ways. It is offered through each practitioner and the way in which he uses his personal-professional self. Hence, it appears important for practitioners to have a good understanding of the tacit, invisible, and perhaps out-of-awareness aspects of self that are the vehicle for delivering service. For it is these nebulous aspects of self that exert influence on the interventions we provide. It is proposed that heightened attention and awareness of self and other can be achieved through mindfulness. Given this perspective, practitioners are encouraged to come to know themselves through their reflections in and after their practice encounters, in three crucial domains: (1) the way they conceptualize their practice and the types of theories and practice models they use to understand phenomena and guide their practice; (2) the way they deal with personal reactions to situations so that they can use their 'self' in an intentional and purposeful way; and (3) what they feel confident about and where they need to seek help and consultation, and ways to develop greater knowledge and skill in order to be helpful.

Empirical Support for Models of Professional Practice

There is little empirical work to support the superiority of either of the two epistemologies of practice reviewed here, especially with regard to their links to competence. An exception is a study conducted by Cheetham and Chivers (2005) to develop and empirically test a model of professional competence across 20 professions. Their research involved approximately 450 participants, and, through an iterative process, led them to propose a new model of professional practice. Their study included presenting the two epistemologies of practice in a variety of ways to participants, who were then asked about the way they operated in their professional practice. For more than a third of the sample, their practice was described as primarily applying specialist knowledge. In contrast was 10 per cent who saw their practice as more art than science. The largest proportion of participants, 46 per cent, viewed their practice as a combination of art and science. Principles from specialized knowledge or theory were used, as well as tacit knowledge and 'gut feeling' (p. 133). With regard to problem solving, only 7.5 per cent primarily used specialist knowledge while the majority (86 per cent) reported using a combination of 'applying specialist or theoretical knowledge to the problem, drawing on a repertoire of previous solutions and using common sense' (p. 133). Of interest was that these practitioners reported using the principle of individualization. They reported that the approach they used in problem solving depended on the type of problem they confronted, as the unique properties of each often required unique solutions. Importantly, most respondents reported consulting with colleagues for problem solving, a dimension missing from Schon's formulations.

With respect to reflection the researchers found around 98 per cent of all participants reported reflecting on their professional work from time to time, and 80 per cent reported that they regularly reflected. From examples of respondents' reflections the researchers conclude that the type and focus of reflection varied considerably, as did the depth and quality. Reflection was largely unstructured, informal, and unsystematic in comparison to the dense frameworks reviewed above, which are intended to guide professionals to examine a wide range of factors in their reflections. The impact of reflection on changing practice was interesting, with 39 per cent stating this occurred regularly and 57 per cent only sometimes. Changes were not necessarily seen in subsequent actions; changes could occur in individuals' ways of thinking or feeling about the situation. Some participants reported that reflection could lead to a decrease in self-confidence, with examples offered of reflection leading to becoming self-conscious, overly concerned with one's own shortcomings, and indecisive.

There were no significant differences found in the frequency of reflection reported in relation to gender or age. Despite small samples in the professions studied there was a suggestion that professionals working with people (for example, health care, teaching, pastoral work) engaged in more reflection than professionals in more routine and rule-bound operations (for example, accounting, surveying). Perhaps in the former professions the knowledge base is contested, problems are highly complex and subject to various interpretations, and there is a lack of generalizable and valid procedural knowledge.

In more routine and determinate forms of practice, reflection may be less crucial than in situations requiring greater analysis, creativity, and innovation (Cheetham & Chivers, 2005).

This study provides some empirical support for the concept of reflective practice but challenges the primacy accorded to it by its proponents. The researchers caution that based on their data neither epistemologies – professional practice as applied theory – nor reflective practice present a satisfactory explanation of the way in which professionals actually go about their work. The participants used both approaches, and in conjunction with each other. They clearly used and valued specialist knowledge, whether gained through their original education or through subsequent experience. Problem solving also included using past repertoires, consultation with others, 'creativity, lateral thinking and common sense,' and, in situations of uniqueness, 'returning to first principles or basic theory to work out a solution' (Cheetham & Chivers, 2005, p. 139).

Based on their findings, the researchers propose a modified epistemology of professional practice termed 'technically grounded extemporization.' This paradigm views professional practice as 'the application of specialist knowledge and rational thought in combination with tacit knowledge and more intuitive forms of thought' (Cheetham & Chivers, 2005, p. 141). Consistent with models of professional expertise (for example, see Dreyfus & Dreyfus, 1986; Hammond, 1980), they propose that as individuals become more expert they rely less on formal procedures and guidelines and more on their own tacit understandings, sometimes referred to as intuition. Nevertheless, even for experts, when confronted with situations that are unique, basic theoretical knowledge, analysis, and judgment form a crucial part of their approach. They also recommend training students to develop reflective skills, but caution that at this early stage of professional development a primary reliance on reflection, in the absence of a solid knowledge base, is not sufficient. Finally, this study demonstrates the need for far more research to examine whether the numerous conceptual and notional writings about reflective practice are more than interesting ideas, but are actually useful in providing a better understanding of the nature of professional practice.

This chapter has reviewed selected concepts about how professionals operate drawing on the work of Cheetham and Chivers (2005), who have integrated aspects of two dominant perspectives: a technical-rational approach and reflective practice. An understanding of professional practice provides a foundation for constructing approaches to professional education. Based on this review it appears that educators, in classroom and field, should ensure that students are prepared with a solid knowledge base and the skills needed to apply concepts in practice. Of equal importance are reflective skills and the conceptual ability to analyse practice situations, to critically appraise potential approaches, and to use judgment in all aspects of their practice. This latter quality may be difficult to teach directly. Students can likely learn from practitioners who are explicit about their reflections, which inform their decisions about their practice.

In the second section of this text the perspectives discussed in this chapter are used to arrive at educational principles for field education. With a view of how practitioners go about their practice, the goals for student preparation are clarified. These perspectives can inform educators as they determine educational objectives for preparing social workers, construct educational programs including curriculum and teaching and learning approaches, and devise methods to evaluate student learning and performance. Before addressing educational principles, however, the concept of professional competence will be presented and explored to offer another framework in which to understand professional practice and the pathways to preparing competent practitioners.

3 Competence

The goal of social work education is to develop competent social work practitioners. Despite the presence of licensing exams, in many jurisdictions university programs serve as the first gatekeeper to the profession. As a result, the quality of their programs and their graduates significantly affects the effectiveness of the services provided in the community. Social workers are committed to service for vulnerable and oppressed populations. Therefore, it is crucial that graduates are well-prepared and able to practice as competent, effective, and ethical social workers, to contribute to productive community building and policy development, and to advocate for and advance the mission of social work.

When professional programs have a clear articulated vision of the type of social worker they wish to develop, then curriculum frameworks and content can be designed in a manner that should ideally achieve this educational goal. For many helping professions throughout the twentieth century, curriculum design focused on input. Input refers to delineating the content and educational experiences that students must be exposed to. Educational programs identify the knowledge domains students are expected to master and the expected amounts of time needed, usually expressed as numbers of courses in a subject area and required hours for practicum attendance. For example, the previous Educational Policy and Accreditation Standards of the Council on Social Work Education (EPAS, 2004) expected students to master knowledge about social work values, ethical principles, and decision-making; diversity and difference; social context, social policy, and social justice; understanding the human condition; social work practice; and research methods. Based on the level of study, undergraduate or graduate, specific numbers of hours for practicum attendance are required to assist students to develop professional competence (EPAS, 2004). Inventories of knowledge and practice expectations reflect the dominant view of the particular profession at a point in time. As well, these descriptions provide an implicit view of the nature of professional practice; in this instance, that acquiring a body of knowledge will lead to the capacity or capability to effectively practice as a social worker. This is akin to what has been described as a technical-rational approach to professional practice (Cheetham & Chivers, 2005; Schon, 1983), reviewed in the previous chapter. It is a view of professional practice as applied theory: professionals use the knowledge base of their profession, including theory, specialist, and technical knowledge, to understand and intervene in the situations they confront.

In recent years competency-based education has been adopted in many fields, especially health and human service professions, including medicine (Carraccio, Wolfsthal, Englander, Ferentz, & Martin, 2002; Epstein & Hundert, 2002) and psychology (Kaslow et al., 2004). In social work, the Council on Social Work Education approved the 2008 Educational Policy and Accreditation Standards (EPAS, 2008) and described it as a competency-based outcome performance model. The shift to competency models in professions is driven by a number of socio-political factors such as the increasing expectations for accountability to the public and to funding bodies, the need to communicate to legislators what particular professions can do (especially if they wish to attract public funding and support), and the desire to facilitate the movement of professionals between jurisdictions and internationally.

Competency-based education shifts focus from input, such as curriculum structure and process, to output or outcomes, expressed as student performance. The outcomes detail what students should be able to do when they complete the program and begin their professional careers. While mastery of knowledge is certainly valued, it is incorporated in the definitions of competence as it should be evident in practice or in conceptualizations of and decisions for intervention. These two curriculum paradigms differ, and educators in many disciplines do not agree about the optimum balance between focusing on knowledge and focusing on competence.

Competency-based education emanates from a framework or blueprint which begins with the program articulating its goals and objectives. Curriculum is then designed to include the content students must master to meet the educational objectives. Learning and teaching strategies and activities are constructed to provide educational opportunities for students to learn to meet those goals. Competencies can be articulated at various levels of abstraction, from concrete atomistic skills to more complex sets of practice behaviours based on students' integration of knowledge, skills, attitudes, or values. Competencies are the educational or performance outcomes expected of students who complete the program. A program will then need to develop evaluation approaches to assess whether students have achieved the specified outcomes.

In a competency model competencies are evaluated based on a number of methods, with emphasis given to directly observable aspects of performance. This requires specification of practice at a level that is not so broad as to render it difficult to evaluate, nor so specific and minute that descriptors no longer reflect authentic practice. Challenges to assessment will be discussed further in this book, in the chapter on evaluation of competence. In a competency-based education framework the content to be mastered must still be specified and taught systematically through courses, special seminars or lectures, in field assignments, and in any other educational activity where faculty members believe students could gain valuable knowledge.

Competency Models in Social Work

As early as the mid-seventies, social work educators became interested in competency-based education as a unifying framework for curriculum planning and student performance evaluation, which would encompass both class and field. Proponents of the competency-based model encouraged educators to identify relevant educational outcomes, to define these outcomes as specific behaviours, to describe indicators that reflect increasing levels of performance, and to create methods of evaluation to ensure that students demonstrated these behaviours at the appropriate level (Arkava & Brennan, 1976; Baer & Frederico, 1978; Clark & Arkava, 1979; Gross, 1981). Entire competency-based programs were designed and provided, largely in undergraduate social work programs (Boitel, 2002). In graduate programs, many schools adopted a competency approach to define educational objectives or outcomes for the field practicum, although university-based courses continued to be designed and evaluated in traditional ways. The hope for field educators was that the broad, vague, and ill-defined goals and accompanying evaluation narratives characteristic of field assessment would be replaced with specific, rigorous, outcome expectations. Clear learning objectives would assist field instructors to assess student learning in an objective manner.

Evaluation was a recurrent challenge to field educators, as evident in two Delphi studies of field experts conducted two decades apart. The panel of field specialists identified the most crucial issue for field education, as the difficulty in achieving agreement on field learning goals and developing objective evaluation approaches (Raskin, 1983, 1994). Despite the initial enthusiasm about competency-based education and the adoption of this framework for field education in many schools, until recently there has been limited progress in articulating agreed upon competencies at a national level and developing effective evaluation measures in North American schools of social work.

In Canada, national organizations have been unable to achieve consensus about standards for the social work profession (Beals, 2003) despite recommendations of an extensive national study on social work. Conducted at the beginning of the twenty-first century, this study highlighted the need for social work to identify competencies at each degree or diploma level so as to better inform the public about the profession, how it serves the community, and what it achieves. National competencies would also facilitate labour mobility across provinces through mutual recognition of standards for professionals, as has occurred in the European Union (Stephanson, Rondeau, Michaud, & Fiddler, 2001; Westhues, 2002). Critics of this recommendation feared that defining national competencies would enable state control over social work activity. They perceived the process of defining competence as a behavioural and reductionistic approach, and feared that this would result in the deskilling of the profession, undermine an emphasis on critical and reflective skills, and weaken the role played by the Canadian Association of Schools of Social Work accreditation standards and review procedures (Rossiter, 2002).

In 2004 the Council on Social Work Education in the United States began to draft a new version of the Educational Policy for use by the Commission on Accreditation in revising the Accreditation Standards. The Commission on Curriculum and Educational Innovation declared a number of working principles (COCEI, 2007). Relevant to this discussion of competency are the following principles. The primacy of practice is underscored through the emphasis in the curriculum on preparing for the *practice* of social work. A competency-based outcome

approach to curriculum design is used, as it provides a vehicle to identify the essentials of professional social work practice. A set of competencies are articulated and programs can decide the content and design
of the curriculum they will offer so that students will achieve these
nationally recognized competencies. Field education's crucial role in
socializing students to the role of social work is recognized along with
a commitment to elevate the place of field education. Consistent with
the emphasis on student outcomes in competency-based education,
promoting accountability through assessment of student competence
is another principle. This approach was adopted, and forms the basis
of the current Educational Policy and Accreditation Standards (EPAS,
2008). The specific competencies will be discussed later in this chapter.

When developing a competency-based educational approach,
accrediting bodies and professional educators must address two broad
questions: (1) What is the prevailing conceptualization of professional
competence and how can this view be defined as educational outcomes? and (2) What processes and methods to assess students' competence will yield authentic, reliable, and valid results? This chapter
will discuss the first question, and evaluation of competence will be
addressed in chapters 8 and 9, on evaluation of student performance.

Conceptualizing Competence

There are many definitions of professional competence, all of which
refer to a set of knowledge, skills, and attitudes or values that are
evident in the *behaviour* of professionals as they perform in the domains
associated with their profession. Some have suggested that a competency-based approach to education and evaluation is less a theory of
professional practice and more a method of establishing national occupational standards that guide the production of a skilled and competi-
tive workforce (Hackett, 2001; Skinner & Whyte, 2004). Theoretically,
the prevailing view of competence as behaviours evident in a practice
reflects a positivist, behaviourist concept or managerial position, and
has been critiqued by educators especially in countries such as the
United Kingdom and Australia, where competency approaches were
developed through central government national initiatives (Eraut,
2004). Social work scholars who have reviewed these experiences argue
that competency-based education is mechanistic, devoid of context,
and loses sight of the holistic nature of practice (Kelly & Horder, 2001;
Skinner & Whyte, 2004). Qualities of professionalism, such as the way

in which problems are understood and framed (Eraut, 1994) and the way in which judgment is exercised (Kane, 1992), are not well captured. Educators argue persuasively that judgment and the ability to decide when and how to precede in particular contexts and situations is a hallmark of effective professionals. Professionals work in complex contemporary environments where they face multi-faceted, complicated situations, and there is uncertainty regarding the best approaches or interventions. Therefore, judgment and professionalism are crucial capacities which may not be well articulated in competency models (Fraser & Greenhalgh, 2001; Schon, 1983, 1987).

Reviewing competence approaches for a range of professions, Cheetham and Chivers (2005) critique the overreliance on 'directly observable aspects of competence, perhaps to the neglect of cognitive processes' (p. 64) and knowledge competencies needed to practice. Similarly, for more complex professions such as social work, competence models do not attempt to define and assess the cognitive or reasoning processes that lie behind professionals' understanding of a situation and choice of interventions (Hyland, 1995).

Parallel concerns regarding the reductionist nature of competency-based education are present in medical education, where it is argued that undue emphasis on procedures runs the risk of negating a deep and reflective engagement with a professional practicum (Leung, 2002; Talbot, 2004). Proponents of postmodern perspectives argue that a more reflective view of practice recognizes multi-perspectives and the importance of intellectual understanding and emotional awareness, as well as skilful behaviour (Ruch, 2002).

Professions in the United States, however, have recently developed more complex definitions of competence that incorporate these higher-order capabilities. For example, the American Association for Graduate Medical Education has developed generic competencies for all medical specialists that include integrative aspects of care, patient-centred relationships, and affective and moral dimensions of practice (Epstein & Hundert, 2002). Six general competencies comprise the framework, which consists of patient care, medical knowledge, practice-based learning and improvement, interpersonal and communication skills, professionalism, and systems-based practice. Recent initiatives of the American Psychological Association for defining competency for clinical psychologists include intellectual, adaptive, and creative capacities (Kaslow et al., 2004). In social work, a competency based approach has been used to define outcomes for students for geriatric social work

(Damron-Rodriguez, Lawrance, Barnett, & Simmons, 2006). Generic competencies have been proposed for all social work graduates by Bogo, Regehr, Woodford, and colleagues (2006) and a similar set of abilities by Gingerich, Kaye, and Bailey (1999); in both models competencies are presented at a level which is not so abstract as to be vague and nebulous, nor so concrete as to be mechanistic.

Implicit in debates about the strengths and weaknesses of a competency approach are the underlying views or constructions of professional practice. In other words, how we define competence reflects the way in which we conceive of a professional practice. An enduring theme in social work has been that social work is both science and art; it involves both intentional use of knowledge, procedures, and techniques, and use of self. The latter term originally emanated from attention to the personality style of the worker and the way in which internal dynamics affected interactions with clients (Brandell, 2004). In contemporary usage the term can incorporate a wider range of factors, including social identity characteristics such as social location, cultural and ethnic group reference, sexual orientation, and so on. Less attention has been given to the way in which the professional's ways of thinking or habits of mind (Epstein & Hundert, 2002) affect the way practice situations are framed and understood. Since our internal constructions of problems presented by individual clients, families, and communities are significantly influenced by multiple factors, dimensions such as critical thinking, reflection, and judgment are essential components of professional competence. And yet, they are not directly evident in observing professionals' practice. To capture the notion of competence in a meaningful manner, both external, observable practice behaviours and skills and internal cognitive processes need to be taken into account.

The definition of competence offered by Kane (1992) is similar to this perspective. Competence is defined as 'the degree to which the individual can use the knowledge, skills, and judgment associated with the profession to perform effectively in the domain of possible encounters defining the scope of professional practice' (p. 166). In this definition the concept of competence unquestionably involves *performance ability* across the range of situations relevant to the scope of practice, and also the *judgment* needed to combine knowledge and skills into effective solutions to particular client problems. For the definition to be useful in social work, attitudes or values would also be added to knowledge and skill. This formulation can incorporate adaptive and creative capabilities that are needed to work in contemporary practice environments (Fraser & Greenhalgh, 2001), capabilities such as 'habits of mind that allow the practitioner to be attentive, curious, self-aware, and willing to recognize and correct errors' (Epstein & Hundert, 2002, p.228). The latter writers note, however, that these characteristics are especially difficult to objectify and hence to evaluate.

It is important to bear in mind that competence is not the same as expert status, which signifies skills attained after years of experience by those who master their fields (Yager & Kay, 2003). Competence signifies some degree of familiarity, achievement, and proficiency, perhaps in the range of 'good enough.' The question for the profession then becomes, What constitutes 'good enough,' and how it can be defined?

Defining Competence in Social Work

A number of approaches have been used to define competencies which involve, to varying extents, using the existing professional and empirical literature and seeking consensus from experts. These projects vary from small local efforts to large-scale, national initiatives. With the growing emphasis in social work on evidence-based practice, it is likely that future efforts will include competencies demonstrated to be associated with effective outcomes for clients.

An example of a small-scale approach is described by Vourlekis and colleagues (Vourlekis, Bambry, Hall, & Rosenblum, 1996). A small working group of expert field instructors worked with Wilson (1981) to generate a checklist of specific characteristics which differentiate beginning students from advanced students. Vourlekis and colleagues (1996) tested the reliability and the content, concurrent and predictive validity of a subset of the checklist – 26 specific interviewing skills with descriptors on a scale that ranges from beginning to advanced skill levels. While these researchers established sound psychometric properties in their scale, the focus solely on interviewing skills ignores other dimensions of practice such as relationship, assessment, and intervention. This small-scale project demonstrates that educators can define general components of practice, such as interviewing skills, in a specific manner, and measure students' acquisition of skills. However, it is an example of the atomistic approach of competency models, which assumes that high scores on one dimension, in this instance interviewing skills, is likely associated with effectiveness in holistic and integrated social work practice.

A commonly used approach to identifying competence is to survey experts and develop a consensus view of what constitutes effective practice. In this approach, practitioners, educators, agency administrators, and, in some cases, clients are surveyed to elicit their perceptions. Delphi methodology can be used to involve larger numbers of participants, who contribute to developing and then ranking a list of necessary competencies in a specific field of practice. A series of rounds are conducted through paper and pencil responses that may be supplemented with individual interviews or focus groups. Numerous examples of this approach exist in social work, and an instance of its success is provided by the California Social Work Education Center (CalSWEC). Clark (2003) describes the process the center used to develop a set of competencies for social workers in child welfare. The initiative involved a consortium of 12 schools of social work with graduate programs and 58 county-level public social service departments. A Delphi method was used to develop and refine a list of child welfare competencies deemed essential and possible to teach, or provide experience for students prior to graduation (Clark, 2003). Participants also identified opportunities for and barriers to the implementation of a curriculum to achieve these competencies in their respective organizations and developed recommendations for solutions. Competencies were refined through consultation with faculty members, practitioners, and those with leadership roles in both organizations (deans and field work directors in the schools, and managers and department heads in the public service agencies). A competency list organized into six categories was generated: multicultural and ethnic sensitive practice, core child welfare skills, social work skills and methods, human development and behaviour, workplace management, and child welfare administration, planning, and evaluation. A similar initiative is described by Drake (1994), who also included clients in the study.

An impressive project in social work is Strengthening Aging and Gerontological Education in Social Work, supported by the Hartford Foundation through the Council on Social Work Education (CSWE/SAGE-SW). This project aims to increase the ability of social work to practice with the aging population and their families. A competency framework for the Practicum Partnership Program of the project has been developed in conjunction with the New York Academy of Medicine, Social Work Leadership Institute. Initial work on defining competencies for practice with older persons began with a literature review and consultation with national experts, and a survey of 945 practitioners and faculty, leading to the CSWE/SAGE-SW professional competencies for social work practice in aging (Rosen, Zlotnik, Curl, & Green, 2000). The Geriatric Social Work Education Consortium (GSWEC), one of the Hartford Practicum Partnership Programs (PPP), conducted focus groups of employers and recent social work graduates in the field of aging, older persons, and their caregivers. Focusing on practice with the aging as a specialization, this project drew from the SAGE-SW competencies as well, to develop and subsequently refine a Geriatric Social Work Competency Scale (GSWCS) (Damron-Rodriguez et al., 2006). The scale consists of four domains: values, ethics, and theoretical perspectives; assessment; intervention; and aging services, programs, and policies. Within each domain there are 10 dimensions of competence expressed as skill subsets, resulting in a manageable 40-item scale. Recently, the competencies were expanded to incorporate practice behaviours associated with community, management, and leadership roles. (The competency scales can be found at http://www.socialworkleadership.org/nsw/.)

The Educational Policy and Accreditation Standards of the Council on Social Work Education, United States (EPAS, 2008) adopts a competency-based framework. The document refers to competency-based education as 'an outcome performance approach to curriculum design. Competencies are measurable practice behaviors that are comprised of knowledge, values, and skills. The goal of the outcome approach is to demonstrate the integration and application of the competencies in practice with individuals, families, groups, organizations, and communities' (p. 3). Ten core competencies for social work practice are identified, with further explanations and an elaboration of each. The competencies are: identify as a professional social worker and conduct oneself accordingly; apply social work ethical principles to guide professional practice; apply critical thinking to inform and communicate professional judgments; engage diversity and difference in practice; advance human rights and social and economic justice; engage in research-informed practice and practice-informed research; apply knowledge of human behaviour and the social environment; engage in policy practice to advance social and economic well-being, and to deliver effective social work services; respond to contexts that shape practice; engage, assess, intervene, and evaluate with individuals, families, groups, organizations, and communities (EPAS, 2008). These core competencies are expected of graduates of both undergraduate and graduate programs. Advanced practice competencies for graduates of master's of social work (MSW) programs are to be identified specific to the concentration.

In common with related human service professional programs, the national and regional examples described above demonstrate that social work professionals and educators can arrive at consensus about competencies for specialized practice and for particular dimensions of practice. These competency models are then used as a framework for curriculum planning and ultimately for more effective and authentic evaluation approaches. The critiques arising from others' experiences in using similar frameworks are noteworthy and instructive as programs move forward to implement competency-based education.

Further Thoughts on Competency in Social Work

Educators at the University of Toronto developed a comprehensive and detailed competency model in the late seventies as part of the initial enthusiasm about this approach in social work education. This competency model was used for all students in a MSW program. Competencies were articulated in six domains: Practice in a Professional Context; Practice in an Organizational Context; Practice in a Community Context; Assessment; Intervention; and Evaluation of Practice. Each domain was then defined in greater detail with the identification of numerous behavioural skills which would give evidence of that competency. Two major critiques arose from the field instructors who used this model. One critique related to the vast number of behavioural skills used to describe each competency and to evaluate student performance. Through the years, as feedback was received from field instructors, skills were added to reflect changes in practice. For example, numerous detailed skills were added related to cross-cultural and anti-oppressive practice. Interviewing skills, written and verbal presentations, and communication skills were also added to further concretize the model. Eventually students and field instructors were confronted with ever-growing lists of behaviours.

A second critique related to challenges in evaluation, particularly the lack of reliability in the use of the competency inventory with graduating students; it did not identify students in difficulty in the final year of the program. Evaluation issues will be discussed further in this text. However, these issues contributed to a growing concern that the competency model, rather than assisting in clarifying field teaching and learning, was not representing social work practice and the objectives of field education in a way that was authentic for practitioners and field instructors.

As a result, a several-year program of research was undertaken in an attempt to better conceptualize social work practice competence and to develop reliable and valid methods to evaluate competence. A full description of the project, the findings, and the new tools developed can be found in journal publications (Bogo, Regehr, Hughes, Power, & Globerman, 2002; Bogo, Regehr et al., 2004; Bogo et al., 2007, Regehr et al., 2007), and on the website of the Factor-Inwentash Faculty of Social Work, University of Toronto, Research Institute for Evidence-based Practice, Competency for Professional Practice Initiative (see http://www.socialwork.utoronto.ca/research/intiatives/competency .htm). Through a series of studies, a complex view of the dimensions of social work practice that expert field instructors use to describe and assess professional competence of students in direct practice emerged. Currently the study is being repeated with field instructors in mezzo and macro practice in community, administration, and policy development practicum sites.

In-depth interviews were conducted with 19 expert field instructors who were engaged in direct practice in child welfare, mental health, and general hospital settings (see Appendix B). The aim of the interviews was to elicit their depictions of a range of students they had supervised: exemplary students, average students, and students with problematic behaviours. All instructors were asked the same questions about how they described competency in social work students. Probing questions were used to obtain concrete examples of student behaviours and interactions in practice, in the setting, and with the field instructor. Following the transcriptions of these interviews, grounded theory research methodology was used by the research team to conduct content and thematic analysis of the data. To assess the transferability of the findings, emerging results were presented to groups of field instructors and to participants in following studies, and to field coordinators, researchers, and faculty at international conferences. These audiences affirmed that these descriptions of competence resonated with their views confirming that the way the field instructors in this sample described levels of student competence was more than a local phenomenon.

Of enormous interest was that a constellation of students' *personal qualities* was perceived as crucial to competent social work practice

(Bogo, Regehr, Woodford et al., 2006). These qualities affected students' ability to learn to become social workers, and included such dimensions as motivation, self-direction, and independence; energy and initiative; commitment; interpersonal ability; and responsiveness to others, including clients, staff, and the field instructor. Field instructors' examples of behaviours related to these personal qualities were not presented as examples of competencies that others might achieve; rather, they were examples of special personal qualities. For example, an exemplary student was described as 'being highly motivated ... going beyond the expectations of the practicum' (p. 583). The behavioural evidence of this quality was taking risks in meetings, producing a resource pamphlet, developing a committee to review a policy on reporting abuse. Conversely, characteristics in students described as problematic included being ill at ease and passive, defensive, judgmental, cynical, or lacking empathy. These negative qualities were evident in the way they performed in the setting. For example, a student described as shy and easily intimidated was poor when presenting client needs at team meetings, infrequently initiated contact with clients, or gave superficial information about the client in field instruction sessions. In the research interviews, field instructors spontaneously spoke about a wide range of student qualities. When the research interviewer probed for specific student behaviours, the field instructors were able to provide these. However, the key point they were making was that behaviours were only examples of more pervasive dimensions, dimensions that affect a wide range of performance competencies. While competency models direct educators and field instructors to focus on behaviours or performance, these behaviours or skills may in fact only be the surface representation of more fundamental and core characteristics of students, characteristics that affect their ability to learn and perform as competent and effective social workers.

This finding is similar to emerging views of competence in related human service fields. For example, personal qualities are referred to as personal intelligences of graduate medical residents by Harden and colleagues (Harden, Crosby, Davis, & Friedman, 1999), and as personal competencies (personality characteristics, intellectual and personal skills) for professional psychology graduate students (Hatcher & Lassiter, 2007).

The way in which students approached *learning* was connected to this view of the importance of personal qualities. Again, displaying initiative was valued. As learners, these students were described as not only wanting to master skills, but also to understand the concepts that provide a rationale for the choice of particular interventions. These students were embarked on creating their own integration of theory and practice through drawing together an approach consisting of knowledge and skill, which 'made sense in a personal way' (Bogo, Regehr, Woodford et al., 2006, p. 585). They were seen as 'good learners ... bright, quick, thoughtful' (p. 585), which facilitated their quick acquisition of new material. Adaptable and flexible, they recognized situations that were novel or complex and did not respond easily to the practice approaches they had already mastered. They took initiative to seek out and learn different approaches through searching the literature, talking to staff members, and consulting with field instructors. These characteristics are described by Schon (1983) in his discussion of reflective practitioners. In contrast were students who were neither self-directed nor highly engaged in learning. The latter students were described as approaching learning in a passive manner, expecting to be taught, and not willing to take risks. Many students were described as 'putting in time' (Bogo, Regehr, Woodford et al., 2006, p. 584) so that they would complete program requirements, get a degree, and look for a job. Between these two ends of the continuum are students who are more reliant on the field instructor to identify their learning needs and ways of meeting them. For some students, as they develop their skills and more confidence in general, they become less dependent on the field instructor.

An important part of learning is the way in which students react to feedback. Students range in their ability to seek it out and use it. Excellent learners were open to feedback and used it in the next interaction with clients. They sought out input about their performance, actively discussed the suggestions field instructors' offered, and examined different ways of intervening. In contrast were students who were unreceptive to input about their interventions, reacted defensively or argumentatively, or experienced constructive feedback in a personal way, feeling depreciated, humiliated, or misunderstood.

Social work practice takes place in organizational and team contexts, and many interventions are based on practitioners' ability to form relationships with a range of personnel and to build alliances, so that advocacy for clients may be successful and new programs and policies can be introduced. Field instructors are conscious of the way the social work role is perceived in their setting and that students can influence others' perceptions. The strongest students were, almost intuitively, able to understand the importance of context, and sensitively and appropriately learned the role of social worker in that setting and ways to carry it out effectively as a student. These students were described as good team players, able to hear the perspectives of others, and able to challenge other team members in a manner that was respectful while still conveying a different opinion. Students on the continuum between exemplary and demonstrating problematic behaviours were those who could understand and carry out the basic procedures associated with the role. Due to feeling intimidated by other team members or unsure of their knowledge and skill, they presented themselves as beginners and were somewhat daunted by other team members. Students with problematic behaviours were not able to engage appropriately with the team. Some missed cues about what was expected and were demanding of team members' time. Others did not engage well with the team, as they were overly confrontational or rigid in arguing for their opinions. Working within a formal organization with rules, procedures, and a hierarchy was experienced in a thoroughly negative way.

Field instructors placed great importance on students' ability to *conceptualize their practice* and identify the values, principles, and ideas that underlie their judgments and actions. This dimension comprised students' understanding of what professional social work was about, and was connected to their ability to use a theoretical framework(s) or concepts to guide all aspects of their practice with clients and interactions in the setting. This element included the ability to see the interrelationships between theory and practice and demonstrate analytic ability and critical thinking. The ability to conceptualize practice seemed to provide the foundation for students to learn a broad range of practice behaviours and know-how, and when to use them differentially based on a broader understanding of the context. Study participants suggested that this ability served as the overarching framework within which the procedural or operational skills, such as assessment, intervention, and written and oral presentations, were developed. Conversely, students who have difficulty understanding the role and the way in which knowledge informs practice appeared to perform in a technical or concrete manner. There was difficulty generalizing learning from one practice situation to another. Instructors observed that assessments had no direction and interventions were 'thrown out' (Bogo, Regehr, Woodford et al., 2006, p. 585). Without an intellectual understanding of the knowledge and value base of social work ethical and boundary issues, working with diverse populations and differential use of self were confusing for these students. Many students struggle with the ways in which concepts are integrated in practice and fall along the mid-range of this continuum. They can learn through their field instruction sessions to examine practice in a critical and reflective manner, to use more than one framework, and to think through practice situations from a variety of perspectives. In the field instructor interviews in this study, the ability to conceptualize practice appeared as an overarching or super-competency that affected the ability to use the procedural skills of assessment and intervention.

Another overarching competency was the student's *relational* abilities. Relational abilities were viewed as related to the qualities discussed above, and influenced students' relationships with team members and the field instructor, as reviewed above, and also with clients. Instructors commented on students' ability to connect, support, and collaborate with clients while also being able to confront, challenge, and set boundaries. These students' were able to empathize with both voluntary and involuntary clients and were not negatively reactive to involuntary clients, understanding their reluctance to engage with the student social worker. Conversely, relationship issues were of great concern for students considered to be demonstrating problematic behaviours. Ethical and boundary issues arose with over-identification due to students' own personal history or current concerns. Behaviour that was too casual or 'too free with hugs' (Bogo, Regehr, Woodford et al., 2006, p. 586) was highlighted. There were other students who could not connect or engage with clients. While field instructors believed this difficulty was related to anxiety, when there was no improvement over the course of the practicum the students were seen as not ready to become social workers.

These findings about the overall importance of competencies such as approach to learning, ability to conceptualize, and capacity for relationships lend support to the importance of *meta-competencies* as proposed in the literatures of the fields of management (Fleming, 1991; Hall, 1986), medicine (Harden et al., 1999; Talbot, 2004), professional psychology (Weinert, 2001), and professional competence in general (Cheetham & Chivers, 1996, 1998, 2005). Meta-competencies may be common across a range of professions, especially the helping professions. They may affect students' ability to learn the specific role competencies of particular professions. The notion of meta-competencies refers to higher-order, overarching abilities and qualities that are of a different order and nature than procedural or operational behaviours and skills. Meta-competencies may be related to individuals' ability to use these discrete behaviours in a purposeful, integrated, and professional manner. The term 'meta-competencies' has been used to refer to mental agility and creativity (Reynolds & Snell, 1988); problem-solving and analytic capacities (Cheetham & Chivers, 1996); and interpersonal communication, self-awareness, and self-development (Hatcher & Lassiter, 2007; Talbot, 2004). Harden and colleagues (1999) suggest that meta-competencies such as the ability to integrate theory, ethics, and emotional intelligence into clinical reasoning and judgment operate through the performance of basic competencies. Weinert (2001) suggests that the development of meta-competencies depends on self-awareness, self-reflection, and self-assessment.

In a series of conceptual and empirical studies, Cheetham and Chivers (1996, 1998, 2005) describe their analysis of existing conceptualizations of professional competence and the activities they undertook to test and revise a professional competence model that cuts across a wide range of professions. They characterize the meta-competencies discussed above as linked and overarching. They define meta-competency as 'a competency that is beyond other competencies, and which enables individuals to monitor and/or develop other competencies' (2005, p. 109). They refer to the capacity and process whereby individuals 'step outside of their own performance, to analyse the competencies they are applying and then modify or develop them further' (p. 109). The similarity with Schon's concept of reflection-in-action is made. The term trans-competency is used and defined as: 'a competency that spans other competencies, enhancing or mediating them' (p. 109). Recognizing the unique and important position of reflection, they term it a 'super-metacompetency.'

Based on the findings from the Toronto study, we concluded that not all competencies are equivalent and that there is a hierarchy of competencies. Meta-competencies are seen as of a first order and procedural competencies of a second order. These two levels operate in concert; first-order competencies enable mastery and performance of second-order competencies. The first-order abilities and qualities appear to involve three interrelated domains: (1) cognitive/conceptual, (2) interpersonal/relational, and (3) personal/professional. Cognitive or conceptual meta-competencies refer to problem solving, critical thinking, and analytic capabilities as well as mental agility and creativity. Professional judgment may be part of this cluster, and connected to an appreciation of the holistic nature of practice, including the self of the practitioner. Interpersonal and relational competencies refer to emotional and social intelligence, the ability to read social situations and respond effectively. These abilities are seen in professionals' communication styles. Personal and professional competencies refer to a cluster of abilities such as an individual's ability to reflect on practice and achieve self-awareness, which contributes to one's ability to self-assess, to know when consultation is needed, and to establish goals for continuing professional development. This cluster can be thought of as performing an organizing function, enabling individuals to use skills in a flexible manner, to transfer learning from one problem to another, and to combine skills differentially based on the needs of the practice situation encountered.

Second-order competencies refer to the procedural, operational, or clinical aspects of practice. This includes *assessment*, *intervention*, and professional *communication*. Generic competency inventories generally list common and broad components associated with *assessment*: for example, the ability to collect and organize relevant data from primary and/or secondary sources, and the ability to define the problem from the perspective of all involved. Competency inventories for special areas of practice list specific skills needed: for example, the Hartford Geriatric Social Work Competency Scale II includes the ability to assess the cognitive functioning and mental health status of older clients, caregivers' needs and levels of stress, and so on. Similarly, with respect to *intervention*, competency inventories may express general skills such as the ability to draw connections between cognitive, behavioural, and affective aspects of a problem, and to seek and use feedback from the client about progress. For specialized areas of practice, competencies are more specific: for example, with the elderly, use educational strategies to provide older persons and their families with information related to wellness and disease management; with child welfare, demonstrate cultural understanding and use of support, and be able to deal with non-voluntary and hostile clients. *Communication* competencies include written skills that are needed to document information about the practice situation, plan, and progress in intervention. Oral presentation skills refer to the ability to convey to team members and colleagues in other settings pertinent aspects of the practice situation.

Ethics and values did not appear as a separate domain in the research interviews; rather, they were discussed in relation to conceptualizing practice, that is, as part of understanding and thinking through client situations and possible interventions. Scholars concerned with professional competence have noted the importance of building ethics into competency models, and the sets of values which enable professionals to make ethical decisions. For example, Eraut (1994) identifies four interrelated sets of values: (1) legal values and those related to mandatory systems, (2) professional values with respect to appropriate behaviour and relationships with clients, (3) organizational values about relationships with others in the organization and the public, and (4) personal values and beliefs. Following the recommendation of Cheetham and Chivers (1996), the ability to make sound ethical decisions should be a part of any competency model.

As noted earlier, the field instructor respondents put a significant emphasis on students' ability to conceptualize practice using theories and approaches consistent with social work in their setting. In this instance they were referring to knowledge competence but not producing lists of concepts or principles expected of students. For educators who wish to develop competency models, since a body of concepts is crucial to practice, it would be important to define the specific bodies of knowledge needed for generic practice and for specializations.

Implications for Social Work Educators

The competency model developed by a profession, a school of social work, or an organization demonstrates the components considered important for effective performance. It reflects a value and belief stance about what is needed to achieve positive outcomes for the clients and communities served by the profession at a particular point in time. To the extent that a competency model is developed by local, rather than national, groups it will indicate the priorities and concerns of a particular context. Hence, the articulated competency model is a product of social, political, and economic forces faced by educators and practitioners who have developed the model.

A conceptual framework for delineating a competency model for social work will include a number of interrelated elements. Elements are defined at varying levels, from general, abstract, or global to specific, concrete, or partial. There is considerable difference in the way competency models are articulated, both between and within professions. Frameworks vary between countries and between specializations; again, highlighting that context is an important consideration when thinking about this construct.

While competency models purport to describe knowledge, atti-

Table 3.1 Meta-competencies

Cognitive/conceptual competence related to a knowledge base, including the ability to conceptualize practice	Interpersonal and relational competence with clients and members of the organization	Personal/professional qualities related to learning and performing in an organization and in a professional role	Ethics and values related to the profession
Procedural Competencies			
Assessment			
Intervention			
Communication and Presentation			

tudes, and skills, based on critiques of this approach and empirical findings, broader concepts of competence may come closer to the lived experience of practitioners. A framework for conceptualizing competence is proposed in the diagram above. Local curriculum developers will find ways of expressing these elements and determining what level of abstraction or specificity is meaningful. This framework of professional competence in social work provides categories or elements which social work educators and practitioners may use as they define the way in which these global dimensions are understood in their specialized or advanced field of practice (see Table 3.1).

The elements recommended fall under two categories: (1) meta-competencies; and (2) procedural, technical, or clinical competencies. The first category – meta-competencies – appears important across human service professions and has enabled competency models to incorporate integrative dimensions critical for practice in complex contemporary environments. Meta-competencies consist of cognitive competence related to professional knowledge, relational competence with clients and colleagues, personal and professional competence evident in qualities that facilitate practice in an organizational context, and ethics and values. The second category procedural, technical, or clinical competencies may be articulated at two levels: generic to the profession, and specific to specializations within the profession. This element is most likely to be broken into its component parts, into smaller and smaller units of analysis. These units can be used to review curriculum and practicum learning opportunities and to ensure that students have strong educational experiences and opportunities to master these competencies. These competencies can also be described as learning objectives, and can form the basis for evaluation of field practicum learning. However, if competency frameworks rely primarily on this level of conceptualization, they become mechanistic and unwieldy.

Conclusion

In summary, educators, researchers, and professional leaders across a number of disciplines are developing a more textured and complex understanding of professional competency. They are aiming to develop competency models which incorporate higher-order meta-competencies that include cognitive/conceptual, interpersonal, and personal/professional qualities. These meta-competencies are reflected in performance behaviours of basic, core, or procedural competencies. This integration involves a view of competence that certainly includes an individual's ability to do or perform. The performance, stance, or activity reflects the student's or practitioner's capacity to use or transfer knowledge, skills, attitudes, and values into action. Transfer is mediated by a reflective, intuitive, less well-understood process in which the practitioner uses meta-competencies such as integrative thinking to analyse and individualize the situation and arrive at the possibilities for action. The challenge for evaluation of student competence is to develop processes and methods that effectively capture these various dimensions of competence.

4 Perspectives on Student Learning

Social work students enter professional education programs with the goal of becoming effective practitioners. Both undergraduate and graduate students choose professional programs to prepare for a career and are generally highly motivated to learn the knowledge and skills required to gain employment upon graduation. There are other pathways to becoming a social worker, as social work agencies frequently employ individuals who do not have social work degrees. In order to progress in their careers and to formally and systematically learn social work knowledge, these individuals enter social work educational programs, often in part-time studies. Social work students also include individuals who are changing careers, having found their initial careers unfulfilling or wanting to redirect their employment paths at mid-life. Therefore, the choice to become a social work student is a highly personal choice as it is directly connected to an important aspect of life, one's career. Adult learning theories, discussed later in this chapter, provide useful concepts for understanding the perspective students bring to their educational experiences and the implications for constructing effective learning environments for these various types of students.

Educational programs provide numerous components designed to provide a comprehensive curriculum to prepare graduates for practice, including academic courses and the field practicum. In academic courses students are exposed to a range of theories, research methodologies, substantive content about issues relevant to social work, and numerous models of intervention for generalist practice; specialized practice with individuals, groups, families, communities, and organizations; and with particular populations. The value base of the profession, emphasizing respect for human dignity and the commitment to social justice, is a theme that runs through course offerings. Programs vary in the degree to which they provide opportunities for mastery of skills in university-based courses, and the degree to which this aspect of social work is left solely to the practicum. The concept of professional use of self is likely discussed in courses. It is in the field practicum, however, where students are most likely to experience, engage, and struggle with this fundamental and challenging practice dynamic. Moreover, the greatest challenge in learning any professional practice involves bringing together the different components learned – knowledge, values, and skills – into some coherent whole. And in social work, this integration takes place through the personal-professional use of self. Both students and novice practitioners frequently express their need to become comfortable enough with what they have learned so that they can use their knowledge and skills to address the unique needs of individual practice situations in particular service settings. Again, learning to become a social worker engages the self of the student in a personally meaningful manner.

This chapter will provide a review of selected intertwined theoretical concepts and empirical findings related to the student as learner. The aim is to illuminate the experience of students and contribute to a broad understanding of the dynamics of learning in the field practicum. The focus is on understanding the student in an environment where new learning can have a profound effect on self-concept and self-esteem. In the next chapter this material and analysis will be used to examine teaching, including facilitative elements for productive learning environments and the role of the field instructor.

The Fundamental Challenge of Learning to Become a Competent Social Worker

Social work interventions are largely delivered through the medium of the practising social worker; knowledge, values, and skills are integrated with the personal self of the social worker (Bogo, 2006). Since practitioners bring their personal attributes and characteristics into their work, self-awareness about personal issues, social identity, and social location are considered necessary. Students receive a consistent message in courses and field settings – what they need to understand how these personal qualities and reactions exert an influence on social work processes. Processes include the way in which practitioners engage with clients, community members, and professionals from related disciplines; how they collect information and make judgments and assessments; and what they deem as important interventions, as well as preferred approaches to achieve goals.

Traditionally, self-awareness referred to knowledge about one's own personality, including feelings, thoughts, reactions, and meanings attributed to or influenced by events resulting from one's own personal and familial experiences. More recently, social identity characteristics and social location have enlarged this concept. Self-awareness now includes attention to cultural influences and the ways in which these values, assumptions, and world views serve as standards and norms which individuals may accept wholly or in part (Ho, 1995). Related is the recognition that in modern diverse societies, culture encompasses more than ethnicity, and refers to the numerous potential sources of identity by virtue of social characteristics such as race, class, gender, sexual orientation, ability, religious affiliation, immigration status, political association, and so on. These characteristics are also associated with views and experiences of privilege, power, deprivation, and oppression. A significant body of pedagogical literature in social work recognizes that the very nature of examining issues related to diversity and oppression can elicit strongly held opinions and intense emotions (Miller, Hyde, & Ruth, 2004; Mishna & Bogo, 2007; Phan et al., 2009; van Soest, Garcia, & Graff, 2001).

While developing increased self-understanding is seen as complex, it is also seen as important, since it will enable practitioners to become cognizant of the subtle and obvious feelings and thoughts evoked in practice. With understanding, practitioners are less likely to react in unexamined and potentially unhelpful ways. Rather, triggered by their internal experiences they can sort out what may be stimulating their own thoughts, feelings, and reactions: what contributions emanate from themselves in interaction with others; and what their responses are to the behaviours of clients, consumers, or colleagues. The goal of self-awareness is to facilitate responses that are intentional and purposeful in manner. Responses can be provided that will serve practice goals, rather than relying on immediate responses to phenomena, which may be experienced as anxiety-provoking, confusing, painful, or threatening.

In summary, students enter social work education motivated to learn how to become effective practitioners. Early on they begin to recognize that social work practice is not a straightforward and linear application of knowledge to practice. Rather, practice is a complex activity where a wide range of components are integrated: aspects of knowledge, skill, and interpersonal ability. The essence of practice involves the worker in collaborative interaction with others, where worker contributions are offered through the professional use of self. This emphasis on self highlights the importance of knowing about the multitude of views about human functioning and social problems one may bring to practice. These views can also elicit feelings in students about the way they see and feel about themselves in general, and in learning environments. Those feelings are likely evoked as they interact in the practicum with clients, staff, and the field instructor.

Adult Learning Theory

Adult learning theory provides a fitting set of concepts for greater understanding of the perspective on professional development presented thus far. This theory values adult students' experience and self-concept, views adult learners as active participants in educational activities, and focuses attention on how adults learn and the implications for the role of the teacher. Adult education theory supports a collaborative stance which draws on adults' views about themselves and their learning needs, as well as instructors' knowledge and experience. Since learning to practice as a social worker is so connected to the self of the student, these principles appear valuable.

The field of adult learning is vast, encompassing topics such as self-directed learning, transformational learning, and informal and incidental learning, with various related theories and models (Merriam, 2001). The greatest influence on social work education comes from the work of Malcolm Knowles, who proposed the term 'andragogy' – helping adults learn – in contrast to 'pedagogy' – helping children learn (Knowles, 1972, 1980; Knowles, Halston, & Swanson, 2005). Some selected assumptions about adult learning proposed by Knowles are presented in the following discussion. There have been critiques of these assumptions; however, their endurance over time suggests their usefulness for understanding how adult social work students approach the field practicum. The assumptions also provide some guidance for field instruction.

Self-concept

The first assumption is that adults have an organized sense of self, a self-concept. Through one's life course adults develop their self-concept, consisting of assumptions, beliefs, and a world view, as a result of an array of characteristics and identities. Included in one's self-concept are feelings about oneself or self-esteem in relation to others and to some ideal. When individuals approach situations that require new learning, such as in social work practice, they may have conflicting feelings. On the one hand, given their career choice they are highly motivated to learn what is needed; on the other, they may experience a threat to their self-confidence. In the field setting students are likely confronted with significant client, community, and social problems. As well, they may begin to recognize what they do not know and need to learn in order to offer some effective service, intervention, or program.

Students are exposed to and learn about theoretical concepts, practice models and techniques, and relevant empirical findings. Despite the mastery of such intellectual content, this knowledge does not easily transfer into actions in practice. A more complex view of professional practice has been proposed for helping professions such as social work (Schon, 1983), a perspective that recognizes that any one theory can only provide a limited lens for understanding, and any one model only limited guides for intervention. Ultimately, students will need to learn how to use a reflective process to individualize practice situations and sift through the various theories and models they have learned to select some that might guide them. Perhaps the greatest challenge for learners in social work is the lack of a precise knowledge base and the need to tolerate the ambiguity and uncertainty characteristic of this type of work.

As students begin to recognize these complexities and difficulties in learning how to practice, they become aware of 'not knowing.' A range of feelings are activated, including feeling incompetent. A paradox in field learning is that the student is expected to provide a service, 'deal with unfamiliar situations, utilize creativity in selecting interventions and determine optimal direction for clients. Indeed, they are asked to begin doing something before they have learned to do so' (Kaplan, 1991, p.106). The ways in which students handle this paradox, the feelings engendered, and the impact on their self-confidence can facilitate or hinder learning to practice.

An illustration of the relationship between self-concept and field learning comes from a number of studies of undergraduate (Sun, 1999) and graduate students' anxiety related to field learning (Rompf, Royse, & Shooper, 1993; Rosenthal Gelman, 2004; Rosenthal Gelman & Lloyd, 2008). While not all students in all studies reported the same sources of anxiety, students were concerned about working with particular client groups and in specialized field settings due to their perceived lack of professional knowledge and skills or lack of related experience. Some students found client problems emotionally overwhelming and reported feeling helpless and demoralized. For example, confronted with a client who disclosed having been sexually abused, an undergraduate student reflected on her lack of specific knowledge for both assessment and intervention (Sun, 1999). Similarly, graduate students were concerned about making mistakes, reported feeling overwhelmed, and were worried that clients would note their inexperience and thus lack confidence in them. Students were also concerned that they would have difficulty engaging clients due to differences in racial, cultural, and socio-economic backgrounds and lack of language skills (Rompf, Royse, & Shooper, 1993; Rosenthal Gelman, 2004; Rosenthal Gelman & Lloyd, 2008).

In Sun's (1999) study, students talked about their struggle to learn how to set professional boundaries for themselves given the ways in which they were drawn in emotionally and responded to clients' problems; they felt sympathy for clients' vulnerability, wanted to rescue them, felt great responsibility for clients' welfare, and, where they had developed strong relationships with clients, especially young children, had difficulty with endings. There was a trend in some studies that indicated that older students, those with related experience and some course work, reported less anxiety and a greater sense of preparedness for entering the field practicum (Rompf et al., 1993; Rosenthal Gelman, 2004).

Of interest in this discussion about student anxiety is the proposition offered by educational theorist Lee Shulman (2005a) that adaptive anxiety is a powerful motivator for learning in the professions and an indication of emotional investment. Educational or pedagogical practices that are pervasive and routine throughout the program enable students to manage their anxiety and 'cushion the burdens of higher learning. Habit makes novelty tolerable and surprise sufferable' (p. 56).

Theoretically, there has been some attention to describing stage models of student development, although there is scant empirical research in social work to support the view of learning as linear, progressive, sequential, and similar for all students. Nevertheless, all development models propose that beginning students have high anxiety, are self-conscious, and lack self-confidence (Deal, 2002). These feelings can contribute to students' becoming more focused on their performance than on clients' needs. As students progress through their first year they begin to develop greater cognitive understanding of practice and the rationale underlying specific interventions. Some theorists observe that students' skills lag behind their understanding; hence, their use of skills may still appear uneven (Holman & Freed, 1987). With a sense of greater understanding, students feel less anxious than at the beginning, and hence feel less need for the field instructor to provide as much support and guidance. Students can then become more autonomous and self-directing. With less anxiety and less self-preoccupation they can engage in learning that is more client-focused (Saari, 1989).

A debated assumption in adult education theory is that adults can direct their own learning, and consequently in learning situations such as classrooms there should be active involvement of students in setting learning objectives and carrying out learning and evaluation activities, and teachers can play the role of facilitator and resource. The classroom climate should be one of respect, acceptance, and acknowledgment of the value of adults' experience, and needs, and support. Teachers' stance in such an environment is to create an atmosphere of shared and mutual inquiry where all are learning. Similarly, field education should offer a respectful and collaborative milieu for learning and teaching.

There remains, however, amongst adult education theorists, an ongoing critique of this perspective and of the original proposition that all adults are self-directing. 'This belief has become part of the mythology of adult education; and as a myth, blinds us to the fact that some adults cannot, will not, or do not perform as self-directed learners' (MacKeracher, 1996, p. 57). Rather, MacKeracher notes that adults change in the degree of direction, support, and structure they desire over the course of any learning event. When approaching a new learning episode where the learner has little previous knowledge or foundation, a higher need for structure and guidance may be useful. As the learner is exposed to new knowledge and is able to integrate information and 'make it her own,' there may be less need for structure and more autonomy in seeking out further education. Similarly, the need for support may vary over time, depending on the learner's self-concept, self-esteem, the nature of the learning environment, and experience with the material to be learned.

Indeed, Knowles (1980) revised his formulations over time. Adult learning was seen as representing positions on a continuum from teacher-directed to student-directed learning, rather than as a contrast between child and adult learners (Merriam, 2001). The importance of the learning context also affected the degree to which teacher or student could direct the learning.

The Role of Experience

Closely related to self-concept is the recognition that adults have a rich reservoir of experience which has been integrated into their self-concept and affects both the way they view situations and their beliefs about what actions will bring about change. Experiences are internalized and serve as a form of tacit or implicit knowledge. This knowledge is used to frame and make sense of subsequent problems and situations encountered, and also to guide interactions. Through their experiences as workers, volunteers, or recipients of service, students have likely learned some aspects of professional knowledge as well as practical knowledge about everyday life. Experience then contributes to individuals' personal models of reality and is invested with emotional energy – energy which may be used to protect or defend our model and our self when confronted with new learning that challenges this model (MacKeracher, 1996).

Experience, therefore, provides a foundation for new learning but can also serve as an obstacle. Since students are bringing into social work education what they already know, it is important for learners to analyse prior experiences so as to identify and make explicit these underlying ideas or schemas. Underlying schemas will exert a powerful influence on whether new information will be accepted, adapted, integrated, or rejected. A critical perspective is proposed by Mezirow and Associates (1990) to uncover the historical, cultural, and biographical basis for our knowledge so as to be open to new learning. New learning involves a transformative process where knowledge and skills derived from our past are examined and may be reconstructed. Transformative learning requires time and effort, as it likely challenges central personal constructs and beliefs about self and others. Obviously it is a process that is better conducted in safe and trusted environments.

In a study of the field experiences of part-time, older, and employment-based students, Hopkins and colleagues (2005) found that students in employment-based field settings reported positive field experiences. These students contracted to have an educational experience in their work setting different from their usual assignment. The researchers speculate that these students were in a setting which they knew and presumably in which they were comfortable. Possibly they already possessed the ability to work with others to develop useful plans for clients, and could use and transfer this knowledge and these skills to design a positive learning assignment and establish a facilitative relationship with a field instructor. Possibly they already shared a similar outlook about social work with professional staff. Consistent with adult education theory, their experience in the agency setting may have provided enough foundation substantive and procedural knowledge that they were able to quickly engage in learning without the 'beginner's anxiety' associated with entering a new setting for an unknown field practicum. Continued practice and learning in a familiar organization presumably created less of a challenge for the issues related to self which are stirred up when beginning a practicum.

From field instructors' perspective, students with life and work experience may not only feel less anxiety but may also learn faster and perform more competently in field education. In an exploratory study, Zosky and colleagues (2003) compared field instructors' ratings of the field performance of non-traditional and traditional undergraduate students (Zosky, Unger, White, & Mills, 2003). Non-traditional students were defined as over the age of 21, out of school for three years or more, or occupying multiple roles (parent, employee, student), and with prior life experience. They found that field instructors rated non-traditional undergraduate students more highly than traditional students on all skill-based activities and on value-based variables such as boundaries and self-determination. They assessed non-traditional students as more prepared for the field.

In discussing the use of past experience in new learning, MacKeracher (1996) notes that many students do not spontaneously perceive connections between past and current experiences, and, furthermore, only some parts of past experiences may be relevant for the present new learning situation. Facilitators and instructors have a role to play in assisting students to draw analogies between cases or situations and to extract and make explicit similarities and differences.

For some students, learning in the field will also involve 'unlearning' attitudes and approaches which may not be consistent with contemporary models of practice. This may be especially so for students who possess an undergraduate degree in social work, have worked as social workers for a number of years, and are now in a graduate program. They may find themselves confronted with new concepts and information which appears to contradict earlier learning and practice wisdom they have developed from their own social work experiences. For example, if in their agency practice a more directive and authoritative style was used, the emphasis on collaboration with clients, strengths, and solution-based approaches, and empowerment strategies may require leaving behind former ways of working. There is a transition period where familiar ways of operating are no longer used and the student does not yet feel proficient or comfortable with new approaches. Reactions to this state of affairs vary. Anecdotally, some students have confidence in their ability to learn, can contain their discomfort, and relish the time and space to practice new skills. Other students become distressed, question whether they have any ability, refer to feeling like a fraud, fearful of being exposed as incompetent. Feeling demoralized, these students may withdraw from field instruction and provide the instructor with few examples of their current practice, or they may become dependent on the field instructor, asking for specific, concrete directions for their practice. Still other students may reject new models of practice, arguing for the superiority of what they are already comfortable with and able to do.

The critical role of experience in learning is a theme in the educational literature, and the work of Kolb (1984) is well respected in schools of social work. Experiential learning theory aims to explain how students learn from experience outside the formal classroom, and is well-suited to understanding learning derived from field and clinical environments. Drawing on earlier theorists such as Dewey (1933) and Lewin (1951), Kolb (1984) presents the following assumptions: Learning is a continuous process which occurs as individuals adapt to the world they experience. This process involves individuals in a cycle which is both active and passive, concrete and abstract. The cycle involves engaging with the environment through concrete experience. This is followed by a reflective period where observations are made and reviewed, leading to the formation of abstract concepts and generalizations. The next phase in the cycle involves testing the implications of concepts derived from abstraction in new situations; the cycle continues as the new situation provides concrete experience to stimulate further learning. Since Schon (1983, 1987) has identified reflection as an essential process in professional practice and learning, experiential learning theory is highly compatible with field education. An important point is that simply having 'an experience' is not necessarily sufficient for new learning to occur. Some period of reflection and identification of ideas or principles is needed to capture the essence of what may be considered new or transformative learning.

There are numerous examples of this phenomenon in the field practicum. Students learn about social work concepts in university courses, and often convey that it is only when carrying out a practice role in a setting that they truly 'get it' and understand nuanced principles, such as: start where the client is, go at the client's pace, demonstrate empathic attunement, and so on. Critiques of experiential learning theory exist based on its proposal of an orderly cycle for learning. Social work educators, however, are likely to agree with the important contribution of 'experience' to learning. This is seen in the century-long tradition of providing students with experiences of 'real life' social work practice through the practicum (Raskin et al., 2008) or using practice experiences in the classroom. The Educational Policy Statement of the Council on Social Work Education (EPAS, 2008) upholds and strengthens this tradition, referring to field education as the 'signature pedagogy' of social work. This term, introduced by Lee Shulman, an education scholar, refers to a way of teaching that has been inextricably identified with the preparation of individuals for a particular profession (Shulman, 2005a). It is the way a profession engages its students to think, act, and be '... preparing them to know, to think, to understand in order to act, to act in order to make a difference in the minds and lives of others – to act in order to serve others responsibly and with integrity' (p. 3). The importance of learning through experience is captured in the following statement in the educational policy: 'The intent of field education is to connect the theoretical and conceptual contribution of the classroom with the practical world of the practice setting. It is a basic precept of social work education that the two interrelated components of curriculum – classroom and field – are of equal importance within the curriculum, and each contributes to the development of the requisite competencies of professional practice' (EPAS, 2008, p. 8).

Readiness to Learn

Adults' orientation to learning is related to their needs to solve problems and apply new knowledge to current life circumstances, including social roles and career activities. Hence, adult learners have, in some sense, a good idea of what they need to learn and can be expected to take some initiative in seeking out learning opportunities to meet their needs. Indeed, the model of the self-directing professional, responsible for her own continuing education and professional development, is founded on this assumption. Although there is conflicting research evidence about professionals' ability to accurately self-assess (see, for example, the systematic review of studies of physicians' self-assessment abilities conducted by Davis et al., 2006), this self-directing model is the core of continuing education in many human service professions where self-assessment is expected to lead to educational plans to address gaps in competence.

Adults are believed to be pragmatic, drawn to learning new information they believe will be useful. Adults perceive that they do not have time to waste, and want to see immediate applications for new learning. Students will express in university-based social work courses the desire to learn today what they can use in the field practicum with their clients tomorrow. Similarly in field learning, students express feeling frustrated with long periods of observation unless the objective and rationale of such observations are made clear and are linked to preparing them for the next stage, where their practice will be more autonomous. As noted earlier, many adult learners, accustomed to steering the direction of their life, appreciate having some degree of control in new learning experiences, as well as collaborating in developing a learning plan and putting it into action.

Active Learning

Another assumption about adult learners is that they learn best when they are actively involved in learning activities rather than passively listening to a lecture or to an instructor providing direction. With the growth of technologically assisted learning, this maxim is true for children who have grown up exposed to highly interactive entertainment and teaching devices. A growing body of neuro-cognitive research emphasizes that the brain does not simply receive information but

rather processes it (Sousa, 2006), with emotional reactions, both conscious and not conscious, integrated with thoughts and actions
(Damasio, 2003; Siegel, 2007). Many senses are engaged in information
processing or learning: hearing, seeing, feeling, and thinking. Active
learning strategies therefore aim to use these different pathways to
stimulate students to connect at cognitive, emotional, and behavioural
levels. Active learning techniques include discussing, reflecting, challenging, questioning, examining, and discovering the personal
meaning of new knowledge. Active learning frequently takes place in
small-group or dyadic interaction where the give and take of ideas
stimulates clarification and understanding for each participant.

The importance of learning to practice social work through delivering service in a field agency arose out of the practice wisdom of the
earliest social work educators (Raskin et al., 2008). The preceding
review of selected concepts from educational theory clearly demonstrates that the propositions offered by adult education and experiential learning theory are congruent with social work's longstanding
acknowledgement of the importance of field learning. In the field, students are personally involved in learning to think and to act like a
social worker and to incorporate social work values. Learning is challenging, as it engages the personal self of the student. Involvement
with 'real life' clients, communities, and social issues provides experiences, immediacy, and activity through drawing students into the concerns of others and offering meaningful opportunities to be helpful or
bring about change – likely the very factors that motivated students to
choose social work as a career. Furthermore, this type of active learning through providing a service is associated with students' perceptions that their field practicum was of high quality and contributed to
their learning to practice social work.

Issues of Self

At the beginning of this chapter the point was made that social work
practice involves the practitioner in the purposeful, intentional,
thoughtful use of self, and that social work education and especially
the practicum provide the milieu for this learning. Use of self relies on
self-awareness: having knowledge and understanding of one's own
personal and social identity characteristics that affect the way one
relates to others, makes judgments, and decides on interventions.
Edwards and Bess (1998) offer a comprehensive approach to under-

standing self from a personality-based perspective. They propose that social workers have a 'systematic inventory of personal traits and characteristic behaviours which come to them as naturally as breathing. They must be able to identify specifically *how they act* and *what they say* that is unique to themselves as persons in relation with others, and that conveys the essence of their inner selves to their clients' (p. 97). Related to self-understanding is some awareness of what provokes one's feelings and reactions. Triggers can be associated with the nature of situations that social workers confront: for example, loss of loved ones, abuse and violence in intimate relationships, experiences of racism and prejudice, abuse of human rights, physical and emotional trauma, chronic and deteriorating physical illness, and living in depriving and harsh environments. Triggers can also be associated with situations similar to those in one's past: alcoholism in the family, immigration or refugee status, living in an adoptive family. Practitioners continuously aim to examine their own personal solutions to the challenges they have faced in their lives, and to determine how these solutions reflect their beliefs about how individuals and society should respond.

The notion of self has expanded in social work to incorporate social identity characteristics that arise from societal, cultural, and familial contexts that shape the values, thoughts, reactions, and behaviours of individuals – both clients and social workers. This involves a recognition of the importance of our underlying world view, and that it may reflect a many-layered personal construction of values from the sociocultural communities of importance to us, to the way our family of origin interpreted their heritage, and ultimately to the degree to which each individual internalizes these perspectives. This social identity is not restricted to ethnicity but also includes attitudes derived from our affiliation with social characteristics such as race, class, gender, sexual orientation, ability, religious affiliation, immigration status, political association, and so on. As practitioners develop they become aware of these social identities and the way in which a range of dimensions operate at surface and depth levels and exert a powerful influence on us in our professional lives. Related to these views are the stereotypes, prejudices, and idealizations that social workers may have about people from specific groups. One observation is that social work students who grew up in white, middle-class communities report they have little experience of interacting with and having close relationships with people of colour, people living in poverty, and people living in dangerous neighborhoods. When receiving such practicum assignments these students need to focus on understanding the nature and origins of the attitudes, expectations, and feelings they bring into these encounters. They also need to review the experience of racism and privilege that accrues to skin colour. Beginning social work students are faced with their own fears and uncertainties about their skills as social workers, and do not feel powerful in relationships with clients. Despite this, they need to attend to the legacy that links colour, power, and privilege, and oppression and disadvantage in society. Foster (1998) noted a range of reactions to the recognition of privilege, including denial of difference, excessive focus on cultural issues, guilt and pity, and ambivalence. When working with clients from a similar background, students may experience over-identification, distancing, ambivalence, guilt about their own success, and hope and despair.

Engagement in learning is also affected by students' personal and social identity characteristics, and affect whether students perceive learning environments as open, welcoming of difference, highly risky, or safe. Safety refers to the sense an individual has that expression of opinions will not be met with dismissal, hostility, humiliation, aggression, and so on. While there is a considerable body of pedagogical literature related to classroom experiences for discussion of self issues and diversity concerns (see, for example, Holley and Steiner, 2005; Mishna and Rasmussen, 2001), there is scant literature on this crucial topic in field education. This is surprising given the wide acceptance in social work of adult education principles pertaining to the importance of self in learning. A brief review of the limited literature on developing self-awareness through field education reveals some salient themes.

Developing Self-awareness

Clinical social work literature addresses the issue of professional use of self, self-awareness, and understanding counter-transference as a practice principle and essential component of practice (see Chapman, Oppenheim, Shibusawa, & Jackson, 2003, for a historical review). For clinical social workers using a psychodynamic approach, engaging in personal therapy is viewed as enhancing effectiveness. Small exploratory studies of social work students' experience with personal therapy found that respondents believed it enhanced their listening skills, understanding of and effectiveness in therapy. Their therapists' empathy appeared to provide a model for them to both connect with and maintain appropriate emotional separation from their clients (Mackey & Mackey, 1994). Graduating students believed that increased self-awareness and a sense of personal and professional identity were the most important gains (Mackey, Mackey, & O'Brien, 1993).

A survey of faculty and students at single track clinical programs found that more students, in contrast to faculty, believed that personal therapy was essential to their social work education (Strozier & Stacey, 2001). Students who had been in therapy viewed it as more important than students who had not. Both students and faculty identified personal therapy as important for developing self-awareness and dealing with one's own issues. Of interest were the mixed opinions of faculty members who noted the decline in these clinical schools of a focus on traditional clinical theory and issues. This was attributed to a new emphasis on social and community issues and theories such as empowerment. Faculty also drew a distinction between the personal and professional life of students, with the need for boundaries. On the other hand, some noted that since more students appeared to present personal problems related to trauma, depression, substance use, and recovery, personal therapy was recommended to help students deal with these issues. Many faculty members were adverse to therapy as a requisite part of social work education, while still noting its usefulness. A perceptive quote about the benefit of students' voluntarily entering therapy is offered: '[we] must know ourselves sufficiently well and have worked through our own issues in order to best serve clients. Otherwise, the self that we seek to use in our work becomes an obstacle for the client rather than a facilitative element' (Strozier & Stacey, 2001, p. 189). Finally, the authors observe that since students seem to want and value personal therapy, it is most likely that field instructors will experience students' needs and pressure for attention to issues of self and identity.

Educational approaches to facilitate the development of self-awareness have been examined mainly in the field education literature. Early writings on field education emphasized that the identity of the learner should be developed and students helped to face emotions and personal value judgments elicited in their practice, along with an examination of those judgments in light of social work values (Towle, 1954; Younghusband, 1967). The focus on developing self-awareness in professional education was always intended to be related to meeting

the needs of client situations, not to be undertaken as personal therapeutic work (Hamilton, 1954). It was seen as a by-product of professional learning and approached on a conscious level, not through
exploration of personal material that is out of awareness. Influenced
by psychoanalytic theory and its recognition of the impact of the
student's or practitioner's personality on the work, an approach to
field instruction and worker supervision developed which gave considerable emphasis to self-development or personal growth as a necessary element in professional development. Studies conducted at that
time found students' experienced this form of supervision as stressful
and objectionable (Kadushin, 1974; Rosenblatt & Mayer, 1975). Others
observed that boundaries may have been crossed due to confusion
between field instruction or supervision and therapy (Siporin, 1982).
The growth orientation approach fell into disfavour, replaced by an
approach that entailed a collaborative relationship between student
and field instructor with clearer definitions and expectations of roles
(Wijnberg & Schwartz, 1977). In this approach the focus is primarily on
case dynamics and student interventions and the skills required. Discussions of student personal reflections are primarily about the needs
of the practice situation.

Despite this trend, it is obvious that practice situations students
encounter in field education can evoke strong emotions and reactions.
Field educators note the importance of assisting students with their
reactions (Grossman, Levine-Jordano, & Shearer, 1990), and the need
for students' to reconcile personal capacity and professional knowledge and values (Collins, 1993), as well as to move towards the development of a professional self (Deal, 2000; Hensley, 2002). Others
observe that students want to learn how to handle their personal reactions in a manner that allows them be authentic, genuine, and professional, so that they experience congruence and integration of aspects
of their personal and professional self (Bogo, 1993, 2006; Hendricks et
al., 2005).

Since social work literature emphasizes the importance of self-
awareness, it is reasonable that students expect their field instructors
to help them learn how to understand and respond to affect and judgments evoked in practice. For instructors there are obvious tensions,
given that educational principles are expressed at a general level to
assist students to enhance their self-awareness and at the same time to
limit the focus and range of such discussions. Anecdotal reports
provide information about both sides of the dilemma. For example,

some students suggest that when field instruction discussions include students' strong reactions, feelings, and judgments about case situations, their personal history and information is explored in relation to these reactions to the practice situation. As noted, this link between highly personal material and practice can be seen as very helpful to some students, while other students experience it as intrusive. Most educators believe that such exploration can cross a boundary between education and therapy, placing the field instructor in a dual relationship with the student as both educator and therapist. Dual relationships become complicated, especially given the responsibility of the field instructor as evaluator and the power inherent in that role.

Self, Social Identity, and Diversity

Earlier it was noted that self-awareness has expanded beyond a focus on personality to integrate social identity characteristics that arise from societal, cultural, and familial contexts. Social identity includes ethnicity, race, class, gender, sexual orientation, religion, ability, and so on. When student and field instructor approach each other, they both present with numerous visible and invisible personal attributes which may or may not make a difference in the way they approach the practice situation, the educational experience, and the learning relationship. An authentic and professional way of discussing issues needs to be found, as avoidance can interfere with achieving a mutual partnership and impede learning. As well, it is necessary to respect privacy and recognize factors that lead to perceptions of risk and work against ease in disclosure and discussion.

Surprisingly, there are few studies that would assist in understanding and responding to these important dynamics in field instruction. Two studies investigated the impact of gender combinations on satisfaction and both found no significant effects. In the first study, same-gender combinations led to higher satisfaction, but this accounted for only a small percentage of overall satisfaction (Thyer, Sower-Hoag, & Love, 1987). A later study employing similar methodology found opposite gender combinations were evaluated more positively, but overall satisfaction was not appreciably affected by gender combinations (Vonk, Zucrow, & Thyer, 1996).

Two studies of field instructors found they were aware of cultural, ethnic, gender, class, and age similarities and differences between themselves and their students, but rarely discussed these issues in supervision (Gladstein & Mailick, 1986; Marshack, Hendricks, & Gladstein, 1994). In an early study of the impact of race and ethnicity on field education, students and field instructors identified students' fear that they would not be supported by their field instructor if they raised issues about cultural sensitivity or cultural conflicts (McRoy, Freeman, Logan, & Blackmon, 1986). However, the respondents reported few actual problems had surfaced. In a similar study respondents generally reported a positive experience in the supervisory relationship (Black, Maki, & Nunn, 1997). Where students had minority field instructors they reported feeling better prepared to work with individuals different from themselves as compared to students with instructors similar to themselves.

More recently, Armour, Bain, and Rubio (2004) developed and pilot tested an approach to diversity training for 11 field instructors, offered in response to field instructors' reporting their avoidance of addressing diversity issues despite their desire to do so. The evaluation of the training found that the participants developed some skills to enhance supervision in this area, such as normalization of discomfort, awareness of retreating from exploring diversity, and permission to talk about concerns related to working with clients. They increased self-knowledge and felt empowered to address diversity issues with the agency, student, or client.

Based on their extensive experience providing seminars for first-time field instructors in the New York City area, Hendricks, Finch, and Franks (2005) note the importance of creating a climate where both differences and similarities between the student and field instructor can be discussed in an open and free manner as a regular part of the field instruction session. Field instructors must take the lead in this regard, and these authors recommend a number of educational practices. They note that it is useful to acknowledge that normally uncomfortable feelings can be stirred up by discussions of difference, given historical societal and structural oppression and 'the taboo against talking about such issues as race and sexual orientation' (p. 180). Of importance is field instructors' willingness not to avoid such discussions for fear of not being able to manage feelings that may surface, such as anxiety, fear, anger, and so on. Field instructor training can assist in preparing educators for this important interpersonal work. When field instructors include diversity issues in all aspects of the field practicum, students are more able to integrate these dimensions as part of their practice. Hendricks and colleagues expect students to identify and discuss

diversity issues in their learning contracts or plans and in their practice learning documentation in process recordings and reflective journals, and to include this competence in regular and final evaluations.

There is an expanding literature addressing lesbian and gay students, which began with a poignant personal anecdote written by two
'sexual-minority' students, who described their struggles when faced
with personal questions from agency staff and clients that included
the assumption that they were 'straight' (Messinger & Topal, 1997).
Their field instructors advised them not to disclose their sexual orientation and to evade questions from clients. This advice left them
silenced and shamed about this deception. They also reflected on the
missed opportunities to assist their lesbian and gay clients in confronting homophobia. Following this paper, Messinger (2004) conducted an exploratory study which examined the experiences of
lesbian and gay social work students in the field. Students reported
heterosexist and homophobic attitudes and behaviours, unwelcoming
agency climates, an absence of discussion of gay and lesbian issues in
the field placement, general feelings of lack of safety or anxiety at the
placement, and challenges related to disclosure of sexual orientation
in the agency. Barriers related to disclosure were found on individual,
interpersonal, and institutional levels: anxiety about disclosure of
sexual orientation to clients and staff and field educators; pressures to
hide one's sexual orientation; and concerns about identity and professionalism as a gay man or lesbian. Of particular concern was the
threat of negative ramifications for lesbian and gay students' evaluations and future employment as a result of self-disclosure to heterosexual field educators.

In a subsequent phase of this research, Messinger (2007) interviewed
matched dyads of 13 students and their field instructors about the students' field practicum. Disagreements in perceptions of the practicum
were common, and related to the field instructors' style and comfort
with discussing lesbian, gay, and bisexual issues, the quality of the
instructional relationship, the perception of the agency climate, and
the student's level of disclosure. Based on an extensive and rich qualitative analysis of the interviews, Messinger recommends that heterosexual field instructors gain more knowledge about sexual orientation
to enhance their ability to discuss sexual orientation-related issues
with all students. They must also take initiative to change the agency
climate and recognize and intervene in homophobic and heterosexist
incidents.

Similar findings of the multi-dimensional and mutually reinforcing factors affecting gay and lesbian students' field learning emerged in a study of field instructors' and students' perspectives (Newman, Bogo, & Daley, 2008, 2009). The eight field instructor participants for the study were chosen based on their considerable knowledge and history of working effectively with lesbian and gay students or their self-identification as lesbian or gay. Six students who were recent graduates of the master's program volunteered to participate. Based on in-depth exploratory interviews, the researchers conclude that students' experiences in the field were influenced by interactions between three factors. First is students' comfort level with their sexual orientation and management of self-disclosure of sexual orientation. Second are the contexts in which students' education occurs, including the university program and ways in which sexual orientation is integrated or omitted from course work. The agency context is a powerful facilitator or inhibitor of students' perceptions of safety. Agency context is reflected in formal ways, such as the presence of agency-wide diversity; human rights policy and clear consequences of violations; staff practices – whether there were 'out' agency staff (Newman et al., 2009, p. 14); and the power of signs and symbols in the setting to convey the agency as a positive and affirmative space. The third factor relates to field instructors and their ability to create a comfortable learning relationship through 'sustained and ongoing dialogue ... you face it, you talk about it, you explore it' (p. 15). Choice and student readiness for discussion were also key factors.

Participants underscored the importance for learning and practice of assisting students to feel enough safety and comfort to raise sexual orientation-related issues and examine how they might respond with clients. Field instructors gave examples of students confronted with clients who ask about students' sexual orientation, and emphasized the importance of instructors' openness to discussing students' feelings and the possible responses to the client. Students in the study reported feeling considerable risk regarding self-disclosure, testing the waters with subtle narratives to determine potential reactions, and the general omission or avoidance of discussion of sexual orientation-related issues. In contrast, the field instructor participants who were not matched with the student participants strongly recommended that field instructors initiate discussions as part of their responsibility as educators, and use 'explicit and direct statements about discussion of sexual orientation, professional identity and practice, rather than subtle comments and cues' (Newman et al., 2008, p. 232).

Since organizational factors exert an important influence on students' learning, the researchers recommend that schools of social work create opportunities for discussion of agency policy and climate with respect to sexual orientation, and diversity issues in general, when contracting with settings. In the absence of such policies, such discussion might lead to positive change or schools may decline the use of the setting. As well, in most communities there are programs specifically designed to serve populations based on sexual orientation, which schools can proactively seek out as practicum settings.

Towards Facilitating Students' Integration of the Personal and Professional Self

An enduring theme in the field education literature recognizes the importance of assisting students to examine and understand how their personal values and reactions are present in their practice, to develop greater awareness of self issues evoked in their practice, and to come to some integration of aspects of their personal and professional self. Generic educational principles emerge from the discussion of this topic and from recommendations in the literature. The establishment of a trusting and supportive relationship with the field instructor provides a context where students may feel comfortable and safe enough to disclose feelings and concerns. Disclosure is balanced with maintaining boundaries through a firm focus on practice encounters. Matorin and colleagues propose that field instructors set a tone for disciplined self-revelation within a comfortable learning environment (Matorin, Monaco, & Kerson, 1994). Engaging in conscious and systematic reflection helps students examine how personal reactions and professional interventions merge in practice (Bogo & Vayda, 1998; Hendricks et al., 2005; Walter & Young, 1999). The importance of boundaries is underscored, and stated as follows: 'Student self-disclosures are primarily important as they relate to the work. Walking this delicate line between treating and teaching entails emphasizing the difference between developing practitioner self-awareness and learning more about oneself through a therapeutic relationship' (Hendricks et al., 2005, p. 7).

Despite these general guidelines, recent empirical evidence suggests that in situations of diversity, students experience numerous barriers and a sense of anxiety and lack of safety about discussion of ethnic and racial issues or disclosure of their sexual orientation. Discriminatory attitudes and experiences in society may be repeated in the agency and school context, and it is understandable that students may approach field instructors with apprehension and hesitancy. Preoccupation with safety and the perception of a need to self-censor is thought to compromise engagement with clients, and with the field learning experience. More explicit statements about field education as a location and process for considering a range of social identities (for example, race, ethnicity, gender, sexual orientation, ability, religious affiliation, and so on) may provide opportunities for educationally focused discussions about personal and professional issues. Social workers are likely to confront a wide range of issues related to social identity characteristics in their careers as they engage with individuals who are both similar and different from themselves. The field experience is a unique opportunity to learn to function in an authentic and integrated manner (Newman et al., 2008). While field instructors need to consider student readiness for discussion and the stage of development of the student and field instructor relationship, in the absence of discussion of salient issues the relationship may remain superficial.

In conclusion, this chapter aimed to examine some of the salient issues students experience when engaging in field learning. A review of theoretical concepts pertaining to the self of the student as adult learner in an experiential setting and ideas about achieving greater levels of self awareness were offered. From this body of literature an evidence-based set of principles for field education can be identified. The next chapter integrates the perspectives discussed in this chapter with empirical findings about what appears to facilitate student learning in the field, and offers some guidelines for field instructors to use in their educational role.

PART TWO

Field Education for Professional Practice

5 Facilitating Student Learning

The information presented in the previous chapter provides concepts and empirical findings that illuminate salient aspects of students' experiences as they engage in learning in the field. Drawing on this body of knowledge, generic principles and techniques for field instruction can be identified, some of which are further supported in research studies. Many of these principles are similar to those developed through the years as dedicated social workers provide and reflect on field learning experiences for countless social work students. Practice wisdom represents the identification of approaches that have been effective. In this instance, theory, research, and practice appear to complement each other.

While generic principles provide guidelines which can be used in ideal circumstances, in everyday education there are likely to be unique individual characteristics and interpersonal dynamics that challenge the effective and straightforward application of these principles. Once again, the integration of theory and practice is not linear; rather, it is based on a reflective process that aims to arrive at interventions (in this case educational interventions) relevant to the particular needs of the situation. This section of the text will cover three major areas. In this chapter the focus is on the student and field instructor relationship as the context for learning. Complex issues related to the interplay between the personal and professional self will be considered, such as how field instructors can work with students within an educational framework to develop self-awareness, how instructors' can take into account students' developmental level, ruptures and repairs in educational relationships, and potential obstacles to collaboration as a result of the ways in which power is constructed, perceived, and used. In the following chapter in this section, more concrete methods for field education are reviewed, grouped under the categories of observation, reflection, and giving and receiving feedback. The final chapter in this section reviews approaches for field education, including structure and process dimensions of each format.

The Self of the Student Is Engaged in Field Learning

Learning and teaching activities are experienced on a subjective or personal level as students strive to integrate knowledge, values, and skills and construct a personal professional identity. In the previous chapter, general student anxiety about the practicum was reviewed. In addition, two exploratory qualitative studies provide insights about the intense personal and emotional reactions field education stirs up in some students. Both studies had small samples of students who chose voluntarily to respond to the researchers' invitation to comment on their difficult or upsetting experiences in the field and the emotional impact on them (Barlow & Hall, 2007; Litvack, Bogo, & Mishna, 2010). Consequently, the conclusions may be particular to only a limited number of students. They do, however, show that for some students the field learning experience is stressful in a highly personal way. This result is in contrast to the finding from a review of quantitative studies of student satisfaction with the practicum, which found that the majority of students reported moderately high to high satisfaction (Bogo, 2005).

While a wide variation in situations which individual students reported as emotionally upsetting were found in the studies, issues identified in both studies could be grouped into similar themes. The main themes related to extremely difficult client situations, professional issues, and tensions in students' relationships with their field instructors. Client situations understandably upsetting were hearing stories of great pain involving death, abuse, and having a client who committed suicide. In many of these situations students said they were ill-equipped to provide help due to their perceived lack of knowledge and competence. Professional-contextual issues included the poor condition of the physical environment of some settings, and observing staff behaviour that students felt lacked respect for clients. In Barlow and Hall's (2007) study, many students reported situations where clients had threatened or confronted them, leaving students fearing for their own safety. Relationship issues with field instructors included the enormously strong positive or negative feelings students had about their instructors. When students experienced a positive relationship, it greatly assisted them in coping with client or organizational stresses (Litvack et al., 2010). Conversely, when the relationship with the field instructor was experienced negatively, it had a great influence on the student's ability to openly participate in learning. Negative experiences with field instructors arose from a wide range of conditions. For example, there were instructors who subtly or directly conveyed that the agency had pressured them to take a student against their own wishes and that this was a burden for them, and some instructors were unsupportive and gave feedback which focused on students' weaknesses and rarely acknowledged strengths. In other instances, instructors crossed boundaries by revealing too much information about their personal or professional lives, and others misused their power.

Individual student reactions to new learning in the field practicum will vary, and while the issues emanating from these studies are useful for understanding potential students' responses, a range is expected. Situations upsetting to one student may not have the same intense effect on others. There is a temptation to refer to 'students,' as if there is such a category, with universal and general characteristics. In new field instructor seminars there can be a tendency to reinforce the idea that there are typical or usual experiences for all students. In fact, as reviewed in the previous chapter, students vary tremendously along a number of dimensions: age, experience, world view, learning, personal and social identity characteristics, and so on. These variations significantly affect the way in which students engage in learning and respond to educational interventions. Reactions to challenges and threats include flight, fight, freeze, and fragment (Carroll, 2009). Similar to practice, social workers use the principle of individualization and recognize the necessity of knowing each student, understanding her unique experiences and perspectives, and particular responses to the pleasures and discomforts which are inevitable byproducts of learning social work practice.

The Student Field Instructor Relationship

Throughout the discussion thus far, the learning environment and relationship between student and field instructor has been described as respectful of the feelings and needs of the learner, supportive, and valuing the mutual contribution of both. Consistent with contemporary values of social work, the ideal-type relationship is collaborative, non-hierarchical, provides for free expression of opinions, and accepts differences. A considerable body of research exists about the factors that social work students value in the field instruction relationship. Based on a critical review of empirical studies on field education conducted recently, Bogo (2005) extracted preliminary foundation principles for evidence-based field instruction, which are discussed below and in the following chapter on principles and methods for field instruction. As noted above, an interesting conclusion from a review of this literature is that across studies, the majority of students report moderately high to high satisfaction with individual field instruction. This finding confirms the observation that students highly value their learning experiences in the field practicum and believe it prepares them for practice.

Before proceeding with a review of the empirical literature, it is important to note the limitations in this work. Most researchers have examined students' perceptions of teaching activities, processes, and techniques in individual field instruction that affect their satisfaction and perception of a quality field experience. These studies rely on students' self-reports to provide data about what occurs in field education rather than in field instructors' reports, or, preferably, observations of what actually transpires. Furthermore, the outcome variable in the studies is student satisfaction, rather than student practice competence. While it is acknowledged that satisfaction is important, as it likely contributes to learning, it falls short of meeting educational programs' responsibility to ensure graduates are competent to practice. Fortune and colleagues (Fortune, McCarthy, & Abramson, 2001) are the only research team to use performance as an outcome measure, assessed by the field instructor's rating of the student on the university's evaluation form. Chapter 8 in this book, on evaluation of student competence, analyses the measurement challenges associated with such evaluations and concludes that these ratings are not as psychometrically sound as needed to provide strong evidence of student learning and progress. Furthermore, the vicissitudes of the interpersonal relationship between student and field instructor create a leniency bias which leads to inflated ratings of student performance (Bogo, Regehr, Power, & Regehr, 2007). The field needs valid and reliable educational outcome measures and approaches if we are to be able to advance research and provide a solid empirically based foundation for our educational practices. Given this caveat we can still use the empirical literature, albeit tentatively, with some degree of hesitation, while cognizant of these limitations.

The following educational principles are presented as generic and the foundation for quality field teaching: (1) field education takes place within an available and supportive relationship; (2) learners benefit from a balance between structure and autonomy in practice and learning; (3) learners need to develop reflective and conceptual capacities; and (4) observation, reflective discussion, and the provision of constructive feedback facilitates mastery of skills. Throughout this discussion is the assumption that the learning and teaching enterprise in the field is collaborative. Students are expected to show initiative and participate fully in all aspects of learning; this stance is consistent with developing professional practitioners who are lifelong learners. These four broad principles of learning and teaching in the field are discussed in two sections. In this chapter, the first two are considered as they pertain to the relationship context of field instruction. The next two principles are considered in the following chapter, as they pertain to the process and techniques associated with the pedagogy of field teaching.

Available and Supportive Relationships

Accessibility and availability provide the basis for a relationship to develop with the field instructor. In a study of undergraduate social work students' relative rankings of desirable field instructor characteristics, Barretti (2009) found that availability was perceived as the most important characteristic. Students in Knight's (2001) study gave positive evaluations to field instructors who offered more frequent and longer sessions. Similar findings emerged from Ellison's (1994) review of nine studies. Clearly, when students feel that their instructors are interested enough in their learning to provide regularly scheduled field instruction sessions and to be available when needed, there is the opportunity for a working relationship to grow and develop.

Students rate highly a group of instructor characteristics that they associate with a supportive climate: honest, likeable, expert, reliable, sociable, prepared, sincere, warm, skilful, and trustworthy (Strozier, Barnett-Queen, & Bennett, 2000). (While the terms 'supervisor' and 'supervision' are used by a number of authors, the educational terms 'field instructor' and 'field instruction session' are used in this review.)

The researchers found these characteristics especially valued by first-year students, although ongoing support was valued by students in both years of a graduate program. In a study of undergraduate and graduate students' views about field instructors, those deemed negative were seen as neither engaged nor supportive (Knight, 2001). Similarly, students in Hong Kong reported the importance of support for their learning by their field instructors (Choy, Leung, Tam, & Chu, 1998).

Another enduring theme in the literature is that students appreciate a socio-emotional climate which is responsive to their feelings (Fortune & Abramson, 1993; Urbanowski & Dwyer, 1988). Instructors who enjoy teaching, who can convey that making mistakes is part of learning, and who can empathize with feelings of demoralization, display character-istics associated with support. In the previous chapter, the dynamics for the 'self' of the student when learning to practice social work were dis-cussed. With the recognition of the impact of this new learning on the self, it is reasonable that students find helpful those field instructors who are sensitive and understanding about students' struggles and their feelings about their competence.

Attachment theory provides a framework for field instructor approaches congruent with this way of perceiving learners' needs. Attachment theory recognizes that learners search for a 'secure base' from which to venture into unfamiliar territory (Bowlby, 1988). Attach-ment theory has been applied to the student and field instructor rela-tionship in social work (Bennett, Mohr, Szoc, & Saks, 2008; Bennett & Saks, 2006). These scholars make the point that individuals' internal working models of attachment serve as templates for adult relation-ships and shape how present-day relationships are experienced and interpreted, how intimacy is experienced, and how one seeks help and guidance from others. They propose that in the field instructor-student relationship these templates will be activated as a student begins to venture into and explore the professional world. These authors under-score the importance of the field instructor providing a secure base so that the student can return 'to the safe haven of supervision for repair of the inevitable ruptures that occur during the field experience' (Bennett & Saks, 2006, p. 671). The field instructor who is attuned to the student's cues can determine what should be offered, when to provide encouragement to venture forth again into the practice situa-tion, and when to use the safe haven of the relationship to examine the vulnerabilities and difficulties evoked in learning. In this respect the relationship is central to student learning in the field practicum, and is the product of the ways in which the two participants provide and respond to relationship cues.

To test their hypothesis, a study examined the relationship between two attachment variables, anxiety and avoidance, and students' perceptions of the relationship with the field instructor, referred to as the supervisory working alliance and supervisory style (Bennett et al., 2008). The supervisory working alliance is defined, following Bordin (1983), as consisting of agreement between supervisor and supervisee on the goals and tasks of their work and the relational bonds between them. Supervisory style is defined, following Friedlander and Ward (1984), as consisting of perceptions of the supervisor as interpersonally attractive and sensitive, and as task-oriented. The researchers found some support for the hypothesis that a student's general attachment styles may influence attachment-related thoughts and feelings about their field instructor (Bennett et al., 2008). In the case of students who were uncomfortable with intimacy in close relationships and had high levels of avoidance, higher levels of avoidance and anxiety in the supervision relationship were reported, in contrast to students who were comfortable with intimacy and had low levels of avoidance. From this finding the researchers recommend that field instructors pay attention to students' general level of comfort and discomfort with closeness in the field instructor-student relationship.

Regarding supervision-specific attachment, both avoidance and anxiety variables were associated with the supervisory alliance and supervisory style, with avoidance and lack of trust in relation to the supervisor considered especially important. While this program of research is in its early stages, and, as the researchers note, does not include significant variables such as field instructors' responses to students, it provides a textured analytic framework for examining the relationship, and for understanding situations which appear disappointing to both participants, or become problematic.

Structure and Autonomy

As adults, learners can engage in a collaborative partnership with instructors, to work together drawing on the experiences of both the student and the instructor. It is the responsibility of the field instructor to provide leadership and structure in designing the learning plan, especially in the beginning stages. Collaboration can involve the student and field instructor in discussion of both the content and the process dimensions of the field practicum. The content dimension will focus on how the competency framework and learning objectives provided by the educational program can be met given the learning opportunities available in the setting. As well, each student has her or his own learning goals, and field instructors likely have unique beliefs about crucial competencies, particularly in their specialized area of practice. Finally, the context of the field practicum needs attention, and there will be a number of topics to cover in a student's orientation to an agency and its various programs and policies.

Capturing the process dynamics of field instruction is more difficult. While it can be uncomfortable, it is useful for field instructors and students to discuss their expectations about the relationship and potentially sensitive topics. The recommendations with respect to diversity issues discussed in chapter 4 are relevant; if these notions are to become an integrated and usual part of the field experience they should be introduced from the beginning. Contracting regarding the process of teaching and learning has been identified as a crucial part of facilitating the student's entry into the field and continued learning. Four interrelated activities are presented by Shulman (1993): the field instructor shares his or her sense of purpose, describes his or her role, reaches for feedback from the student about the student's perceptions about the teaching and learning relationship and educational activities, and discusses the mutual obligations and expectations about the authority of the field instructor. When discussing purpose and role, the field instructor will likely describe some of the methods she will use to help the student learn. The instructor will try to provide some examples of her teaching style. At the same time there is also likely to be some discussion about the student's preferred learning style.

While a collaborative relationship has been recommended throughout this text, this is not to imply that field instructors are not experts. In fact, they are appointed to this role because they have expertise as social work practitioners. It is their knowledge and skill which give them the authority to be seen as an expert and teacher, and ultimately to evaluate the student's learning and progress. Field instructors are also socializing agents through directly and indirectly showing and telling students about expected professional behaviour, values, and attitudes. As well, there is the role of socializing students into the agency culture and climate.

Using adult learning theory, most field instructors also play the role of coordinator of learning opportunities for students, and link them to others in the setting from whom students can learn through sharing assignments, observation, and discussion. It is unrealistic to expect that all learning will come directly from the field instructor. Especially in team settings, students can have rich experiences with a range of staff members and colleagues from related disciplines. Field instructors play the role of 'resource,' and assist students to seek out pertinent materials to add to their learning, not only formal written material but also agency materials such as manuals, workshop presentations, and similar unpublished information.

Direct discussion of the authority of the field instructor can be uncomfortable for both parties, and yet the student is likely to be concerned about how much responsibility and autonomy she or he will have regarding making decisions about clients and preparing written material for the agency record. As Shulman (1993) notes regarding new staff, students want to know what they can do on their own and what must be first vetted with the field instructor. Evaluation of their field performance is understandably of concern to students. Many schools use a pass or fail grade in the field practicum with an evaluation form that includes a rating scale. Students are likely to want to know the process that will be involved in arriving at these ratings and how much input they might have. It is uncomfortable to directly discuss these issues, especially at the beginning of the practicum when the field instructor-student relationship is still at a very early stage of formation. The hope on both parts is that both parties will work well together and the relationship will progress smoothly. However, since authority issues are of concern, in the beginning stage of the practicum some discussion is preferable to ignoring them.

Through mutual discussion and reflection, student and field instructor can begin to formulate some preliminary ideas about how they will work productively together. These ideas can be documented in an initial learning plan, which describes the learning assignments, types of practice data for use in field instruction (for example, live observation, working together, review of audio or video records, written reports, or process recordings), and structure of field instruction. Structural factors include the frequency, time, and duration of field instruction meetings and the respective responsibilities for preparation and setting an agenda. Arrangements and expectations for ad hoc consultation, with the field instructor and in her absence, should be clarified. At the beginning the stage is set for the degree of openness and collaboration in the relationship. Through the behaviours of each over time, the actual working relationship will develop and both parties will have clearer ideas about how to provide each other with the information and cues about what is needed to facilitate learning for competent performance.

Connected to structure is promoting student autonomy. Studies find that while students value available instructors they also wish to move to more independence as their learning progresses (Fortune et al., 1985; Urbanowski & Dwyer, 1988). Behaviours associated with autonomy involve students in designing the learning plan and encourage expression of students' ideas. Deal (2002) proposes that in the second year of graduate programs, while students might want more autonomy their still limited knowledge and skill require careful balance of support and guidance with their move towards autonomy. An astute observation is that students' feelings about how much independence they want or need at this point will fluctuate, and field instructors need to stay 'available, connected, and non-defensive' (p. 133) in the face of students' push and pull towards increasing independence in practice.

An interesting study of critical incidents in field education was conducted by Giddings and colleagues (2003), with a national random sample of social workers who were asked to recall problems with their former field instructors. Four factors emerged: (1) a lack of supervision, including lack of structure, direction, and feedback; (2) a harsh and unyielding style that was rigid, authoritarian, overly challenging or accusatory, and lacked empathy and sensitivity to student needs; (3) unprofessional behaviour with moderate ethical and boundary violations; and (4) extreme violations such as physical aggression, sexual harassment, and racial bias. These findings provide additional empirical evidence for the principles discussed thus far with respect to the importance of a supportive relationship and a balance of structure and autonomy.

Similar findings emerged in a study which examined the preferences of students in a macro practicum. The great majority of studies on student satisfaction in field education and preferences for field instructor behaviours are conducted on students in undergraduate programs; in the foundation-level, generalist-type practicum; and in the advanced clinical practicum. Few studies of students in mezzo and macro practicum, where they are learning community practice, administration and management, social policy and planning, are available to guide instructors in such settings. A recent study provides useful information to address this gap. A comparison of 148 macro and 329 micro students' experiences of the field practicum was undertaken, and the researchers found similarity in student preferences, although macro students reported less positive experiences than did clinical students (Deal, Hopkins, Fisher, & Hartin, 2007). Both groups of students reported the same reasons for judging the experience less positively, such as few relevant learning assignments, and field instructors who were unprepared, failed to provide positive feedback, were overbearing or autocratic, and who were often unavailable.

A Developmental Perspective

Earlier we noted that viewing students' needs from a developmental perspective could be useful in understanding issues students may be struggling with at various points in their personal and career pathways. Such insights can be used to tailor the dimension of support and autonomy and provide a relationship appropriate to the students' level of development. Counselling psychologists have developed models of supervisee development to capture this notion; most notable is the work of Stoltenberg (2005). While empirical work has not always supported the model's contentions, and education of psychology students (referred to as supervision of trainees or supervisees) is different contextually and substantively from field instruction, there may be some useful insights gleaned from this literature. Stoltenberg and colleagues propose that students proceed through three developmental levels as they progress from beginners to experts as counselling psychologists (Stoltenberg, McNeill, & Delworth, 1998). Changes occur in three areas: self-other awareness, motivation, and autonomy. Beginners are characterized as motivated, but with high anxiety and a focus on acquiring skills, wanting to know how to do the best thing for clients, seeking the right approach. With respect to self-awareness, the focus is on the self at an early stage in developing self-awareness. Students are responsive to a didactic approach, dependent on the supervisor, and need structure and positive feedback rather than critical confrontation or feedback.

At the next stage of development, which is referred to as intermediate, students vacillate between feeling confident and feeling confused. They are also conflicted about wanting more autonomy and at other times still wanting dependency. With respect to awareness, there is a greater focus on the client, although there is great interest in their own personal development. Supervisees are learning to develop alternative conceptualizations of the client situations they encounter, and deriving a cohesive theory (Stoltenberg, 2008). Since confusion and movement backward and forward characterizes this stage, supervisors with 'considerable skill, flexibility, and perhaps a sense of humor' are recommended (Stoltenberg et al., 1998, p. 87). Supervisees express wanting more guidance and help with issues in cases they overlook, and assistance with conceptualization rather than with a didactic focus on specific skills.

In the advanced stage of development the supervisee is more confident about her effectiveness, with only occasional doubts. Belief in one's own judgment enables the practitioner to advance to independent practice, and supervision becomes more collegial. A more complex examination of personal development is evident, with considerations given to transference and counter-transference, parallel process, and issues of defensiveness and resistance.

In social work, Deal (2002) reports on an exploratory study of 15 second-year master's students in a clinical practicum, and provides data to support development over the year in students' ability to address interpersonal processes occurring between the students and their clients, an increase in students' receptive capacities, and a greater differentiation of the personal and professional self. Receptive capacity refers to the students being able to experience and be with processes in the interview, such as slower pacing, patience with the rate of client change, greater attentiveness to clients, and not imposing the student's thoughts. The study also found that student performance at the beginning of the second year had decreased compared to their field instructors' ratings at the end of the first year. Deal (2002) uses Stoltenberg and Delworth's (1987) model of development to explain this 'period of uncertainty leading to a temporary lessening of skills … consistent with their increasing ability to understand the complexity of client dynamics and theoretical concepts' (Deal, 2002, p. 11). Through increased study of development through the course of field education teaching, interventions to facilitate specific development phases can be articulated and tested.

Challenges to Maintaining the Relationship: Communication

Directly and indirectly, both field instructors and students give each other information about their experience of the relationship. Through discussions of expectations, contracting, and learning and teaching styles, each participant gains a sense of the other's preferences and approaches. Usually, initial agreements require some degree of further exploration so that clarification of roles, expectations, and objectives is achieved. Educators recommend that field instructors take the lead and introduce these notions related to both the process dimensions and learning objectives of the practicum. What is more difficult is drawing attention to concerns arising in their relationship.

Most students have been exposed to hierarchical educational systems and recognize that field instructors have power by virtue of their role as evaluators. Hence, students are not likely to initiate critical feedback unless they perceive a high degree of safety in the relationship with the instructor, that their perspectives will be heard and listened to seriously, and that some positive resolution may result. Effective social work practice requires practitioners who are able to give direct feedback to clients, colleagues, and superiors. This feedback is provided within the context of a relationship, and is successful when given in a way that is not hostile and confrontational, and invites discussion, joint problem solving, and resolution. The field instructor and student relationship can provide a context and model for learning these important communication skills (Bogo, 1993). Students learn through observing, modelling, and participating in a mutual process. Through seeking regular feedback, field instructors can gain useful information about needed teaching strategies and receive information to further develop their abilities as educators (Power & Bogo, 2002).

Through offering numerous workshops for students and field instructors on communication, Power and Bogo (2002) identified a number of crucial dimensions. Conceiving the relationship as a two-person interactional system, they propose that students' comfort in providing regular feedback to instructors is highly dependent on instructors' responses when such feedback is offered. 'If students' issues are ignored, labeled as personality problems, or responded to with defensiveness, students are likely to remain silent in the future. Similarly, if students express feedback in an attacking or hostile manner, it is not surprising if field instructors respond with defensiveness or withdraw' (p. 43). Power and Bogo present the following process for instructors who are interested in gaining ongoing feedback from students: explicitly state that feedback is valued; attend to students' non-verbal cues, as well as statements about the practicum; and encourage the expression of opinions and approaches that differ from the instructors. When students are able to provide critical feedback, instructors are urged to explore the issue, ask for specific and concrete information in a non-defensive manner, and identify alternatives the student might find more helpful. In discussion it is important to clarify the instructor's understanding of the student's concerns, and to follow up on any agreements reached.

Students also have responsibility for communicating in a manner that can facilitate the working relationship. Students are encouraged to provide feedback in a manner that is clear, identify what is helpful, and offer suggestions of other useful means for assisting the student's learning. Students can also share their concerns about giving feedback to someone with the power to evaluate and determine if the student will pass or fail the practicum. Such a discussion can help to clarify expectations – whether the field instructor expects and values student feedback, when and how this feedback should be given, and how differences may be resolved. These aspects of contracting about the process of teaching and learning were discussed in general terms earlier in this chapter. Contracting, clarifying agreements, or developing learning plans are ongoing activities. They may begin in the pre-practicum stage, and certainly are addressed in the beginning and throughout orientation. It is important to revisit these agreements as students and field instructors work together and gain a better understanding of what is actually involved through the 'give and take' of daily interactions. Periodic and mid-term review and evaluation provide a structure to more formally renew and document the process and focus of learning.

Ruptures in the Relationship

For some individuals, despite clear statements that feedback will be both positive and constructive, hearing negative comments is felt as personally hurtful, humiliating, or wounding. Efforts at protecting the self from further negatives can include avoidance of the instructor, aggressive disagreements, or becoming immobilized, and the dynamics in the relationship become a barrier to learning (Bogo, 1993). At such times it may be necessary to engage in reflection and discussion about the educational nature of the relationship. Such explorations can heighten students' feelings of vulnerability or assist them to partner in identifying previously unspoken thoughts about the learning process. With better understanding of how feedback is evoking negative feelings rather than promoting learning, both participants can search for more productive ways of achieving field expectations. Bogo and Vayda (1998) note that students in such a situation will likely struggle with whether they can trust an instructor's request to work jointly on relationship issues through expressing concerns. Trust cannot be automatically gained; rather, it is established over time, through interactions which confirm the genuine nature of the request to openly discuss and explore together better ways of working. Differences and conflicts can be resolved to some extent, especially when instructors are relationally focused and acknowledge the contributions of both parties to any impasse. Differences in histories and encounters with those with power, as well as personal, learning, and teaching styles can contribute to harmonious or discordant interactions. While not all relationship situations can be ideally resolved, some more effective ways of interacting can result. An important consequence of an approach that is openly committed to resolving a rupture is that students experience an aspect of interpersonal relationships which they in turn can use as a model for their practice with clients, committees, and staff groups encountering obstacles or ruptures. Involving the liaison can also be useful when student and instructor find themselves stuck in their work together.

Challenges to Maintaining the Relationship: Power Dynamics

Social work practice literature is increasingly attending to power dynamics in the relationships between social workers and clients and empowerment approaches for practice (Gutierrez, Parsons, & Cox, 1998). In this approach, workers aim to collaborate and share power with individuals, families, and communities. The difference in power between workers and clients are acknowledged, as are the extent and limits of workers' authority. Since clients are seen as the experts in their own lives, goals and issues are mutually defined. When students are engaged in learning how to practice in this approach, it is understandable that they will be sensitive to power dynamics in their relationships with classroom teachers and field instructors.

Field instructors, often front-line social work practitioners in complex and hierarchical organizations, do not generally experience themselves as having power. By virtue of their appointment as field instructors, the social work educational program delegates power to them. Power accrues because they are recognized as having professional knowledge and skill which confers authority. In the setting, they have access to assignments for students' learning. Their role as educator also includes evaluator, with the power and authority to recommend a grade to the liaison and educational program. As a result of these features, students realistically recognize the dominant role their instructors play in the teaching and learning dyad.

Students' perceptions of instructors' power will be influenced by a range of factors, including individual student's histories with persons in positions of power in educational settings, in employment, and in general. Depending on personal and familial experiences of power, privilege, oppression, and marginalization, students and instructors bring into their relationship and work expectations, perceptions, and behaviours about the use and misuse of power by those in positions of authority. Field instruction is generally offered in an individual model with the creation of a tutorial dyadic relationship. When this relationship becomes highly valued and intense, it can also stir up feelings from past significant relationships with authority figures. Thoughts and behaviours may arise which appear unrelated to the present educational milieu. They may be reminiscent of past relationships of vulnerability, mistrust, and abuse of power, or of protection and support by those in power.

Societal Influences on Power

Perceptions of power dynamics may be influenced by events associated with factors such as class, gender, race, sexual orientation, religion, citizenship status, ethnicity, ability, and similar characteristics. For example, the studies of gay and lesbian students' field education concerns, reviewed in the previous chapter, found that while students varied in their individual readiness and decision to self-disclose their sexual orientation, experiences in their relationships with their field instructors and the agency climate profoundly affected this decision. A particular concern related to the power of the instructor, the threat of negative ramifications for lesbian and gay students' evaluations, and future employment as a result of self-disclosure to heterosexual field educators (Messinger, 2004; 2007; Newman et al., 2008, 2009). In one study students identified that while self-disclosure enabled them to be freed up for learning, considerable energy was devoted to determining whether the relationship with the field instructor and the agency milieu were safe or unsafe places to do so. Despite positive space signs and anti-discriminatory policies in the agency, staff practices were highly significant. Where there was an open and accepting attitude in staff discussions about diversity, where sexual orientation was discussed in general, and where there were 'out' staff or board members, a more positive climate prevailed (Newman et al., 2009).

The relationship with the field instructor and the topics addressed in sessions was a crucial facilitator of student disclosure. Students reported that even in 'safe' settings and with 'open-minded' field instructors there was no discussion about sexual orientation and self-disclosure in practice (Newman et al., 2008). Students described feeling that in the absence of field instructor-led discussion, the onus was on them to address sexual orientation-related issues and self-disclosure. Even when an instructor opened the door in subtle ways, if the student did not readily respond, the issue was not pursued. A gay-identified field instructor suggested that lesbian, gay, bi-sexual, and transgendered students may require direct statements rather than subtle gestures from field instructors and other agency staff in order to successfully receive messages of openness and acceptance. 'I think because they hear the field supervisor name it ... you create an environment that says you don't have to come out, but if you want to, we've had students before that are queer' (p. 224). The absence of any direct statements by field instructors indicating their openness to discussing sexual orientation contributed to lesbian and gay students' uncertainty about a field instructor's or agency's openness and acceptance.

These studies provide insight into the ways in which societal attitudes about identity, in this instance sexual orientation, affect field education in agencies and maintain power and oppressive structures and situations for lesbian, gay, bi-sexual, and transgendered students. Consistent with the theme of this chapter, the field instructor relationship has tremendous power to influence the student's readiness to fully engage in learning, in this instance related to disclosure of sexual orientation in professional practice. These studies also remind us of the significant impact of context, and that field education takes place in organizational contexts which also provide messages about power relations and oppressive attitudes and behaviours, and contribute to perceptions of safe or unsafe climates. Researchers recommend that these factors can be better addressed through faculty support and mentoring, supportive field education staff who are knowledgeable about the issues students are experiencing, gay and lesbian social work professionals as mentors, out gay and lesbian agency staff, education, and supportive heterosexual coworkers. In addition, institutional resources were recommended, such as resource information for lesbian and gay students, information about sexual orientation issues in placement, lists of gay-friendly agencies, gay and lesbian agencies as placement sites, and resources for gay and lesbian clients (Messinger, 2004; 2007; Newman et al., 2008, 2009).

Use and Misuse of Power

Power can be used in constructive or destructive ways. The positive use of power involves the ability to influence decisions and provide support. For example, a well-respected social worker perceived as having access to senior administrators in a hospital setting can more easily negotiate with her team to provide time and opportunities for a social work student. A new social worker who has not yet established her reputation and is in a peripheral position may have more difficulty gaining her team's agreement to include a social work student.

Instances of field instructor misuse of power are reported in the literature and in anecdotal reports to field coordinators and liaisons. Power can be imposed directly, indirectly, and subtly when the field instructor exceeds the expectations of their role and its limits. Some examples of abuse of power are using the student as an unpaid worker rather than a learner, not honouring the learning agreement, ignoring student feedback, crossing students' personal boundaries into quasi-therapeutic conversations, speaking to students in negative and disrespectful ways, and engaging in sexual harassment. In Giddings and colleagues' (2003) national study of critical incidents in field education, former students reported abuse of power such as unprofessional behaviour with moderate ethical and boundary violations and extreme violations such as physical aggression, sexual harassment, and racial bias.

Studies of student reactions in field education reveal that many contentious and stressful events relate to the relationship with the field instructor and how power is used with the student. For example, in Barlow and Hall's (2007) study of tensions in field education, a student found the 'authoritarian, militaristic style of her field instructor, quite different from her own' (p. 406) difficult to cope with. This finding is similar to Giddings and colleagues' (2003) report of negative incidents due to a harsh and unyielding supervision style that was rigid, authoritarian, overly challenging or accusatory, and lacked empathy and sensitivity to student needs. Barlow and Hall's (2007) respondents also related feeling powerless when they witnessed social workers' behaviour towards clients which students saw as rude, insensitive, or unjust. The respondents felt helpless, recognized the instructors' 'power over me. So ... I always felt threatened at every moment that she'd be failing me, even though I felt I was achieving' (p. 407). Similarly, in Litvack and colleagues' study (2010), student participants were acutely aware of the power dynamics, and even confident students, with life experience and self-perceived practice competence, reported a sense of vulnerability. Those in a positive relationship could manage their feelings of powerlessness. Those in a negative relationship experienced it as a source of great stress and discomfort. Students related that they were not only fearful of the grade the field instructor would provide, but also viewed instructors as having enormous power to affect their future – instructors could provide a reference for employment. Especially in geographic locations with limited numbers of social work agencies there was a sense that social workers knew each other, and that a poor reference would follow students into their career and affect their choices and options.

Misuse of power can also result from abdication of power. For example, Giddings and colleagues' (2003) national study of critical incidents found concerns about a lack of supervision, including lack of structure, direction, and feedback. Other examples of abdicating power are expecting the student to construct their own learning experience, hence relinquishing the responsibility to provide structure and assignments for the practicum. When students' practice is not observed or recorded and reviewed, when there is little feedback given, students must find others in the setting willing to provide input or become overly reliant on their own reflections and self-assessment. In such situations students may be treated as colleagues as if this position were more favourable than the student role; unfortunately, they are also deprived of the teaching they have every right to expect. Students in such situations are usually reluctant to complain to the liaison, and simply perform as best they can.

There are examples of field instructors who share excessive personal information with students, either in a deliberate or a spontaneous attempt to reduce the power differential. However, inappropriate self-disclosure can be burdensome for students. For example, students who learn their instructor is experiencing personal problems become reluctant to add to the instructor's difficulties and may lessen requests for observation, co-working, or review of their work. There are also instances of instructors who share too much personal or negative information about the agency and the instructor's feelings about other staff early in the practicum. When the instructor realizes the error and then attempts to pull back from such disclosures, the student is left confused and wondering about what is and what is not appropriate for discussion.

Other examples of abdicating power arise from field instructors' discomfort with the authority inherent in their role. They may give feedback that is mainly positive, and avoid negative or critical constructive comments. Reluctant to disturb the equilibrium in the relationship with the student, they avoid dealing with difficult performance issues and focus on safe topics. The term 'demand for work' is used by Shulman (1993, p. 104) to describe the supervisor's intervention when staff members show some ambivalence or resistance to direction. This may occur in response to meeting a difficult demand or expecting new learning that involves more risk for the staff member. The desire to grow and develop may be counter-balanced by pulling back from the challenge. Shulman strongly points out that 'Effective work requires staff members to deal with troublesome subjects and feelings, to recognize their own contributions to a problem, to take responsibility for their own actions, and to lower their established defenses' (p. 104). This sentiment is true for students as well when they encounter difficulties in learning more complex practice interventions, such as relating to hostile and challenging clients, or making or assisting clients to make difficult decisions such as those concerning child protection, end of life care, and domestic violence.

Recognizing that learning is not linear, but involves forward and backward movement, the sensitive field instructor can be attuned to both sides of students' messages – the desire to maintain the status quo and the desire to move ahead into unknown and uncertain territory to master new skills. Offering empathic responses about students' ambivalence within the context of a supportive relationship while confronting the impasse or obstacle with the student, is recommended. Using skills of partializing the student's concerns and focusing on the practice situation allows the instructor to use knowledge, expertise, and power effectively, and to support the student in moving forward.

The Student Role

Recall the discussion of the student as adult learner and the emphasis on field learning as a collaborative process. Given this perspective, students are expected to engage in an active manner with initiative, consistent with a view of professional lifelong learning and continuous development. Carroll (2009) observes that individuals are not necessarily good at self-evaluation, and hence supervisors of staff and field instructors of students need to ask others: How can I enact my role differently? How can I enact my role in a better manner for you to learn? and What should I stop doing in this role? Recognizing the complex dynamics in the relationship, Carroll further comments that supervisees and students need to be allowed to tell their supervisor and field instructor what it is they need in order to learn and progress. Only through the active participation of the learner in fashioning the learning relationship can the field instructor customize the learning process. With the student's collaboration they can identify learning style and learning blocks, in the broadest sense of the meaning of these terms. This recommendation is supported by Fortune (2001), who compared 69 master's students' initial reactions to the field agency, field instructor, and perceptions that their learning goals could be met, and found these impressions were correlated with their satisfaction at the end of the practicum. Since these early impressions were not changed by subsequent experience, this finding supports the importance of explicit discussion at the beginning and throughout the field experience of student's perceptions and satisfaction with the processes of teaching and learning in the field.

Returning to the theme of power in the relationship, while students may feel vulnerable and powerless with their field instructor, they in fact do have power, which may be expressed directly or indirectly. Student reactions to perceptions of field instructors' power vary considerably. There are those individuals who feel extremely vulnerable in the relationship and feel they are 'at the mercy' of the instructor. In these instances they may become very watchful of the instructor's behaviour and try to do what will win them favour in the relationship. Other students may react to their perceptions of the instructor's power by feeling in a 'one down' position, and challenge the instructor. When instructors are attuned to these potential dynamics they can respond in a purposeful manner. Power dynamics can be discussed, and with overly compliant students instructors can encourage more student autonomy; and with challenging students they can engage in discussion and debate in a professional manner.

Students can abuse their power when they do not follow through on learning and service agreements, do not attend scheduled field instruction and staff meetings, or do not provide access to observe their work directly through audio or video records or written reports. Speaking inappropriately with agency staff about their perceptions of their field instructor is a way in which information can be used destructively (Power & Bogo, 2002).

As university students, learners have the capacity and power to pursue and master new knowledge and skills. Abdicating this power is seen when students rely excessively on the field instructor, refrain from exercising their own judgment about next steps in practice, and require frequent concrete and specific directions. Students are sensitive to the dynamics in the working relationship and are likely to be attuned to difficulties or obstacles. Understandably, most students are hesitant to raise concerns directly, and will try to accommodate instructors and extract as much learning as possible. When, however, they see that there is little improvement and the situation is detrimental to their own learning, it is important that students discuss issues directly with the field instructor or faculty liaison so that there is the possibility of change or resolution. Such an action takes some courage, and recognition that to avoid doing so is to minimize and abdicate the legitimate power the student does possess. Field faculty report hearing examples from students, after the practicum grades are submitted, about negative experiences where learning was severely compromised as students decided that the risk in dealing with difficulties was too great. Instead, students attempted to just get through it. In such instances, students are denied the active teaching they deserve, and the university has neglected its responsibility to provide quality education for competent practice. In part, these situations are a reflection of the problems in the structure of social work education, specifically the heavy reliance on field instructors to provide practice education, and the limitations of the field liaison role. These structural issues were discussed earlier in this text, but remain a concern and an area for further consideration and change.

Conclusion

To recapitulate, the examination of studies of factors affecting students' experience in field learning provided the basis for identifying a number of principles for field education pertaining to the relationship context between the student and field instructor. As well, many of these principles derive from the practice wisdom of field educators. From this discussion, it appears that a number of factors related to the relationship must be present for students to experience a quality field practicum. First, similar to social work practice, valued field instruction emanates out of the relationship between the student and instructor. In the context of an available and supportive relationship, students believe they can receive and use critical feedback about their practice; that they can learn within an environment that is attentive to their needs for structure and autonomy, especially as they progress through various stages in learning and growth as professionals. Since the relationship provides the context for learning, much attention has been devoted to discussing the need for collaboration, the challenges to effective communication between the student and instructor, the effect of the different roles and positions of the two participants, and how power is constructed, perceived, and used.

This chapter concluded with an examination of challenges to effective processes of teaching and learning, and focused on communication and power dynamics. Drawing from exploratory studies of the experiences of gay and lesbian students, the impact of social identity was examined. Similar dynamics may exist for students and instructors with respect to a range of characteristics, and these await further study and explication. The increasing research base is adding to a more in-depth understanding of teaching and learning in the field, and is leading, ultimately, to more effective educational approaches.

6 Principles and Methods for Field Instruction

In the previous chapter, principles for field education were discussed which relate to the interpersonal dimensions of teaching and learning, specifically the relational context of student and field instructor collaboration. The aim of the teaching relationship described is to develop an environment conducive for students to fully engage in learning. Of special interest are interactions which build trust, foster transparency, and are sensitive to power dynamics. The presence of these dimensions appears foundational for open discussion to occur, including giving and receiving useful feedback. To clarify, the teaching relationship is not an end in itself. Rather, the extensive discussion of relationship factors is due to its primacy as a means to achieving the objectives of field education – developing students' practice competence.

In this chapter attention is on concrete methods of teaching, such as providing opportunities for observation of practice, reflective discussion, and feedback about expected practice behaviours and skills. It is believed that these teaching methods build towards students' achieving competence in social work practice. Recall the discussion of competence presented earlier in this text. Competence is defined holistically as integrating higher-order meta-competencies and procedural competencies. Meta-competencies refer to three dimensions: (1) cognitive and conceptual abilities such as conceptualizing practice or using theory and practice in an iterative manner, and exercising professional judgment; (2) interpersonal and relational abilities as they are present in ones' behaviour with colleagues, staff members, the field instructor, and clients, including the intentional use of self; and (3) personal and professional competencies such as reflection on practice, knowing when consultation is needed, and self-direction for continuing professional development. While presented as three distinct dimensions, in fact there is interplay and overlap between them. These meta-competencies perform an organizing function, enabling individuals to use skills in a flexible manner, to transfer learning from one situation to another, and to combine skills differentially based on the needs of the practice situation encountered. Holistic competence obviously includes generic and specialized procedural skills of assessment or analysis, intervention or implementation, and professional communication in oral and written forms.

To achieve such holistic competence students need opportunities to practice, to reflect on their practice, and to receive feedback about their practice. Meta-competencies and procedural competencies are developed through multiple sequences of practice, reflection and conceptualization, and gaining feedback. Subsequent interactions in practice provide opportunities to use new insights and information and fuel further sequences of action-reflection-conceptualization-action. While some of these activities can be conducted on one's own, field instruction provides a unique opportunity for discussion in an open and safe environment, one in which students can consider their achievements as well as their 'mistakes' and confusions. With supervision in agencies less available for new and experienced staff members (Gilbert, 2009), field education may be the only time in a social worker's career where so much focused attention is devoted to her learning and practice. The principles for field instruction discussed in the previous chapter provide the context for such direct and unguarded explorations. In this chapter this discussion continues and focuses on principles and methods for field instruction which facilitate student mastery of meta-competencies and competencies.

As stated above, the goal of field education is to prepare students for professional practice as competent social workers. In this regard, recall that earlier in this text two dominant perspectives about professional practice were reviewed: the technical-rational approach and the reflective-practitioner approach. Educators do not need to feel compelled to choose between these paradigms. Rather, following Cheetham and Chivers' (2005) recommendations for integrating the strengths of both approaches, this chapter begins with educational principles for developing students' reflective, analytical, and critical capacities. Methods of teaching are then reviewed, including direct observation of experienced practitioners and students, and giving and receiving feedback.

Developing Reflective and Conceptual Meta-Competence

Conceptual Frameworks for Bridging Knowledge and Practice

Conceptual frameworks can be used to link learning from classroom courses and learning from field experiences. It is clear that social work students need to learn the knowledge base of the profession, and learn it in a way they can use in practice. As noted earlier, theory and concepts that underlie how social workers view the world, and frame and explain individual and social problems, are fundamental to social work education. Students also need to learn generic social work practice principles and practice behaviours and skills, which are likely part of most practitioners' repertoire. In addition, students need to learn the specialized practice models dominant at any particular point in time, especially those associated with best practice with the populations and social problems with which they are working. Currently, the emphasis on evidence-based practice is a proposed method for accessing such procedural knowledge.

In the beginning of this text the first chapter discussed the context of social work and the unique challenges due to the structure of social work education. The division of two domains of social work education, university-based courses and the field practicum, can present a schism where a technical-rational approach is primarily used in classroom courses and a reflective practitioner approach is used in the field setting. It is proposed that learning is facilitated when there are educational devices which serve to bridge these two domains. The Integration of Theory and Practice (ITP) Loop Model developed by Bogo and Vayda (1998) provides one such device to assist field instructors in linking these two sites, and to assist students in examining and using the contributions of knowledge to practice and practice to knowledge-building. This model is described in detail in chapter 2, The Nature of Professional Social Work Practice. To briefly recapitulate, the model includes four phases which are described using a loop metaphor to depict the cumulative and ongoing nature of reflection and action (Bogo & Vayda, 1998). Repeated activities of engaging in practice, thinking, feeling, and doing, or taking some action, again and again, in a practice situation comprise the phases. Each phase of the loop affects the next in an iterative fashion. The four-phase model includes (1) retrieval and recall of the salient facts of a practice situation; (2) reflection on the practitioner's personal subjective associations and reactions to all or aspects of the situation; (3) linkage of both the facts and reactions to various concepts or models derived from the profession's knowledge base; and (4) professional response, which involves a reconsideration of the situation based on the previous steps, and planning for action in the next encounter with the situation.

Reflection and Analytical, Critical Thinking

Reflection and analytical, critical thinking is needed to creatively use and potentially adapt knowledge for local situations. In field instruction there is a tendency to focus on 'what the problem is and what to do about it.' This is understandable, as workplace activities are pragmatic and focus on action-oriented processes. The educational focus in workplace learning, however, emanates from the crucial phases of reflection and linkage in the Integration of Theory and Practice (ITP) Loop Model (Bogo & Vayda, 1998). The reflective practice paradigm discussed earlier offers principles for facilitating reflection, which mainly apply to reflection-on-action – looking back at experiences. As noted in the review of this body of literature, approaches to enhancing reflection-in-action have received less attention and study.

Field instructors are encouraged to appreciate the nature of the reflective process as somewhat nebulous and not easily boxed into stages and steps. This is similar to the notion of practice as complex, messy, and indeterminate. While reflective models reviewed earlier are presented in a linear fashion, in actual practice and teaching, they are likely less systematic; and until there is more research on the topic, this may be appropriate. The objective of reflection is to incorporate into professional action a thoughtful, introspective, attentive dimension – at the time of practice and after the event. It is not possible or desirable to be reflective about all that transpires. Rather, the scholars reviewed all make the case for adopting a mindful, reflective stance and making intentional decisions about what to be thoughtful about (Langer, 1989).

Field Instructors Teach and Model Reflection

Teaching techniques to help students learn to become reflective practitioners involve the presence of a coach, mentor, or teacher who guides, questions, probes, and models the reflective process. As in any teaching situation, rapport between teacher and student is crucial, and this topic is explored in detail in the previous chapter on facilitating learning. Modelling involves the instructor making transparent her own internal process in relation to her practice of social work and also to her practice as an instructor. This level of self-disclosure rests on instructors' comfort with exposing their own vulnerability and struggles to achieve and maintain professional competence.

Field instructors can provide some structure for learners' reflections. The literature is replete with techniques for fostering reflection, including reflective journals and writing portfolios, learning partners, learning contracts, and self-assessment inventories (Boud, 1999; Boud & Walker, 1998). Examining critical incidents and debriefing following structured questions is also proposed (Brookfield, 1998). In peer groups a facilitator made a difference in guiding members in their work settings to stay focused on reflection and to extract learning from sharing experiences (Marsick, 1990). Ground rules and an agreed upon framework for reflection were considered necessary for effective learning from group formats by the participants in Cheetham and Chivers' (2005) study of professionals' continuing development.

Bogo and Vayda's (1998) guidelines for reflection include encouraging students to 'identify their feelings, thoughts, and assumptions regarding the practice data' (p. 111), and to recognize the impact of their behaviour and actions on the evolving interviews or meetings. When students spontaneously draw associations between their own experiences and issues in the practice situation, they recommend assisting students to compare and contrast psychosocial and organizational factors, and societal contexts of the student's and the client's or community's experiences. Such recognition of similarity and difference can help students tease out instances where their assessment of practice situations is overly interpreted through the lens of personal experience, rather than professional knowledge.

Finally, for meaningful reflection to occur, learning environments must be attentive to the socio-emotional climate. Since reflection tends to be very personal, when conducted in dyadic field instruction (student and field instructor) or in group settings, attention to the socio-emotional learning environment is important. Especially in the early stages, before trust and comfort with instructor or peers has developed, a balance of challenge and support of students' thoughts and feelings are facilitative (Rogers, 2001). The importance of the learning environment is a theme throughout this text, emphasized in the previous chapter in the discussion of the instructional relationship and examined in relation to group instruction or supervision in the following chapter.

Before leaving the discussion of reflection it is worthwhile to examine the potential of mindfulness to increasing the capacity to be reflective in practice. The contributions of mindfulness are receiving attention across a variety of professions as well as recognized for reducing stress in everyday life. The cultivation of an observing self is recognized as an aid to interpersonal processes and for self-regulation. An observing self is especially pertinent to the ability to reflect. In order for reflection-in-action to occur, students and practitioners are confronted with a unique challenge: to be fully engaged and active in the present moment with the professional situation, and simultaneously to maintain a level of awareness and attention that enables them to observe important information. It is thought that regular engagement in contemplative practice increases attention, awareness, and intentionality, and is recommended as one of the few approaches for achieving reflection-in-action. Such reflection may yield changes in practice behaviour in the moment, since reflection about practice after the fact can only have an impact in the future. The approach developed by Kabat-Zinn (1990) has been recommended for educating health professionals (Epstein et al., 2008) and can assist social work educators. Mindfulness has been used successfully in a range of populations, to enhance the effects of medical and surgical treatments for individuals suffering from chronic pain and stress-related difficulties (Kabat-Zinn, 2003) and in treatments in mental health (for example, for relapse prevention in depression, see Segal et al., 2002).

Mindfulness involves training practitioners, field instructors, and students for a particular type of attention. The intention is to learn to attend to the moment-to-moment flow of experience with a receptive and non-judging awareness and entails 'cultivating and refining our innate capacity for paying attention and for a deep, penetrative seeing/sensing of the interconnectedness of apparently separate aspects of experience, many of which tend to hover beneath our ordinary level of awareness regarding both inner and outer experience' (Kabat-Zinn, 1990, p. 15). It is thought that recognizing the ubiquitous and automatic nature of reactivity helps to disengage the linkages between perceptions, interpretations, and responses, and then allows an individual to respond through choice rather than to respond in a habitual and 'mindless' manner. Thus, mindfulness enables individuals to respond creatively and skilfully to the particular moment, situation, interaction, or relationship (Alper, 2005).

Since mindfulness supports reflective practice and a stance that enables practitioners to face rather than avoid challenges in practice, to acknowledge rather than suppress discomfort, and to reflect in practice rather than react in a habitual way, it is likely to become part of training for human service professional practice. Proponents recommend practices such as meditation to develop the necessary habits of mind and being.

Teaching Linkage to Social Work Knowledge

The term 'linkage' in the Integration of Theory and Practice (ITP) Loop Model (Bogo & Vayda, 1998) refers to identifying and using the theoretical concepts drawn from social work and relevant related disciplines to explain information gleaned from retrieval and reflection and to guide future interventions. The knowledge base includes foundational explanatory theories, specialized practice approaches, empirically supported models, and generic social work principles. In each phase of the loop, attention is directed towards factors which are consistent with social work's ecological-systemic framework, incorporate notions of power and structural oppression, and encompass the individual, the social context, and the transactions between these various domains. This perspective is a hallmark of social work: that various phenomena at micro through macro levels reinforce and mutually influence each other and are included in the analysis of practice situations. The ITP Loop directs attention to four factors: (1) psycho-social factors specific to the particular client system, group, committee, or project team; (2) interactive factors related to the system created between the worker and client, group, committee, or team; (3) organizational factors consisting of agency policies, programs, and practices that affect the practice of the social worker; and (4) contextual-societal factors such as attitudes, values, and beliefs, which also impact social policy and practice (Vayda & Bogo, 1991). These factors are embedded in the multi-dimensional theoretical and practice frameworks presented in schools of social work.

Psychosocial factors refer to salient features of thinking, feeling, and behaviour that enable understanding of human and social function, dysfunction, and change. These include elements such as, for example, individual and family development and dynamics, the presence of stress and trauma, unique reactions to crisis and life challenges, and individual and family adaptations, needs, and difficulties. Important are the social identity characteristics related to a range of diverse cultural and individual features. Advances in neuroscience will likely have an increasing impact on social workers' understanding of human behaviour in the future, so that more complex bio-psycho-social formulations will emerge.

Interactive factors refer to the nature of the system developed between the social worker or social work student and the client system, the group, or the community. The acknowledgment of the impact of the practitioner's values, attitudes, personality, and stance on the nature of the working relationship has long been a feature of social work based on contributions from psychological theory and casework practice (see, for example, Brandell, 2004; Hollis, 1964; Woods & Hollis, 2000). It has received renewed interest through the contributions of postmodernism and social constructionist theory (Dean, 2001; Gergen & Davis, 1985). Such theories lead to the recognition that views of reality and the self are co-constructed through interactions with the social environment, and affected by language, culture, and power.

Organizational factors refer to the mission, policies, and programs of the agency within which social work practice and the practicum take place. The services and nature of intervention the student will offer reflect the organization's position in the local or regional context. Furthermore, many students are likely to be learning in an interprofessional team, and the assigned roles, work habits, and processes of the team will affect the service provided to clients and the community.

Contextual-societal factors refer to structural issues and features that systematically oppress individuals and serve as impediments to maximal social functioning. Factors that enable or prevent equitable access to resources and opportunities are considered, as they powerfully affect individuals' ability to participate fully in the society and achieve their full human potential.

While all four factors or levels cannot be systematically examined in depth for each client or practice situation, this template provides a framework for examining both personal subjective associations and cognitive theoretical associations. The assumption is that over time, as field instructor and student together examine numerous practice situations, students will come to reflect on their practice using a social work perspective which integrates micro and macro levels.

Studies of students' opinions about factors associated with their field learning provide support for the importance of linkage activities. For example, Fortune and colleagues (2001) found that explanations by field instructors were among the most valued learning activities for first-year students (along with conducting co-therapy and feedback on process recordings). For second-year students, explanations and making connections to theory were most valued (along with critiquing one's own work and observing others in professional roles). A similar finding is reported by Choy and colleagues (1998), that students rated as most important field instructors who provide examples of application of theory to real situations. Knight (2000) found that amongst the most influential teaching activities were integration of theory and practice, including instructors' awareness of the student's classroom learning (along with reviewing and analysing cases, and helping the student understand how the agency functions). There is certainly enough evidence from these studies to support the conclusion that an important teaching activity is that of linkage to a knowledge base, and providing conceptual frameworks for students to understand intellectually what they are observing and why they are intervening in specific ways in their field assignments.

Integrating Evidence-Based Practice

Evidence-based practice (EBP) recognizes that findings from the best empirical studies must be thought through for use in conjunction with clients based on their particular needs and characteristics. While students are expected to learn how to access the best evidence, they will need the help of field instructors to determine whether an approach is feasible in the setting and how to work with clients to gain agreement about interventions.

Once an intervention approach is chosen, the next challenge relates to how the student can learn the competence and skills necessary to provide the intervention effectively. 'Knowing about and knowing how are different, and it is unclear how the EBP approach helps to bridge general knowledge acquisition with specific skill application' (Adams et al., 2009, p. 176). If the field instructor is not conversant with the approach, acting as a resource and coordinator, he may be able to locate a practitioner in the setting or in a related setting who may be willing to train and supervise the student in learning the particular model. Without proper and systematic training in complicated new approaches, it is questionable whether students can develop the level of competence and confidence to provide the empirically supported treatment in a manner that produces change for the client.

Both critics and proponents of evidence-based practice recognize its limitations, including the fact that many forms of practice have not been subject to study and hence are not represented in the available literature. However, that an approach has not been studied should not automatically result in rejection of its potential usefulness for the particular practice situation (Adams et al., 2009). Classroom and field instructors can assist students in developing the critical skills they need to locate and evaluate the strength of the existing evidence to inform selection of possible interventions (Zayas, Gonzalez, & Hanson, 2003), and to examine the relevance of the current literature and identify gaps based on the actual experiences of the practice challenges they confront. In a study of field instructors in a school committed to evidence-based practice, the researchers found a majority of field instructors (87 per cent of 235 instructors) perceived it as a useful idea for practice (Edmond et al., 2006). However, less than half the sample used this approach in practice on a consistent basis, with almost all respondents reporting that practice experience guides their decisions about the selection of interventions. Participating field instructors reported a lack of time as the greatest obstacle to implementing evidence-based practice. The authors recommend that schools assist field instructors in adopting an evidence-based approach through developing resources such as internet access to scientific articles, and in forming collaborative research partnerships with instructors and the field agency sites.

It is also important to remember that extensive research on the common factors across models has overwhelmingly demonstrated the importance of developing and maintaining a positive relationship between worker and client in achieving positive outcomes across different models and approaches (Norcross, 2002; Wampold, 2001). In an insightful discussion of evidence-based practice, Adams and colleagues (2009) highlight that the interviewing and relationship-building skills in generalist social work practice, coupled with this compelling evidence about the importance of relationship factors, lead to the conclusion that these non-specific factors are evidence-based. They note that some social work scholars writing about evidence-based practice appear to ignore this crucial body of empirical literature, which supports the importance of fundamental knowledge and skill in interpersonal processes.

Developing Procedural Competence

Returning to the discussion of teaching methods, thus far the crucial nature of a particular type of relationship for field instruction has been identified as the foundation for teaching, based on the conceptual and empirical literature. Principles about teaching reflective practice and linkage of practice, research, and theory have also been identified. In this section we will examine guidelines from the empirical literature about the educational activities that lead to learning and competent practice performance beyond these methods.

Fortune and colleagues (Fortune, McCarthy et al., 2001) conducted a series of studies on graduate students' perceptions of quality field instruction, referred to earlier, which provide invaluable information for field instruction. They found first-year students valued three learning activities: conducting co-therapy, explanations by field instructors, and feedback on process recordings. Also of importance were the linkages made between the practice situation and the classroom material. The more often these methods were used, the greater was students' satisfaction and perception of quality in their field education. For second-year students the researchers found valued learning activities were: explanations from the field instructor, critiquing one's own work, making connections to theory, and observing others in professional roles. The researchers conclude that students respond positively to learning activities that provide opportunities to see and work with professional role models and that offer a conceptual framework for understanding what they are doing in their field placement. A similar finding is reported by Choy and colleagues (1998), that students rated as most important field instructors who provide examples of application of theory to real situations. In Fortune and colleagues' (2001) study, while the identified learning activities were associated with students' perceptions of quality instruction, no differences were found on the final evaluation of students' performance by virtue of learning activities received .The lack of relationship between learning activities and educational outcomes may be due to the problems with evaluating student competence. These issues are explored in great detail in the chapter on evaluating competence, and relate to the construction of evaluation instruments, measurement issues, and the dynamics of evaluation in the context of the field instructor-student relationship (Bogo, Regehr, Power, & Regehr, 2007; Regehr, Bogo, Regehr, & Power, 2007).

In a study in New Zealand, Maidment (2000) compared students' and field instructors' perception of the effectiveness of a range of teaching methods, such as observation of others' practice and observation of students' practice via direct observation and audio- and videotapes, co-working, live supervision, and role-play, as well as the use of written reports, verbal presentation of cases, and discussion. The researcher found that students and field instructors valued similar activities, although students found the use of audio- and videotapes more effective compared to field instructors' ratings of these activities. The methods students reported as most utilized, however, were observing other workers and discussion of case notes. Hence, there was a discrepancy between the methods students believe promote their learning (and that field instructors rated as effective) and the degree to which these methods were reportedly used by the field instructors. Student responses indicated that they were most likely to experience teaching and learning activities that offer a once-removed view of the student's competence, such as discussion of case notes, even though they valued more direct learning approaches.

Knight (2000) found the most influential teaching activities were: reviewing and analysing cases; helping the student understand how the agency functions; and integration of theory and practice, including instructors' awareness of the student's classroom learning. With respect to process recordings, the way they were used by field instructors in teaching was important, rather than simply how often or how many recordings students were required to submit.

Methods for field education have been grouped by various authors. Bogo and Vayda (1998) presented learning activities that field instructors use to facilitate learning, divided according to whether the field instructor had direct or indirect access to students' practice. Activities that provide direct access include observing students' practice through being present in the room, through a one-way mirror, through reviewing audiotapes, videotapes or DVDs, and through co-working. Role-play, where practice is simulated, would also be included in this list. Methods that provide indirect access to students' practice are verbal reports and reviewing process records, summary records, or agency case notes and recordings. All of these methods provide information which the field instructor uses in discussion, reflection, analysis, and as a base to provide feedback to students.

Fortune and colleagues (2001) organize learning activities into two categories: observation-participatory and conceptual linkage. Observation-participatory includes activities that require 'doing,' such as observing others in their professional roles, co-counselling, direct observation of students' practice through a one-way mirror, and role-playing. Conceptual linkage activities include explanations provided by the field instructor, linking theory to practice, linking classroom work to practice, suggesting readings, having the student critique his or her own field work, providing feedback on an audio or video recording of student work, and feedback on process recordings. The following presentation of methods of teaching and learning incorporates the activities referred to in the studies reviewed, and likely represents the range used in contemporary field instruction.

Practice and Observation of Practice

As reviewed above, research in field education supports the importance of observation and practice for students to acquire procedural competencies (Fortune et al., 2001). In related health professional education, such as medicine and nursing, students are expected to have numerous opportunities to practice using the various skills and competencies they are learning, to be observed by their instructors as they use those skills, and to receive feedback. Sequences of practice, observation, and feedback provide learning about the 'nuts and bolts' of practice. This approach is one valued by social work students as well.

Fortune, Lee, and Cavazos (2007) examined the premise that more practice of skills leads to better performance of those skills. Six categories consisting of 38 skills were selected from the usual field evaluation instrument, and included student as learner; development of professional attitudes, values, and ethics; knowledge and skills for agency-based work; communication skills; assessment skills; and intervention skills. Students rated their frequency of use of each of the skills. The findings indicate that practising professional skills more frequently was positively associated with students' self-evaluation of the skills that were practiced, and with their overall evaluation of their performance. As well, students who practised skills more frequently reported higher satisfaction with the field practicum and received higher field instructor ratings for their performance. The researchers conclude, 'In short, greater practice may not make perfect but certainly is associated with performance and satisfaction' (p. 256).

Fortune's findings are supported by empirical work in related disciplines. Malcolm Gladwell (2008) has drawn popular attention to the importance of deliberate practice in order to develop expertise. Drawing on the theoretical and empirical work of psychologists Ericsson, Krampe, and Tesch-Romer (1993), he summarizes their studies of elite musicians and the findings that once students were good enough to be admitted to a top music school the distinguishing feature for developing expertise was how hard each student worked, and how much they practised in a deliberate effort to improve. Neurologist Daniel Levitin (2006) comments on the findings from numerous studies of expertise, and observes that researchers have concluded that 'ten thousand hours of practice is required to achieve the level of mastery associated with being a world-class expert in anything ... It seems that it takes the brain this long to assimilate all that it needs to know to achieve true mastery' (p. 40). This conclusion provides compelling evidence for the importance of ensuring that social work students have numerous opportunities to engage in actual practice. This involves seeing many clients, working in numerous group sessions or committee meetings, and writing enough reports so that the hours spent in the practicum are used productively towards developing competence and ultimately expertise.

Observation of students' practice by field instructors assists in clarifying learning goals and identifying which skills are targeted at specific times. For example, it is not unusual for students in beginning stages to quickly develop skills for information gathering while the skills for responding with support or empathy to emotionally laden comments by clients are overlooked. A considerable empirical literature has demonstrated the importance of such skills in relationship building in general (Wampold, 2001), and in cross-cultural encounters (Tsang, Bogo, & Lee, **in press**). These crucial skills constitute an important dimension of competence; establishing their presence or absence, and coaching learners to improve effective communication and decrease dysfunctional behaviours, can only be achieved when the instructor has a clear view of the student's actual performance.

Not only is observation of crucial importance in direct practice, it is also important for students learning to practice in community, administrative, and policy planning practicum settings. In all these forms of social work practice, skill in interpersonal practice behaviours is a core competency. In mezzo and macro settings students must learn how to engage with others, including staff in the setting and in other agencies, community members, government officials, and those in powerful positions. Engagement involves learning to maintain focus on key topics and the purposes for the interaction, and to listen for explicit and implicit messages. Students may find themselves confronted with different positions expressed in emotional terms by highly involved stakeholders. Competence in conflict resolution, negotiation, and mediation are important practice behaviours to master to bring about effective new programs and policies (Mertz, Fortune, & Zendell, 2007). And yet, students in both mezzo and macro settings more frequently report a lack of available and regular field instruction sessions (Deal et al., 2007).

In summary, theoretically it is hard to understand how one could learn a professional practice behaviour or skill without observing others in practice and being observed and receiving feedback on that practice. It is inconceivable that one would allow a surgeon to perform an operation if that surgeon had learned about surgery in classroom courses and had only reported on her surgical skills to a supervisor or teacher. Empirically, studies of students' reports of activities that help them learn universally find that observation and being observed, followed by feedback, are highly valued. We can conclude, therefore, that field education must involve numerous opportunities to learn practice through watching others, and to practise those skills oneself while being observed. Both these activities can then be subjected to reflection, linkage, and analysis, with ample feedback from an experienced instructor and other learners if they are also present. And yet, social workers confronted with increasing productivity expectations by their employers may not have the time needed to observe students in practice. As noted in the discussion of the context of field education, best practices for teaching and learning may be compromised by limited resources available for field teaching.

There have been enormous developments in technology over the past few decades, so that educators and students now have easy access to devices to record, in audio or video formats, client or committee sessions. Viewing interviews through one-way mirrors is a hallmark of training in counselling and clinical psychology and in marriage and family therapy. With the ability to directly view the raw material of students interacting with families '... no longer is supervision a largely inferential process wherein the supervisor tried to ferret out what "really happened" through the scrim of the therapist's later reconstruction of it' (McCollum & Wetchler, 1995, p. 155). As a result, most settings that employ and train a range of professionals have such facilities and equipment for observation, recording, and playback readily available. In settings where such equipment is not present, good-quality audio recorders are sold at reasonable prices.

Over 25 years ago, Barth and Gambrill (1984) studied students' opportunities to observe and be observed in the field practicum. They found that field instructors rarely provided a model of interviewing, rarely had students record their interviews on audiotape or videotape, and rarely provided feedback on students' practice behaviours in interviews. Where this still remains the case, their conclusions bear repeating: 'Trial and error is a slow, frustrating and ineffective instructor. Boosts to interviewing effectiveness are less likely to result from repeated and solitary practice, or even from supervisors' critical responses to after-the-fact reports of interviews, than from specific feedback based on observation of students' performances' (p.9).

Despite advances in and access to technology, field instructors still appear to rely on verbal or written descriptions (for example, summary or process recordings) of practice as the primary data for learning about students' assignments and practice behaviours (Maidment, 2000; Rogers & McDonald, 1995). There is a human tendency to reconstruct events, with inherent distortions in recollection of what has transpired, as well as the desire to present oneself in a desirable manner. These factors render the process record too flawed for teaching about observable practice interventions. Process records and journals do have a place in an array of educational methods and can be used to stimulate self-reflection, critical thinking, and improve written communication skills, but they cannot replace the direct observation of interaction as an effective method of retrieving information about the practice situation.

As noted at the beginning of this text regarding the context of field instruction, in many settings social workers have less and less time available for teaching given increasing expectations for client contact. As a result they may not have extra time to review interviews which were recorded. Hence, observation and feedback opportunities may need to occur in a manner more integrated with the instructor's and the student's everyday practice. Learning theorists support the usefulness of learning in the actual situation where knowledge is applied. In Lee Shulman's (2005a) description of medical rounds, teaching and learning happens in a seamless way as senior physicians simultaneously provide patient care and interact with students. Eraut (2003) recognizes that experienced practitioners cannot be expected to fully and explicitly communicate all that is needed to understand and intervene in a situation in a reasonable period. When students participate with experienced practitioner-teachers in episodes and events, there is common ground for discussion, teaching, and learning. Students in such situations also learn through modelling, a method reported as helpful by students (Mumm, 2006).

The social work literature comes closest to this approach in referring to teaching through 'co-working.' Co-working refers to arrangements where the field instructor and student share the work, for example with an individual or family, a group or committee, or a project (Bogo & Vayda, 1998). Both field instructor and student are active in all phases of assessment or analysis, planning, and intervention or implementation, and pre-plan if possible how they will divide up particular tasks and deal with unanticipated conflicts or difficulties in the moment. It is important to acknowledge to each other that the level of expertise between student and field instructor varies, as well as their respective roles regarding evaluation. These dynamics can present potential barriers to the openness and risk-taking required for new learning, change, and growth. However, both participants are exposing their work to discussion, reflection, analysis, and feedback. Field instructors can demonstrate their receptivity to having their ideas challenged and to questioning their rationale for a particular intervention. Indeed, field instructors have identified these types of interactions as motivating factors for working with students. They report that they feel energized by student's questions and the resultant self-examination of their practice (Globerman & Bogo, 2003).

As previously noted, review of audio or video recordings is another way to access the actual performance of a student. Reviewing the entire interview is extremely time-consuming, and creative ways of using the material are needed. To maximize learning, field instructors and students can identify in advance what approach they will take to reviewing and discussing recordings. Generally, a more focused examination of segments is recommended. Field instructors and students can jointly listen to and discuss an entire first interview. Or, they can listen to or watch segments selected at random by the field instructor or chosen by the student. The student can, in advance, identify sequences where she or he perceives that guidance is needed, or where the student wishes to demonstrate progress in learning. Following some agreed upon structure, students can provide a written analysis of the recording. This activity will promote self-assessment and self-critique capacities. The written analysis can focus on conceptualizing issues in the practice situation or in the interaction between the student and client, group, or committee. Written analysis can also include identifying and evaluating the interventions the student is using, and providing, verbatim, alternate preferred responses.

Dettlaff and Wallace (2002) present a format for field journal entries for students which can be used to review recordings. The purpose of the journaling is to facilitate students' drawing linkages between social work literature and their field experiences. Students are expected to identify social work skills, knowledge, and values used or required in an interaction, and identify specific references from the social work literature on these dimensions. Additional questions relate to self-evaluation of the way in which these components were used in the situation analysed. Such a format could be used to guide students in reviewing recordings of specific practice encounters as well as in regular analysis of some or all of their practice interactions. Dettlaff and Wallace report that students benefit from this procedure, as it helps them make connections between knowledge learned in both class and field experiences. Since the journal experience requires continuous referencing of relevant social work literature, students who reviewed readings increased their knowledge base.

It is not uncommon for some social work students to raise concerns about the anxiety they experience when their work is observed by others, including other practitioners, other students, and the field instructor. This does not appear to be the case in related human service fields. For example, in a review of studies of supervision of counselling trainees, Ellis (2009) found no evidence to support the 'myth of supervisees as anxious' when their sessions were monitored or recorded. While studies that used role induction to explain the purpose of observation for learning and the role of the supervisee and supervisor decreased anxiety, overall initial supervisee anxiety was minimal or low. Ellis concludes that supervision theories in counselling psychology which attribute anxiety to trainees are inaccurate. Similarly, research in the related field of family therapy found that observation and live supervision are experienced positively by supervisors and trainees (Haber et al., 2009). Since observational approaches to learning are well entrenched in these fields, it may be that students quickly learn to adapt to these training conditions. Other research found that trainees value supervisors' actions that are perceived as supportive, including 'phone-ins' that provide guidance, especially when trainees were faced with intense sessions and uncertainty about how to proceed (Mauzey, Harris, & Trusty, 2000). Not valued are lengthy explanations and directions that leave trainees feeling that they have erred and the supervisor is trying to correct their mistakes.

Referring to Shulman's (2005a) concept of signature pedagogy, adaptive anxiety is presented as a strong and important motivator for learning. Anxiety is seen as a product of visibility, accountability, and the uncertainties of practice. Shulman notes that visibility of practice and accountability to peers is a hallmark of education in medicine and law. In clinical settings or in the law classroom students are expected to respond and perform, to contribute actively to discussion, debates, presentation of information, and decision-making. According to Shulman, anxiety provides necessary emotional investment in learning and practice.

Wayne, Bogo, and Raskin (in press) review social work field education through the lens of signature pedagogy, and note the invisibility of students' practice, that (as the research reviewed earlier shows) field instructors do not generally observe substantial segments of students' practice and they note that students rarely observe each others' practice. Field education may overly rely on invisibility and lack of accountability to peers, despite the fact that in actual practice most social workers will work in organizations, with teams, and with other professionals where their practice will be more public. With respect to anxiety, the literature demonstrates concern about students' anxiety, and the focus is on how to reduce this anxiety (Gelman, 2004; Zosky et al., 2003).

Learning to handle anxiety in a productive and adaptive fashion, to perform practice behaviours in front of others, and to provide well-articulated and clear rationales for decisions and directions, are important skills for professional practice, especially practice in inter-professional teams. Conceptual understanding and resulting decisions may be based on theoretical explanations, empirical evidence, or well-developed practice theory. Experiences of observation and discussion between student and field instructor provide fertile ground for the type of integration of theory and practice recommended throughout this book. Teaching in this manner links all aspects of practice: individuals' subjective reactions, use of knowledge, and practice behaviours. When both field instructor and student have observed the same practice content, less time is needed for reporting on events or for reviewing written materials or recordings.

Providing Feedback

Given the recognition that the experience of learning is highly personal, receiving and using feedback about actual behaviours, stances, and interventions can be fraught with tensions and dilemmas. On the one hand, students value an instructor who takes the time to observe their work and comment on it. On the other, feedback that points out what has not been successful can, to varying degrees, have a discouraging affect. Students need support and challenge, and, as noted repetitively, a positive relationship provides the milieu in which students can receive critical input about their performance.

From the empirical studies it is apparent that students value feedback that is based on observation of their practice – specific, close in time to the practice situation, and which offers alternate ways of performing (Fortune & Abramson, 1993; Freeman, 1985). Offering feedback in a positive learning environment, balancing negative and positive comments, brainstorming solutions together, and encouraging student self-critique are also important (Abbott & Lyter, 1998). If critical feedback is delivered in a demeaning, harsh, or angry way; when it does not appear to have the goal of promoting growth; and when it is offered without appropriate preparation, students find it can interfere with and block learning (Abbott & Lyter, 1998).

A useful approach to feedback would follow a number of steps, including discussion of what the skill is and observation of experienced practitioners using the skill. The next step would involve enough practice opportunities for students themselves to use the skill in role-play or in simulated practice. Many social work programs systematically teach interviewing skills in practice courses or in special interviewing courses (Bogo, 2006). When in field settings, students should not be expected to automatically transfer what they have learned in a university course into a new and different context, an agency, or an institutional setting. Indeed, a major part of learning in the field is to learn how to transfer one's knowledge and skill to a new situation.

The opportunity to observe experienced practitioners using the skill in the setting and in the context of a particular social work role is an invaluable step in this re-learning or transfer process. This prepares the student for his own interactions with clients. When the field instructor observes the student performing the skill, feedback can then be based on actual, not reported, observation. Ideally, feedback is given immediately, in a concise and direct manner. (When this is not possible, audio or video recordings can provide the data on which to base feedback, as discussed above.) When providing comment it is important to balance positive and negative information and to ensure that the student understands the critical comments. The intention is to guide the student towards new or changed behaviour. Since feedback includes suggestions for alternative ways of using the skill, it is important that follow-up on the feedback take place. Follow-up could include observing students' performance on a subsequent interview, either directly or through reviewing an audio or video recording. Tracking students' progress on a regular basis, rather than solely at mid-term or final evaluations, offers a systematic approach to field learning.

Specific feedback is important for learning and to validate and reinforce gains. Bogo and Vayda (1998) observe that students often comment that they do not know what they are doing that is 'right.' Praise is frequently global and non-specific, or comments about their work are simply not given on an ongoing basis. When comments are only of a critical nature, some students may become demoralized and question their ability to learn to become a social worker. Hence, balanced and specific feedback is important, noting areas of mastery and progress as well as areas for growth.

When a field instructor has observed a student's interventions with clients, committee members, or in staff meetings, she has a firm grasp of the student's actual skills as a beginning point for feedback. It is useful to begin the discussion about a student's practice by eliciting the student's perception of his comments or interventions, and aiming to understand the frame of reference used by the student and his view of his own behaviour. In this way the student is encouraged to engage in self-critique and reflection, as well as learn from the instructor's input. Students will observe other professionals if they are working in teams and may model behaviours not necessarily consistent with social work values and presentation styles. Students may also be receiving guidance from other staff, formally and informally. Since interdisciplinary teamwork is likely a feature of most practice settings, it is important to openly discuss different approaches used by others on the team and their underlying professional perspectives and goals.

Finally, based on the value of collaboration in learning, feedback is ideally reciprocal. Students are encouraged to openly ask field instructors about the rationale for their choice of interventions, why they enact skills in particular ways, whether they have considered alternate approaches, and so on. An open exchange makes it possible for students to question the instructor's feedback about the student's work. This questioning can be seen as part of learning, developing critical and reflective capacities, and the importance of professionals' understanding the reasons underlying judgments, assessments, and intervention choices. The ability to have reciprocal feedback brings us back to the discussion in the previous chapter about the student and field instructor relationship, ways to create an open learning environment, and ways to handle challenges to maintaining a productive working partnership.

Use of Written Records

Before concluding this chapter on learning techniques it is relevant to review the use of written records. Historically, written records were used as a major teaching tool in social work field education. The process record was developed and intended to provide a written description of the interactions between the student and the client or others with whom the student was interacting. Wilson (1981) recommended that the student record 'verbatim' as much as possible what took place in an interview, including client content, interactions with the student, and the student's impressions and feelings. Over time, more structured recording of the process has been recommended. For example, Urbanowski and Dwyer (1988) recommended recording the following: purpose of the encounter, observations, selected content (such as pertinent facts, responses of the client and student to those facts, the feeling content), preparation for the next meeting, the ending, and impressions. Graybeal and Ruff (1995) present five categories for the recording: student's pre-engagement thoughts and feelings, a summary of the interaction, an assessment of what occurred, plans and next steps, and questions for discussion with the field instructor about the content or process of the meeting.

More recently, Black and Feld (2006) proposed a learning-oriented thematic model that aims to focus the process record in relation to specific themes defined by the school's curriculum, field expectations, and the student's learning goals. Themes serve to define what material in a session should be recorded and examined in greater detail, and what material is peripheral at a particular point in time (in relation to teaching and learning) and can be recorded briefly. The authors provide examples of learning themes such as beginnings, helping skills, and cultural competence, and agency-based themes such as clarifying a particular agency policy (Black & Feld, 2006). This approach can be used effectively with all levels of practice. The following categories guide the recording: (1) statement of learning themes and purpose of the session; (2) background information about the client/problem; (3) analysis of the encounter, including description, reflection, and reaction; (4) evaluation of the session; (5) future plans for student and client/situation; and (6) questions to be discussed during supervision.

As noted earlier, the major difficulty with using process records as a proxy for the student's interaction with the client, group, committee, or community member is that it is commonly known that recall is subject to personal omissions, distortions, and errors. Furthermore, it has been observed that 'Generations of students have laboriously struggled to recall the details of practice encounters and prepare a process record' (Bogo & Vayda, 1998, pp. 1323). Anecdotally, there are many examples of students spending huge amounts of time trying to reconstruct the session, and record and analyse it, only to find that it received cursory or incomplete attention in their field instruction sessions. As Knight (2000) found in her study of students' perceptions of effective teaching methods in the field, the significance of process records was the way in which field instructors used them in teaching, rather than simply the frequency with which students were required to submit them. A field instructor and student can focus on issues presented in the record and use the integration of theory and practice loop to reflect on these issues and examine, analyse, and link them to conceptual frameworks. Planning and preparation for the next encounter can result from such discussions.

Students can benefit as well from the thoughtful recall of a situation, and the insights that may surface through the concentration, attention, and focus involved in constructing a written record. The practice of writing in journals, increasingly used in social work education, is similar to the process record, and is seen as an aid to developing reflective and critical thinking and to linking observations to social work knowledge. The journal method described earlier in this chapter, developed by Dettlaff and Wallace (2002), appears to be one such useful vehicle for assisting students to draw linkages between social work literature and their field experiences. Hence, such records can play an important part in field education. They should, however, not be viewed as a suitable alternative to observing students' actual practice behaviours in social work situations.

Social work students must also learn how to record their work in a way that is consistent with agency or project purposes. In the field practicum, students may need to produce initial and periodic assessments and summary notes, or minutes of committee meetings, project reports, an executive summary, and so on. Such records require considerable thought, and represent a cognitive and intellectual process of recalling a significant amount of information, sifting through it to select that which is most salient, analysing the information through the lens of one or more frameworks, and synthesizing the information into a succinct report, often with a set of recommendations (Bogo & Vayda, 1998). Attention must be paid to the purpose of the written document and the anticipated audience. For example, when assessment reports will be used in court decisions about apprehension of children or child custody, or in forensic situations regarding readiness for probation or parole, authors of such reports must provide the factual information to support their recommendations and conclusions. This type of recording is different from case notes on a chart in a health setting, which will be read quickly by other members of the interprofessional team.

Learning the skill of writing such concise and informative reports requires a degree of 'hands-on' training by the field instructor. The practicum agency will have an approach to record keeping and report writing which the student will be expected to follow. Students are likely to have mastered the skills needed for writing in an academic setting and also the writing skills for process records and journals. But this style of writing is likely not easily adaptable to the range of professional writing required in service settings or government policy work. As in learning the interpersonal skills of practice, students will benefit from seeing models of excellent records and reports, from writing such materials, and from receiving feedback about the specific areas that are well done or that need improvement or change, with suggestions for alternate ways of writing. The material in these written records and reports may also be useful in field instruction sessions, especially with respect to conceptualizing or synthesizing large amounts of information. As with process records, summary recordings are not an alternative to teaching about interpersonal practice and observing students' actual practice behaviours.

In conclusion, this chapter, along with the previous chapter on the student and field instructor relationship, considered principles and methods for field teaching. Studies of students' preferred learning activities and field instructors' teaching approaches in field education provided the basis for identifying pedagogical principles and techniques. Where it existed, empirical support from the social work literature was included. As well, many principles derive from the practice wisdom of field educators. From the material presented it appears that three dimensions must be present for students to perceive a quality field practicum.

First, similar to social work practice, valued field instruction emanates out of the relationship between the student and instructor. In the context of a supportive relationship, students believe they can receive and use critical feedback about their practice. They can learn within an environment that is attentive to their needs for structure and autonomy, especially as they progress through various stages in learning and growth as a professional.

Second, reflective and conceptual learning occurs when field instructors provide theoretical frameworks and explanations for understanding practice, and help students use concepts they have learned to analyse their practice assignments with clients and committees, in the community, and in projects. Encouraging students to self-critique their work is relevant. While a staged view of student development was not fully supported in studies reviewed, there is some support for a greater emphasis on orientation in the beginning stage, and greater focus on conceptual and self-assessment activities at later stages.

Finally, a range of learning activities are also valued, especially those that provide opportunities to observe practitioners and to be observed as students carry out practice roles. Observations of practitioners provide role models as well as concrete examples of what concepts 'look like' in practice. Observations of students by field instructors, with opportunities for immediate feedback and discussion, provide the immediacy associated with active learning as well as rich examples to draw the links between theory and practice. The key message is that students develop a holistic competence of conceptual, professional, and practice capabilities and skills through multiple sequences of practice/action, reflection, critical thinking, and analysis of practice/conceptualization, observation and feedback about their practice, and further opportunities for practice/action. Field instructors have available to them a number of teaching methods to facilitate this cycle of learning, and through creative innovation will likely add to this repertoire over time.

7 Approaches and Formats for Field Instruction

The individual student and field instructor dyad is the most prevalent approach used in social work for field education. There are, however, other formats for instruction that have been used, studied, and reported in the literature. These include group supervision, task supervision (both of which should actually be called group or task field instruction to be consistent with the way in which terms are used in this book), rotations, and field units. In addition are field arrangements which are defined temporally, including concurrent, block, and delayed-entry. In social work, approaches to field instruction to date generally consist of general, broad ideas about structures and methods based on a number of educational theories and practice wisdom. In contrast, in counselling psychology distinct models of supervision have been described which emanate from specific theoretical perspectives and provide sequential steps. See, for example, Stoltenberg and colleagues (1998) developmental model and Bernard's discrimination model (Bernard & Goodyear, 2008). The only social work field education model with such specificity is the Task-Centered Model for Field Instruction and Staff Development developed by Caspi and Reid (2002). In this chapter, approaches and formats for field instruction will be presented, with emphasis on the key processes for field learning.

Individual Field Instruction

It is likely that the individual approach of one student with one field instructor was adopted early in social work field education as it mirrored the predominant practice modality of the time, that of social casework. In individual field instruction one student is assigned or matched to one agency-based field instructor, who serves as the primary and central educator, resource, coordinator, and evaluator of field learning. The student and instructor proceed through a set of activities in the beginning, middle, and end stages of the practicum. The steps and tasks in these phases are described in some detail in texts for field instructors, such as Bogo and Vayda (1998) and Hendricks and colleagues (2005), and a specialized approach to teaching group work in the field practicum is offered in Wayne and Cohen (2001). As well, most programs of social work will provide a Field Practicum Manual that includes policies, procedures, and clear expectations for students and field instructors, with tasks and associated timelines.

The following is a brief summary of the fundamentals of individual field instruction which draws from the literature (Bogo, 2005; Bogo & Vayda, 1998; Fortune, 2001; Fortune, Lee, & Cavazos, 2007; Fortune, McCarthy, & Abramson, 2001; Shulman, 1993) and guidelines presented in this book. In the beginning stage the field instructor prepares the team or other staff for the student's arrival, and orients the student to the setting and the practicum learning experience. Expectations of each person's role, agency procedures and recording requirements, and the school's learning objectives form the context and framework for developing a learning contract, agreement, or plan.

The notion of a learning contract has been well accepted in the social work literature (Fox & Zischka, 1989). Essentially, a contract represents the instructor's and student's individual and joint assessment of the student's level of competence in relation to the objectives or educational outcomes for the practicum, the specification of learning goals, and the identification of learning activities to meet those goals. Learning activities include practice assignments, the ways in which the field instructor will have access to the student's practice data, and the methods of field instruction that will be used, as discussed in the previous chapter. The nature of the learning plan and activities chosen is based to some extent on a mutual assessment of the student's predominant approach to learning, or learning style, and the field instructor's approach to teaching. Any learning plan is influenced by the nature of the setting and the feasibility of providing enough relevant assignments and teaching inputs to facilitate the student's learning to practice. While a learning plan or contract is typically developed in the beginning stage, it is not seen as a rigid and fixed document. Rather, as the practicum proceeds, greater understanding of learning needs occurs and new objectives may be added with different assignments and teaching methods incorporated.

Attention to developing the socio-emotional climate in the student-field instructor relationship is important in the beginning stage. Chapter 4, on perspectives about student learning, and chapter 5, on facilitating student learning, review pertinent research pertaining to these topics and offer guidelines for all approaches and formats, including individual field instruction. Further support for the importance for beginnings comes from a subset of data in a larger study conducted by Fortune (2001). An examination of the initial reactions of 69 master's students, after two weeks in the practicum setting, were compared to these students' reactions at the end of the practicum. At the beginning of the practicum the researcher assessed students' perceptions along a number of dimensions: their satisfaction or dissatisfaction with the field agency, field instructor, and field learning; whether the setting was the type desired; and whether the students expected that they could meet their learning goals in this setting. These initial reactions were compared with responses to the same questions about satisfaction at the end of the practicum. Findings revealed that students' impressions at the beginning correlated with their satisfaction at the end of the practicum; and that findings were similar for both first- and second-year students, although stronger for first-year students. Fortune concludes: 'Students make quick judgments that are unlikely to be changed by subsequent experience. Students who do not value a practicum to begin with or do not see it meeting their goals are unlikely to "come around" and be satisfied later' (pp. 501). While satisfaction in this study did not correlate with performance, the researcher points out the importance of student satisfaction in contributing to an environment conducive to learning.

Based on these findings, it is useful for field instructors, early in the field experience, to identify and discuss with students their perceptions about the field setting and its potential to meet their learning goals. Shulman (1993) recommends that field instructors tune into students' feelings, respond directly to thoughts and feelings expressed through indirect communication, and clarify the purpose of field instruction and the role of each participant. Furthermore, field instructors need to encourage students to discuss their perception of the roles and activities of both field instructor and student, what each will do, and how the student expects learning will occur in field education. Through open and transparent discussion mutual expectations can be clarified, including issues related to authority, such as evaluation of learning.

Students can be prepared by both field faculty at the university program and field instructors to take a proactive role in all aspects of the practicum. In a guide for students, Birkenmaier and Berg-Weger (2006) discuss the importance of students preparing themselves to enter the field. They recommend students learn about the expectations of adult learning; identify their own learning style; identify what they already know and what they need to learn about the agency and culture of the organization; what knowledge, skills, and values they already have and those that need to be mastered; what strengths they have; and the typical role of students at the site. Students are urged to take responsibility for their own learning, to use the field instructor and other staff as much as possible, to seek out and welcome feedback, and to be prepared for field instruction sessions.

In the middle phase of the practicum the field instructor and student will carry out the activities detailed in the learning plan or contract. Methods of teaching and learning will be put into action, some or all of the methods discussed in the previous chapter will be used. Based on the nature of the field assignments, the setting, and the population served, a range of appropriate and possible methods for observing or recording students' practice will be used, including written records. Sequences of practice/observation/recall, reflection, analysis and conceptualization, gaining feedback, and planning for future interactions will form the content and process of instruction sessions. Periodic evaluation of student learning and progress will be structured, usually following timelines set up by the school.

Focusing on the dynamics of teaching and learning requires instructors to remain sensitive and open to issues the student may be experiencing and struggling to express. This guideline is consistent with findings from studies about the student as learner, reviewed earlier in the text. For example, qualitative studies revealed that some students have strong emotional reactions to learning to practice, to the organization, and to the instructor, reactions which they may not readily share for a range of reasons (Barlow & Hall, 2007; Litvack, Bogo, & Mishna, 2010). As noted earlier, in the studies of lesbian and gay students, they reported being attentive and concerned about the agency climate and environment, whether it was open and safe. These perceptions affect their decision about self-disclosure of their sexual orientation (Messinger, 2004; 2007; Newman et al., 2008; 2009). Hence, again the importance of listening for indirect communication of cues that an issue, interaction, or situation is troubling to the student.

Shulman (1993) described the middle phase as the 'work phase,' and recommended contracting for the topic and focus of each meeting. The agenda for the session may be initiated by the student or by the instructor, and should include issues previously agreed upon that required follow-up, or reviewing specific pieces of work agreed upon in an earlier meeting. Shulman notes the ways in which engagement in learning can be undermined, and proposes that field instructors use the skill of 'demand for work.' This refers to facilitative confrontation, where instructors expect, ask, and hold students to engage in the work agreed to in their learning plan or contract. This skill is useful when topics are discussed in a superficial way, creating an illusion of learning, or when key issues are denied or inquiries about important issues are met with silence or minimal responses.

The ending stage of field instruction involves evaluation of learning and termination of key relationships. The next chapter in this book discusses content and process issues in evaluation in great detail. The essence of this phase is to review the student's practice and progress in learning, assess strengths, and identify areas where further learning and growth are needed. Depending on the evaluation tools and format used in each school, the field instructor is expected to complete an evaluation report summarizing the practicum and rating the student's performance. Students have considerable involvement and input in this process.

In the ending stage students are also assisted in reviewing and evaluating the service provided to clients, communities, committees, projects, and others with whom they have been working throughout the practicum. In project assignments, ensuring that summary or final reports are completed is a crucial aspect of ending. Written records and reports for agency purposes must also be finalized. Relationships formed with a range of individuals are also brought to closure. The extent of review and discussion about ending reflects the level of involvement with the student.

Given the nature of the student and field instructor relationship throughout the field experience, feedback from the student to the field instructor and the organization may be more or less fulsome. In situations of tension that were not successfully addressed, feedback may be minimal or may be filled with strong unresolved feelings of disappointment or anger. As the studies reviewed throughout this book indicate, the great majority of students rate their field practicum experience highly, and endings generally consist of expressions of positive sentiments. It is not unusual for students to be hired by the practicum agency for summer, contract, or permanent employment.

Group Field Instruction

Group field instruction has been used for decades in social work education and is usually referred to as group supervision in the literature. It consists of small learning groups of students who meet with one field instructor on a regular basis. The literature tends to describe examples of group teaching provided to students in addition to their own regular individual sessions with the field instructor (Walter & Young, 1999). Rarely does it appear that all instruction takes place in a group format.

The hallmark of group learning is thought to be the knowledge acquired from peers as well as from the group leader or field instructor. The format involves students presenting examples of their practice followed by group discussion and input from the field instructor. In this manner, students benefit from the exposure to a wide range of practice situations, and the perspectives and information offered by their peers (Abels, 1977; Cowan, Dastyk, & Wickham, 1972; Mayers, 1970). The group format is recommended as an economical alternative to the resource-intensive, traditional individual tutorial model (Tebb, Manning, & Klaumann, 1996). Groups can provide emotional support and mutual aid, and the group milieu can be used for self-reflection and learning about group process, stages, and roles (Geller, 1994).

Proponents of group instruction base their recommendations on their practice and teaching experience. There are few empirical studies of its impact or effectiveness conducted in social work. Walter and Young (1999) studied 12 master's students who received a combination of individual and group instruction. The students, who were experienced case managers in child protective services, reported varied positive and negative experiences in group supervision, in contrast to their uniformly positive evaluation of their individual instruction. These students acknowledged greater comfort in discussing crucial practice learning issues related to forming relationships with clients, exposing their own vulnerabilities, and developing self-awareness in individual instruction. In the second term, as these participants gained comfort and increased practice skill, they began to perceive the group learning format more positively. Similar to the observation of Tebb and colleagues (1996), when there is a supportive and validating milieu, students can learn from each other through exchanging information and hearing about similar assignments and others' work.

In a study of group supervision of three cohorts of undergraduate social work students in Israel, in each of three years a pilot group of approximately 16 to 26 students received group supervision, and were compared with the rest of the class of approximately 66 to 93 students, who received individual supervision as usual (Zeira & Schiff, 2010). The researchers found no difference in the students' perception of their experience in relation to learning about intervention with clients, in developing professional values, and in their overall satisfaction with field practice. Significant differences were found, however, in the students' perception of their field instructors – the relationships they had with them and the content covered in supervision. A general question about overall satisfaction with the field instructor found lower satisfaction for students in the second cohort in group supervision, but no difference for the first and third cohorts.

In 2001 at the University of Toronto we studied the experiences of all students and field instructors who had participated in group supervision in the master's program over the previous two years (Bogo, Globerman, & Sussman, 2004a, 2004b; Sussman, Bogo, & Globerman, 2007). The sample consisted of 18 female recent graduates of the program, and five female field instructors. Over the two years these students and field instructors were in seven different groups in hospitals, focusing on micro practice, a community-based, mezzo-macro setting, and a combined micro-mezzo practicum in a school board. The field instructors were experienced social workers and experienced instructors, having used both individual and group formats frequently. Despite learning different levels of intervention and in different agency contexts, the themes emerging from in-depth exploratory interviews with students and field instructors were the same across settings.

Similar to Walter and Young's (1999) findings, students and field instructors reported that varied positive and negative experiences in group supervision related to a number of factors which can contribute important information towards an emerging model of group field instruction (Bogo et al., 2004a, 2004b; Sussman et al., 2007). Four key elements were identified as necessary for successful group learning. First, as in the studies of relationship factors reviewed in the chapter on facilitating student learning, available and supportive field instructors were key to providing a foundation for learning. Students valued regularly scheduled sessions that were uninterrupted and long enough for all important student practice issues to be discussed. The second element related to the rationale for using the group format. When the perception was that the group was used for pragmatic or administrative reasons – for example, to save time rather than being based on an educational rationale – students felt short-changed. The remaining elements associated with perceived helpfulness were related to group dynamics and the instructors' competence in leading groups and creating a group climate where mutual aid, rather than competition, was paramount.

Of special interest was the importance of trust and safety being established in the group. The key reason for group instruction is the assumption that students learn from each other through processes of mutual aid, giving and receiving feedback, and discussion with each other. In order for these processes to occur and flourish it appears that students need to be actively engaged in the group and able to share their work with each other, including exposing their mistakes and uncertainties. Therefore, a group climate must be established where students feel respected, and perceive they can trust each other with their vulnerabilities. This finding is consistent with contemporary group work theory. These all-female groups progressed through stages of group development only when a relational base of safety emerged (Schiller, 1995, 1997). 'Safety must be established as a prerequisite to greater intimacy or self-disclosure' (Schiller, 1995. p. 123). Schiller proposes that a fairly high degree of trust must be established where 'women have sufficiently experienced connection, empathic attunement, and respect for differences' (p. 130), before members can challenge authority and each other.

In a number of the groups studied, natural and easy openness and trust did not spontaneously arise (Bogo et al., 2004a). Factors that undermined the establishment of mutual aid were members who had negative histories with each other from previous classroom experiences, members who only presented positive aspects of their practice rather than difficulties, members who appeared concerned with demonstrating their competence and superiority. Where such dynamics were present and not addressed, managed, or contained by the field instructor, group members' energy became invested in self-protection, and they became guarded when presenting their practice. We observed 'these respondents struggled, more or less actively, to find a supportive environment and were generally unable to deal directly with conflict and competition' (p. 22), and learning was compromised.

Since a positive group climate is crucial for learning, the third key element for successful group instruction is the competence of the instructor in leading learning groups. The instructor's leadership style includes orientation not only to the setting and the practicum, but especially to participating as a member of a learning group. Effective group leaders modelled expected behaviour such as risk taking and well-framed feedback, and facilitated group interaction to promote mutual aid between members, rather than simply providing individual instruction with the group serving as an audience. They also engaged the group members in establishing group norms, and actively intervened when group members' behaviour was not consistent with those norms. This involved assisting group members to recognize behaviour contrary to the norms, as well as encouraging reflective discussion about the group's process, progress, and difficulties in maintaining the learning climate they desired. These findings about group interaction appear similar to Lee Shulman's (2005a) concept of accountable talk between students. Students are expected to offer focused and cogent comments, to build on others' statements, to offer counter-arguments or new data. This type of dialogue is in contrast to students' reports of feedback from their peers that 'consisted of multiple ideas and opinions that were not grounded in their own practice experience and not linked to the context within which they were practicing' (Bogo et al., 2004b, pp. 209–10). Such unconstrained feedback led to students feeling overwhelmed, inadequate, and incompetent. In contrast, students reported as helpful focused discussion that included feedback and helped plan for the next client intervention or meeting with a committee on a project. Students repeatedly identified the need for the instructor to provide leadership and structure so that the group discussion was directed.

Related to students' ability to function as members of a learning group is their understanding of group process. This later dimension relates to the fourth element for successful group instruction: the instructor's ability to assist the members in processing group dynamics. Consistent with the literature on group supervision of social work staff and of students in the related field of counselling psychology, successful group development and functioning depends on the establishment and maintenance of group norms and rules, the expression and resolution of group conflict and competition, and the development of group cohesion (Bernard & Goodyear, 2008; Proctor, 2000; Shulman, 1993). When conflict existed and operated in overt or covert ways, the student participants in the study wanted instructors who could respond directly to indirect cues that tension or conflict existed; they wished that instructors would explicitly identify interpersonal issues, and help group members resolve their differences (Bogo et al., 2004a, 2004b). In contrast were the perspectives of the field instructors and the researchers' observation that what seemed rather benign to the field instructor participants were concerns for the student participants (Sussman et al., 2007). How the different levels of skill and competence of individual student group members are perceived by their peers, and how divergent learning styles and needs are experienced and responded to, were important to the students.

Another important finding in this study was the challenge of meeting some students' individual needs in a group context (Sussman et al., 2007). Some instructors offered ad hoc individual sessions for students who could not discuss specific issues in the group, as these issues led the particular student to feel extremely vulnerable. Inevitably, however, group-related themes emerged in these individual sessions, which, despite instructors' best efforts to have students redirect their concerns to group meetings, did not happen. Balancing individual and group needs was also found to present problems in a study of group supervision of social work students in Ireland. Using quantitative methods to study the experiences of 38 students in group supervision, with a follow-up qualitative study of 11students and five practice teachers (field instructors), Lindsay (2005) found that some students disliked instructors' attention to meeting individual student's needs in the group when this involved discussion of issues they experienced as irrelevant. This researcher concludes that a system that alternates group and individual instructional formats is best, to capitalize on the benefits of both. Given the dearth of studies on group learning in social work field education, there is a need for more empirical work to provide information about a mixed method or blended approach.

Based on the themes that emerged in the Toronto study, a range of best practices for facilitating group instruction were delineated. The following is offered as an emerging approach which would benefit from further study of its implementation and effectiveness. In the beginning phase it is highly recommended that instructors begin teaching the attitudes and skills for effective participation as a member of a learning group, including the notion of 'accountable talk' (Shulman, 2005a, p. 57). Instructors can orient students to the group learning environment, including the following: (1) the rationale and goals for providing instruction in a group format; (2) the multi-purpose nature of the group, such as learning from each other as well as from the instructor, and meeting administrative and informational needs; and (3) the basic operational procedures, such as the allotted time for each student for presentation and how feedback will be given.

Instructors can actively and transparently request members to join in creating the optimum learning environment by asking students to describe the type of group they envision needing so that they could take risks, expose their practice to others, develop a sense of commonality and cohesion, and promote mutual aid. From these images members will begin to identify norms, and the instructor can also contribute her perspectives. Norms can be articulated in a manner that makes clear the expectations for group procedures and process and the productive behaviours of group members, such as turn-taking, avoiding monopolizing time, and giving feedback in a helpful manner. Students can be taught how to summarize case or project material so that time to present is used efficiently. Regarding feedback, general principles presented in chapter 6 on methods of instruction should be followed. To repeat, feedback should be specific, close in time to the practice situation, and offer alternate ways of performing (Fortune & Abramson, 1993; Freeman, 1985). It should be focused, concise, and related to the questions of the presenter. Instructors should ensure that feedback balances negative and positive comments, involves all members in brainstorming, and encourages student self-critique (Abbott & Lyter, 1998).

In the middle phase, ideally the structure and process of group instruction has been well-established so that a sense of bonding and cohesion becomes evident, enabling members to move beyond only offering each other support to including challenge and the expression of difference in their discussions. With respect to structure, a clear procedure for presentation and discussion is recommended. Students are provided equal opportunities for presentation and response so that all members may have their learning needs met.

The focus in discussion is not only on feedback about practice behaviours; as in individual field instruction, there is also opportunity for critical reflection on practice and linkage to theoretical concepts of relevance to all student cases. In this instance the instructor may need to play more of a teacher role and provide information on the population and community served or on organization policies and programs, as well as intervention models or implementation approaches pre-

ferred in the setting. Such information will assist students in conceptualizing their practice in the particular setting in relation to a range of
theoretical frameworks. Students in both the mezzo and macro
practicum in this study valued linkage of project development and
implementation to relevant literature studied in their courses or provided by their instructor.

As noted, in the middle phase group process dynamics are crucial,
and field instructors must remain vigilante to overt and covert cues
about the way the group is progressing. Instructors' modelling and
transparently commenting on desired behaviours such as risk taking
and providing constructive feedback is suggested. When group
members are presenting their practice, the instructor serves as group
leader and facilitates focused discussion and feedback following best
practices, as noted above. Members are encouraged to respond to each
other's concerns in an attentive and helpful manner.

Regular review of group norms that identify what is working and
what needs attention is recommended. When group norms are clearly
being violated instructors need to actively intervene, without shaming
members but demonstrating commitment to a particular type of group
interaction and process. Instructors can also encourage open communication about current and immediate issues between group members,
and facilitate focused discussion of any key group issues. Having
noted that in some groups instructors found students reluctant to
provide feedback about the group, field instructors can use direct
questions that draw on previous experiences. For example, rather than
ask how things are going, a more targeted question would be: '...
sometimes students can feel overly criticized in group supervision; are
any of you having that experience in this group?' (Sussman et al., 2007,
p. 76).

In the final stage of group field instruction, as in individual instruction, review of assignments and learning takes place along with review
of the process and progress of the group. The importance of regular
review of these dynamics, as recommended above, is underscored. It
is disheartening when only in this final phase do members express
what has not worked, and field instructors only learn after the fact
what could have made the learning process more productive for students. Sharing the responsibility for group learning with students,
through setting and reviewing group norms and discussing overt and
covert cues about blocks to learning, appears to offer strategies for
effective group instruction.

Task Field Instruction

In contemporary field education it is recognized that students can learn invaluable practice knowledge and skill not only from the primary assigned instructor but also from other social workers in the setting and team members from a range of professions. In addition, some staff social workers may not have the time to provide fully for a student, but are motivated to offer instruction on limited projects, intervention approaches, or practice assignments. A range of terms is used to capture these arrangements, including 'task supervision' (Abram, Hartung, & Wernet, 2000) and 'co-supervision' (Coulton & Krimmer, 2005). Perceived benefits include students' learning more than one perspective and having greater access to potential role models and available instructors. The primary instructor benefits from needing less time for teaching, and also from having colleagues to consult should issues arise regarding student performance.

Task or joint instruction is usually prearranged based on the school's learning expectations, students' learning needs and goals, available assignments in the setting, and schedules and availability of staff. While there is scant literature on this topic, the general guidelines offered underscore the importance of clear, regular, and consistent communication about the various roles and responsibilities of the primary field instructor and other instructors, especially with respect to the final evaluation of student learning performance. In their research on co-supervision Coulton and Krimmer (2005) found that trust between all the instructors that the student was receiving a quality educational experience in each assignment was critical. The researchers also identified the importance of all instructors' commitment to education and a working alliance between the instructors. They recommend that contracting should produce clearly stated goals and objectives, and periodic review and evaluation, to identify what is helpful and what is not helpful in the 'co-supervision' process. While the researchers are generally positive about this approach, they note the importance of coordination and communication, especially in the event that significant differences arise between the student and one instructor or concerning instructors' opinions about the student's level of performance. The potential for splitting is acknowledged.

It has long been a practice in schools of social work to use innovative settings that provide relevant learning opportunities despite the absence of a staff member with a social work degree. An on-site task supervisor is appointed to oversee administrative issues and an off-site MSW field instructor to provide social work education. In an exploratory study of four non-MSW task supervisors and five MSW field instructors, the researchers found the perception of a high-quality experience was in some respects related to student qualities. For example, when students assigned to such settings were self-confident, experienced, active and prepared, took initiative, and had good communication skills, the approach worked well (Abram et al., 2000). As in the previous study, good communication between the on- and off-site instructors was important, as was the ability to work cooperatively and to clarify roles and responsibilities. The agency involvement was important – that there was commitment to and time for student education.

Rotations in Field Education

Despite the prevalence of rotations in training students in health professions, social work field education literature offers only a limited number of reports on the use of this format. A series of studies and reports of rotational models in social work in the health field are instructive. As early as 1976, social work educators described a format for students to rotate through three medical departments in an academic health care setting, and concluded that this approach provided high quality and appropriate preparation for practice in the health field (Dalgleish, Kane, & McNamara, 1976).

More recently, Cuzzi and colleagues compared social work students in a traditional year-long format and students in an experimental rotation consisting of three 10-week assignments in different patient care areas in hospitals (Cuzzi, Holden, Chernack, Rutter, & Rosenberg, 1997; Cuzzi, Holden, Rutter, Rosenberg, & Chernack, 1996). Key components of these models are well described by Spitzer and colleagues (2001), and include: assignment of a primary field instructor and associate field instructors, detailed initial orientation, monthly meetings of all the students, specific learning tasks, and regular meetings of the instructor group for planning and education. As Dagleish and colleagues (1976) observed, the rotation format appears well-suited for learning to practice in health institutions. Students benefit from learning how to practice with a wide range of diverse health problems and client situations, and learn short-term and crisis-oriented approaches to practice since clients are usually admitted for short periods. Since care and planning occur in interprofessional teams, students learn about other professionals' expertise and roles and the dynamics of team functioning, and they develop some competence in team work. While some students reported difficulties with the pace of rotations, overall, statistically significant increases in students' ratings of self-efficacy were found (Cuzzi et al., 1997; Cuzzi et al, 1996). Field instructors also perceived benefits for students from the rotation format, and noted students' improved perceptions of public hospitals. Spitzer and colleagues (2001) note that rotational formats may encourage students to pursue careers in these settings, which were previously seen as less interesting or attractive than social work agencies or private settings.

The field of geriatric social work practice has produced creative and innovative development and study of rotation models for field education. Netting and colleagues (Netting, Hash, & Miller, 2002) describe rotations developed where students followed clients through various health and human service organizations. Students had a primary instructor and a home base in one agency and rotated through other settings in an effort to expose them to the continuum of care in which geriatric clients may find themselves. The Geriatric Practicum Partnership Program of the Hartford-sponsored project referred to throughout this book stimulated the development and study of rotation formats for field education. A thorough review of six demonstration programs is provided by Ivry and colleagues (Ivry, Lawrance, Damron-Rodriguez, & Robbins, 2005). While models varied, students moved through two or more programs or agencies where geriatric clients might be served. Most arrangements consisted of one primary practicum site with rotations to an associate site for a period of time, from a year, to a semester, to several weeks. Another format involved sequential rotations of equal time. Instruction was given by a primary field instructor as well as task supervisors or preceptors. Students received orientation in didactic sessions, had the opportunity to accompany staff in a range of practice activities, and observe intake and assessment procedures, as well as work with their own clients (Scharlach & Robinson, 2005). Student satisfaction with the program was very high, and students perceived the rotations positively, as assisting them to learn about the range of services for older adults.

In these studies and in reports of rotation formats in health and geriatric services, it is clear that these approaches evolved out of efforts to build strong university-community partnerships. Community relationship-building, collaboration, and joint planning led to effective field education programming (Ivry et al., 2005). These findings are

consistent with the factors associated with university-field relationships reviewed in the first chapter in this book, on the context of field
education.

These innovative rotation projects provide a model for experimentation in offering the field practicum and are welcomed and encouraged.
Surprisingly, while curriculum development and change has occurred
over the years in classroom-based courses, there is less innovation in
field models despite the identification of problems with the current
format and regular calls for unfreezing the status quo and developing
and testing new approaches (see, for example, the analysis and pro-
posals offered by Raskin, Wayne, & Bogo, 2008; Wayne, Bogo, & Raskin,
2006; Jarman-Rohde et al., 1997; Reisch & Jarman-Rohde, 2000).

Field Units

Field units were established in many schools of social work in the
sixties and seventies, in part to provide field settings for greater
numbers of students given the need for more social workers and the
expansion of social work education programs. Government funding,
particularly in under-serviced social service and mental health programs, enabled schools to become more directly involved in field education. Schools established field units in existing settings, experimented
with field units in settings where there were no social work services,
and designed innovative projects in community practice. Some field
units were located in fledgling front-line community organizations
serving populations with special needs, and others in agencies serving
specific ethno-racial communities. In the absence of a firm source of
funding, such settings would not typically have enough resources to
provide education for students. Universities employed faculty-based
field instructors to lead these units, and many published reports of
these projects. For example, Singer and Wells (1981) described units in
residential and nursing homes for the elderly, Benavides and colleagues
(Benavides III, Lynch, & Valasquez, 1980) described a unit to educate
students with specific competencies for culturally relevant practice,
and Ruffolo and Miller (1994) described a community practice initiative. Since faculty-based field instructors were employees of the university program and might also teach practice courses, the field instruction they provided could more easily bridge classroom and field
learning through using conceptual frameworks taught in classroom
courses to analyse phenomena students confronted in the field.

In a review of an initiative to provide field units in school systems, Bronstein and Kelly (1998) note the many positive outcomes of these units, including improved field education for students. Field instruction was offered through both individual and group approaches with the potential for students to learn from each other in a supportive learning environment. These units were also able to bring social work services into under-serviced areas and provide a useful service to clients, the organization, and the community. The unit instructor worked in close collaboration with personnel in the host agency to ensure that students had access to relevant learning assignments and that the setting would benefit from the presence of the unit. The authors concluded with the observation that field units are a cost-effective and mutually beneficial way to meet the needs of schools and communities. For communities, additional services become available; for social work schools, they offer a way to provide quality field education when agency cutbacks result in fewer available practicum sites. The costs, however, of hiring field instructors to lead these units must be borne by schools of social work that are also likely facing competing resource demands and budget constraints.

A recent report of a field initiative similar in many ways to the field unit demonstrates that innovative formats can respond to contemporary field education issues. Poulin, Silver, & Kaufmann (2006) also describe challenges for providing quality field education as a result of changing agency context. For example, they note that many agencies have less time for field instructors to provide intensive instruction due to managed care. Also, highly specialized agencies do not lend themselves to the goals of undergraduate generalist and master's foundation practice learning goals and field assignments. Consequently, a faculty-initiated and faculty-led agency was organized to meet the needs of the local community, to develop partnerships with grassroots community organizations, and to involve students in field education through civic engagement. An evaluation of the project found students were involved in assignments at all levels of practice, including direct practice, developing services, conducting needs assessments, community organizing, and developing organization policies and procedures. Student satisfaction was high, and this type of project seemed to foster a commitment to practice with disadvantaged and disenfranchised communities and populations.

Structural Arrangements and Temporal Formats

Two dominant structures for field education exist: the concurrent format and the block format. In the concurrent format students attend classroom courses and field settings at the same time, with two to three days in class or field, depending on whether the student is in an undergraduate program or in the first or second year of study in a graduate program. The intention of concurrent structures is to facilitate the link between learning social work in two domains. The assumption is that simultaneous involvement furthers integration of theory, research, and practice. In the practicum students gain authentic experiences which can be examined through the lens of concepts and information learned in classroom courses. Their analyses, assessments, and interventions may be guided by the knowledge they are exposed to in practice courses. In many courses, assignments are structured so that students are expected to apply material learned in the course to their practicum. As well, theoretical knowledge and practice models can be analysed and critiqued based on actual transactions gleaned from practice situations and service settings. The field seminar, offered in almost all undergraduate social work programs, is another vehicle to assist students in integrating theory and practice. In seminars, students meet with the faculty field liaison to review the field experience and draw links to their coursework. While some students find it difficult to juggle the two domains of learning, this format is likely the one most used.

A variation on this structure occurs when the program delays the entry of students in the field by a number of weeks or a semester. Instead of directly beginning field learning when the semester commences, other educational experiences of a preparatory nature are provided, such as skills-based courses or special seminars related to the practicum.

The block placement format involves students exclusively in field learning, preceded by or following a portion of coursework. This format may have originated for practical reasons. University social work programs located a distance from large urban centres did not have enough available agencies and field instructors for their student body to easily move between class and field, as in the concurrent model. Hence, an alternate format involved students in some amount of coursework followed by a block in a field setting. Part-time students' schedules may also necessitate some deviation from the concurrent structure. Based on program resources and numbers of students in a particular geographical location, some schools provide integrative seminars or practice courses along with a block arrangement. For schools offering an international practicum experience, obviously the block arrangement is the only feasible method.

The educational issues related to these two structures are concerned with the integration of conceptual material taught in the university with field experiences. As noted, seminars may be offered or the faculty field liaison role may focus more on integration in the block arrangement. Other concerns involve the way in which the student as learner is perceived in concurrent and block formats. In the concurrent arrangement it is clear to the student, field instructor, and agency staff that the student is also attending university courses. In the block arrangement, there is greater likelihood that the practicum is viewed as a work experience by all, including the student, where the educational primacy and purpose can become somewhat compromised.

As noted earlier, some students must continue to work at their place of employment during their studies for personal and financial reasons. Employment-based practicum assignments are offered where students can remain in their program or unit for their practicum; however, their assignments and the field instructor must be different from the students' usual employment tasks and supervisor. Such a practicum may also be offered in non-traditional times such as in the evening or on weekends. These structural arrangements have yet to be studied in depth to examine how potential dual roles of student and employee affect student learning.

There is a dearth of studies on the impact of structural factors on field learning. In a review of studies that do exist on the effect of structural arrangements on student learning, Fortune (1994) found that students in the concurrent format, when compared to the block format, appear to maintain or increase the conceptual aspect of their learning. No gains or losses in student learning were associated with the few studies on delayed-entry compared to immediately entering the field. No significant difference in student outcome in employment-based settings were found when compared to usual practicum settings, although student learning was better if the field instructor participated in training and provided conceptual input when reviewing process records.

While the studies that do exist report few significant differences when various formats are compared, it is important to recognize that the outcome measure, student performance on field evaluations, is viewed as subject to measurement problems such as lack of reliability and validity. Evaluation is considered in depth in the following chapter. In the absence of psychometrically sound outcome measures, the findings of studies which compare various educational formats and activities must be viewed with great caution.

In a meeting of 33 field directors from northeastern states, participants identified shared concerns and proposed possible new approaches for field education (Wayne, Bogo, & Raskin, 2006). These include new partnerships with agencies that become accredited permanent educational centres similar to those found in university-affiliated teaching hospitals for students in the health professions; separating field learning from social work education with a required internship supervised by professional regulatory bodies; a hybrid model of simulations and observational agency visits in one year, followed by a second-year practicum in an accredited setting; and an individualized model where students with social work-related experience could receive educational credit if they already had mastered competency requirements. Clearly, all approaches suggested are 'food for thought,' and would need extensive examination to determine their feasibility.

The authors advocate for unfreezing rigid compliance with traditional practices in the face of new realities. In a further analysis of the development of some field education standards and the lack of empirical support for them, these authors again propose creative thinking that will lead to innovations with well-designed evaluations that demonstrate student mastery of competence (Raskin, Wayne, & Bogo, 2008). The Council on Social Work Education has provided great impetus for such developments through the (EPAS, 2008), and the designation of field education as the signature pedagogy of social work. It is likely that new and tested approaches and formats for field education will be available in the coming decade.

The International Field Practicum

While interest in international social work has long been a feature of North American social work educators, increasingly globalization further supports offering the international field practicum for students. In a survey conducted in 2004, Panos and colleagues (Panos, Pettys, Cox, & Jones, 2004) found one in five schools in the United States placed students internationally, and in 2002 Caragata and Sanchez reported over half of Canadian schools did so as well. While the numbers of international practicums are generally quite modest, a number of investigators are examining the conditions needed for productive learning to occur. The stated goals for the international practicum are many, and include increasing students' understanding of international and cross-cultural factors (Panos et al., 2004); preparing for practice in non-governmental organizations across the globe (Caragata & Sanchez, 2002); exposing students to views of human behaviour and social problems, community and institutional social welfare programs and policies different from those found in their own country (Barlow, 2007); and increasing awareness of global poverty and their commitment as global participants to social justice (Lough, 2009). All scholars note that in order to achieve these goals institutional capacity is necessary, capacity comprising attention to practical matters, accountability and support for students, and curriculum integration.

Practical matters pertain to the many details of developing and maintaining inter-country relationships so that practicum sites can be used in an ongoing manner. Necessary criteria, such as language skills, must be established so that the student can engage in a meaningful service role and not only observe the setting's work and the community. Numerous logistical issues regarding transportation and housing must be addressed.

Accountability refers to preparation and on-site teaching and support. Pre-departure work includes discussion of expectations for the international sojourn and the practicum so that students have realistic goals. While in the setting students must learn about a range of historical, political, economic, and social factors to understand the context of service issues. As well as content information, students need the same input as discussed throughout this book. Intense emotional reactions to conditions and social issues can be expected, and critical reflection is noted as a hallmark of extracting meaningful learning from cross-cultural experiences (Barlow, 2007). Hence, there is a need for skilled field instructors who can work with students in an intensive manner to help them process and learn from their reactions to phenomena in the host country, as well as to learn the social work competencies in the field program. In the absence of an on-site field instructor, video conferencing and web-based communication has been suggested as necessary to undercut the isolation students have reported (Panos, 2005). Two papers offer extremely useful ideas for illuminating aspects of the international practicum. Lough (2009) provides an insightful theoretical framework for examining such a practicum based on lessons learned from the literature on service learning and international volunteerism. Barlow (2007) presents interesting qualitative data from interviews with 11 Canadian students who had completed a practicum in India, and shows how they negotiated tensions inherent in trying 'to integrate their personal values and beliefs with the stark issues of class, race, gender, sexuality and culture in ways that were professionally and personally meaningful to them' (p. 245).

When students return from the practicum they need opportunities to debrief their experiences, to highlight their new understandings and practice learning, and to reflect on how they may transfer that learning into their local practice. Guidelines for integrating these educational placements into the curriculum need consideration, especially for programs with significant numbers of students in international settings.

Although anecdotal reports suggest that positive international field experiences are transformative for students, there are also challenges. Some have observed that such placements, when not effectively facilitated, can lead to poor cross-cultural understanding, less tolerance, and greater prejudice (Lough, 2009). It is worthy to also question the benefits to the host country agencies, communities, and personnel when receiving international students, and whether reciprocal exchanges exist for students from these communities to in turn have field practicum in North American settings. Finally, while social work practice bears similarities globally, there are significant national differences. The implications for students' ability to achieve the competence expectations of their school's program in an international practicum warrant examination and study.

Technology in Field Education

Social work educators are using a range of technological innovations in teaching, including in field education. At the most basic level, e-mail now allows faculty members who are field liaisons to stay in contact with students and field instructors and to respond quickly to a range of questions. Field programs can make effective use of Internet technology through the use of course management software such as Black-Board or WebCT to communicate with field sites and field instructors, to provide information and materials such as policy manuals and other documents, and to transmit and receive learning contracts and evaluation reports (Birkenmaier et al., 2005). The online site can offer support to students to discuss relevant field issues, or to field instructors for exchange of perspectives about field education. Technology can facilitate the use of field settings that are distant from the university. For example, video conferencing can be used to conduct faculty field liaison visits for sites that are more than one hour away from the university (Birkenmaier et al., 2005).

Studies of the use of technology to support field education find benefits identified by students. For example, students appreciated the ease and timeliness of access to information about the field program through receiving online announcements, and some used the online support site to discuss their concerns and experiences in the field practicum with other students (Roberts-DeGennaro, Brown, Min, & Siegel, 2005). Regehr, Bogo, and Regehr (in review) have developed and tested an online evaluation tool which is independently completed by field instructors and students though a password-protected secure system. This tool is discussed in the next chapter on evaluation.

Projects are reported that use online methods for field seminars to accommodate students who live a considerable distance from the university (Wolfson, Magnuson, & Marsom, 2005). Evaluations of undergraduate student reactions found that students valued the convenience of participating on their own time, although some resented the requirement to respond to others' postings. In this project, faculty observed that some students did not participate fully while others were more forthcoming with their opinions and ideas than when in class settings. Both students and faculty recommended some in-person meetings so that participants can have an interpersonal basis for their communications. Synchronous live chats can also be part of the seminar. Birkenmaier and colleagues (2005) describe the use of online seminars in a graduate program as a supplement to three times per semester, face-to-face sessions. These authors note the time efficiency of posting cases for others to read, review, and develop questions and comments prior to meeting in the seminar. Previously, more time was used for oral case presentation with less time available for discussion and learning. These educators have also instituted an online integrative seminar which includes the first class in a face-to-face meeting for orientation to the quantity, quality, and timeframe for postings. Students use the bulletin board feature to comment on others' cases and to further develop their ability to integrate theory and practice. The authors note the increase in the amount of feedback to each student due to the use of technology.

Webcam and video conferencing are described for use in international field sites so that university personnel can interact with students and the field setting (Panos, 2005). Both provide a vehicle for support of students and undercut their feelings of isolation by allowing them to interact with faculty and discuss any issue they are not comfortable raising with local field instructors in the host country, for a range of cultural reasons.

While no published reports yet exist, anecdotal discussion on the baccalaureate program directors listserve reveal great interest in field instructor training modules offered through the Internet. Field directors describe powerpoint presentations for field instructors with voice-over narration, links to recommended readings, and materials such as checklists and guidelines for field education.

All faculty who have written about the use of technology for field education note the importance of available technical assistance for students, and the availability of the required equipment and sufficient computer bandwidth in agencies for transmissions to be of high quality and speed. Also, it is imperative that agencies and faculty members have the technical support to learn how to install and use the equipment. Clearly, field educators are introducing many novel approaches to increase the capacity for quality field learning and teaching through the use of technology, and new methods will certainly be designed.

This chapter reviewed the dominant approaches and formats for field education in the light of current contextual issues and extant empirical support for various approaches. Technological advances offer promise of new, efficient, and effective methods. From this review one can observe that social work educators have expended tremendous energy in describing and offering a particular type of practicum, one largely based on tradition and practice wisdom, with some elements supported by a strong empirical foundation. There appears to be a need for change, given contemporary realities at universities and agencies. The educational policy introduced in 2008 provides the impetus, expectation, and hope that we are entering a new era of experimentation and research for field learning.

PART THREE

Evaluation and Beyond

8 Evaluation of Competence in Field Education

It bears repeating that in social work, university programs play a significant gatekeeping function for the profession and are expected to determine that students are competent to practice social work when they graduate. In jurisdictions where simply holding an undergraduate or graduate degree from an accredited school of social work is not sufficient for legal registration as a social worker or for gaining a license to practice social work, this responsibility is shared with regulatory bodies. Licensing requirements, however, most often consist of candidates' successful completion of a written examination, which is primarily a test of knowledge rather than of practice ability and skill. In some jurisdictions a prescribed number of supervised hours are also required. There is a dearth of empirical studies about the effect of supervision on workers' practice competence, or on client outcomes, although there is considerable evidence that workers highly value the supervisory relationship for receiving support, gaining skills, and promoting professional growth, and that positive perceptions of supervision are associated with job satisfaction and employee retention (Bogo & McKnight, 2005; Collins-Camargo, 2006; MorBarak, Travis, Pyun, & Xie, 2009). While accreditation of social work programs and success in licensing examinations theoretically should assure the public that a social worker is competent to practice, the literature reflects that educators are not universally comfortable with this assertion.

Student learning outcomes are evaluated in schools of social work through assessment of students' work in two domains: classroom courses and the field practicum. Classroom evaluation is largely based on assessing students' conceptual and written abilities in essays, tests, examinations, and journals (Crisp & Lister, 2002; Lister, Dutton, &

Crisp, 2005). There is a common perception that success in academic courses does not necessarily predict competence in practice. And yet there are no descriptions in the literature of comprehensive assessment systems that include evaluation of conceptual, written, and practice competence.

It seems reasonable to assume that the most valid evaluation of practice ability is observation of students as they carry out social work practice roles and functions. Such evaluation occurs in the field practicum, where field instructors have the front-line primary responsibility for evaluation. Schools of social work vary in the degree to which faculty members, assigned as faculty field liaisons, participate in direct observation and evaluation of students' practice.

The Challenge of Evaluation

Many concerns have been raised about the ability of field instructors to effectively evaluate and report on students' competence and to identify differences in performance. These concerns include the lack of specificity in criteria used (Alperin, 1996; Kilpatrick, Turner, & Holland, 1994), the questionable reliability and validity of evaluation instruments (Bogo, Regehr, Hughes et al., 2002; Raskin, 1994; Wodarski, Feit, & Green, 1995), and the data used to assess performance. As noted earlier in this text, studies have shown that many field instructors do not regularly observe students but rely instead on students' written and verbal reports of their practice (Maidment, 2000; Rogers & McDonald, 1995) and students' reflections in field instruction sessions (Bogo & Vayda, 1998).

As discussed in the chapter on conceptualizing competence, the early attempts to use a competency-based framework in social work education aimed to provide a new and more rigorous approach in order to define educational objectives and evaluate outcomes for educational programs in general as well as for the field practicum. When first introduced in the mid-seventies, field learning goals at that time were generally ill-defined. Field instructors were required to write narratives that discussed student learning and performance on a number of broad and general dimensions. With the introduction of competency-based education, the hope and expectation was that a set of specific, observable behavioural outcomes would dramatically change evaluation of field learning. Writing of the British experience, Skinner and Whyte (2004) note the belief amongst educators that an emphasis on observable performance would produce more equitable evaluation of student competence, rather than evaluation of student qualities, and also that inter-rater reliability would increase.

Despite progress in using a competency approach to define components of social work practice, the goal of achieving objective, standardized outcome measures of student learning has remained elusive. Reliable and valid evaluation approaches, those that differentiate between those students who possess the knowledge, skills, and judgment necessary for safe and effective practice and those that do not, have been more difficult to develop and implement. With the adoption of a competency-based educational framework, the Council on Social Work Education provides the impetus for schools to develop comprehensive and continuous systems of assessment (EPAS, 2008). It is likely that this policy will usher in experimentation and research on methods of evaluation. Developments in the field of medicine show that the introduction of a competency-based framework for graduate medical education in the United States produced experimentation and research on a range of evaluation methods. This activity has led to further understanding of the theoretical concepts associated with the articulated competencies, as well as recognition of the measurement challenges (Ginsburg, Regehr, & Mylopoulos, 2009; Lurie, Mooney, & Lyness, 2009). In this chapter the literature on evaluation of competence and the program of research on this topic undertaken at the University of Toronto are reviewed in an attempt to highlight where progress has been achieved and the need for further research and development. The tools discussed in this chapter can be found in the appendices.

Evaluation Methods

Professional practice in any discipline is a complex and intellectually demanding activity that, due to this essential character, makes it difficult to describe precisely and measure accurately. Practice situations and hence outcomes are affected by a multitude of variables: client and problem complexity and difficulty, and level of risk, as well as contextual factors such as the availability of needed resources, the effectiveness of team functioning and coordination, and the amount and quality of supervision the student receives (Eraut, 2003). Hence, as Kane (1992) observes, educators should attempt to clarify and understand competence; it is unrealistic to think we can eliminate the difficulties in trying to evaluate it.

Scholars support the authenticity of using observed performance in actual practice settings as the most direct approach to evaluation. Referring to evaluating the competence of graduate medical residents, Whitcomb (2002) strongly argues for the necessity to 'critically observe the resident caring for patients in a variety of clinical settings and under different clinical circumstances' (p. 359). Evaluators can determine whether the resident has both mastered the knowledge, skills, and attitudes associated with individual domains of the specialty, and also has the ability to 'translate and integrate' those knowledge, skills, and attitudes into a set of complex behaviours that result in the delivery of high-quality care. Programs must have ways to critically observe the resident's practice with patients in a variety of settings and circumstances (Whitcomb, 2007).

Social work educators have implicitly recognized the importance of conducting evaluations of competence in real settings, as evidenced by the central role given to field education and the designation of field education as the signature pedagogy of social work (EPAS, 2008). However, as will be reviewed in the following section, the complex and diverse nature of practice has made it difficult to create meaningful criteria and evaluation instruments. Moreover, there is little documentation about whether there is pervasive use of repeated observations of student practice, or whether inter-rater reliability in assessing quality of student performance has been achieved.

Evaluation Tools in Social Work

Surprisingly, there are few reported studies on the reliability and validity of the assessment tools used in social work programs to evaluate student competence or performance in the field. Despite the observation that most programs have likely used some form of evaluation rating scale for at least two decades, a review of the literature revealed only three studies on developing and testing scales that rated student acquisition of practice behaviours: the Practice Skills Inventory (O'Hare, Collins, & Walsh, 1998), the Wilson checklist (Vourlekis et al., 1996), and a scale developed by Koroloff and Rhyne (1989). Each of these scales has strengths; as well, there are universal challenges. First, while progress has been made in identifying and measuring core micro social work practice skills, it is more difficult to incorporate professional dimensions that reflect conceptual and integrative capacities that lead to differential application of skills. A second challenge is the need to measure not only the presence, absence, or frequency of the student's use of the skill, but also the quality of the skill performance. Adequate criteria are needed to provide greater specification of performance behaviours along a continuum.

Both of these issues are related to the critique of the manner in which competency in social work, and related human service professions, has been conceptualized. Specifically, highly detailed descriptions of practice attitudes, behaviours, and skills do not adequately capture the many dimensions of competence – how values and critical thinking contribute to the holistic nature of social work practice (Kelly & Horder, 2001; Skinner & Whyte, 2004). As noted in the discussion on competence earlier in this text, overly specific inventories portray practice in an atomistic and mechanistic manner that does not authentically capture the integrated nature of competence. Furthermore, social work is practised in a wide range of settings, and the breadth of learning and the diversity of practice situations and roles pose a challenge for definitions of competence. Therefore, how can essential elements in social work practice be reflected in competency models that lend themselves to meaningful evaluation?

In a similar discussion regarding competence models for graduate medical education, Leach (2006) states, 'The relevance of the work [on competency] is dependent on an integrated version of the competencies, whereas measurement relies on a speciated version of the competencies. The paradox cannot be resolved easily. The more the competencies are specified the less relevant to the whole they become' (p. 3). Social work educators may wish to think about defining components at a general and broad level meaningful to the wide range of practice contexts and nuances; however, this renders their measurement more challenging. In addition, unlike medical practice where there are numerous specific procedural competencies, a considerable component of social work practice is interpersonal in nature. Practitioners engage with and provide interventions or bring about change through intentional dynamic interactions with clients, groups, communities, organizations, and professionals in related disciplines. It is a challenge to capture the essence of producing and maintaining effective relationships. When these complex processes are broken into ever-increasing discrete behaviours, these descriptions become progressively more remote from the practice situations they are intended to represent.

Beyond issues related to what should be evaluated is the concern about how frequently student practice should be observed. Consistent with a competency model, there should be extensive opportunity for the rater to observe the student's practice in the field. This is necessary to establish the confidence to conclude that a student demonstrates competence in general, over some period of time, and in some range of situations. Findings from studies and anecdotal reports raise questions about how systematically evaluation is carried out. For example, it appears that field instructors and field liaisons more frequently access students' practice through reading process reports (students' post-hoc written reconstructions of what has occurred in an interview) or students' verbal reports of what transpired. Consequently, evaluation of students' practice would be based on data that is one step removed from their actual practice. As noted earlier, studies find that the more direct teaching methods, such as observation of students' practice, reviewing students' audio- and videotapes, or co-working, were used least frequently and less consistently than written or verbal reports (Maidment, 2000; Rogers & McDonald, 1995). In Rogers and McDonald's study, when respondents used more direct approaches and actually observed student performance, they rated students as less ready for practice than respondents who used indirect methods. Clearly, observation is preferable to report; however, observation is resource-intensive. Finding feasible methods for time-strapped field instructors, to enable them to devote more time to evaluation, remains a challenge for social work educators.

Another factor that confounds our confidence in field evaluations results from the recognition that social work practice is both generic and specific. As Eraut (1994) points out, the context of practice and of evaluation has a significant impact on the nature of the competencies expected. This is true of social work with respect to the field of practice, the population served, the employing agency's mandate, and the social work role. Moreover, practice approaches differ; for example, practice behaviours deemed necessary for competent use of a short-term, task-focused approach in an acute care hospital may not reflect the competencies needed to engage a resistant adolescent in a group foster home who is in difficulty with the justice system. Students engage in field education in a wide range of diverse settings – a reality of practice, and yet one that contributes to the difficulty in developing representative and agreed-upon views of competence for field evaluation tools.

Beyond specialization of practice, the nature of the educational experiences in the setting affects students' learning and ultimately their level of performance. For example, some settings are crisis oriented in nature, professionals are busy, and students may receive less support and educational feedback than in settings designated as learning centres with dedicated staff time for teaching. In addition, the acuity and complexity of client and community situations vary, and affect students' ability to engage and intervene, making equity in evaluation more difficult to establish. Commenting on these circumstances, Eraut (2003) recommends viewing evaluation as part of a trajectory that could 'include some progression from easier to more difficult working contexts' (p. 179).

Recognizing that context affects learning and performance, educators can balance authenticity and standardization (Eraut, 2003). Greater authenticity seems to come from evaluations in clinical contexts in which students have practised and with which they are familiar. Greater standardization, and hence equity, seems to come from identical evaluation experiences, such as those offered in written or oral examinations of the same case or practice situations. While these evaluations may not meet the authenticity criteria, they are closer to achieving equity for students who are exposed to the same conditions, and there is likely to be more reliability between raters. Programs should strive for some balance between these various evaluation methods to arrive at overall assessments of graduates' competence.

There is little empirical work on inter-rater reliability in assessing student performance. Only one study was found: Reid, Bailey-Dempsey, and Viggiana (1996) compared field instructors' ratings of student performance in the field with an expert's ratings of the students' audiotapes of interviews. The researchers found significant correlations between these raters. However, they note the limitations of their study, as the students were using a task-centred intervention model with clear interventions and a structured recording form. The field instructors, while not directly observing students' practice, were teaching the students to apply this specific practice model, guided by a written protocol, and they evaluated students' work based on the model's components, which students reported via a structured recording form. It is possible that inter-rater reliability was achieved due to the highly specific nature of the intervention. When criteria are well specified it may be easier to achieve greater agreement about the presence or absence of these behaviours in practice. Conversely, when criteria for evaluation are more general and broad, ratings become more reliant on the subjective judgment of the evaluator, and there may be less agreement between raters. Given comments above about the diversity of settings and approaches, field evaluation tools tend to be expressed at more general levels and agreement on specific criteria harder to obtain. However, in the absence of a substantial body of empirical studies about the validity and reliability of field evaluations, at this point one can only speculate about these factors.

Testing an Existing Competency Evaluation Tool

Through the Educational Policy and Accreditation Standards (EPAS) of 2008 and the adoption of a competency-based framework and system for evaluation of student learning, educators may come to experience more confidence in asserting graduates' readiness to practice. Another reason for pursuing more reliable and valid outcome measures than those currently available is that education research in social work has been limited due to the lack of such tools. As noted earlier, field evaluations reveal little variation in student scores, making it difficult to assess the effect of a range of field learning models and activities. Best practices in education can only be developed with solid outcomes used to measure their impact. The current almost universal reliance on student satisfaction and student perceptions of a wide range of educational factors and processes limits our ability to build evidence-based knowledge for field education.

These issues led to the first project in a several-year program of research conducted at the University of Toronto. The aim was to develop innovative and sound approaches to evaluation of students' learning and competence in field education. In the first study the researchers were interested in establishing the reliability and validity of the competency-based field evaluation tool used for students in direct practice in the master's program (Bogo, Regehr, Hughes et al., 2002). A competency-based evaluation tool was developed in the early eighties as part of social work educators' initial interest in this approach. The tool was used by field instructors, in discussion with their students, to evaluate student performance along a five-point scale that identifies stages in skill acquisition (from understanding to behavioural integration). Seven dimensions of practice were examined: (1) practice within a professional context; for example, competencies related to values and ethics, learning and professional development, relationship with clients and colleagues; (2) practice within an organizational context; for example, knowledge about organizational policies and programs and the ability to work on clients behalf within those parameters; (3) practice within a community context; for example, knowledge about the characteristics of a community, its resources and needs, and the ability to work with community members to bring about change; (4) assessment skills; for example, competencies such as ability to collect data from a range of sources, to organize and present data in well-written assessments; (5) planning skills; for example, develop a mutual agreement between all parties involved in problem definition and resolution, use best practices to develop an intervention plan; (6) intervention skills; for example, competencies such as ability to use a range of techniques and roles to achieve planned outcomes; and (7) evaluation skills; for example, competencies such as the ability to assess one's own level of effectiveness and to use feedback to improve ability to evaluate client progress and outcomes.

Feedback from field instructors over a 20-year period had revealed a number of difficulties. The language of the competency model was at a level of abstraction that could theoretically include students focusing on direct practice with individuals, families, and small groups; community practice; and organization practice, especially administration. Field instructors in community and administrative practicum struggled with this language and did not feel that it represented the learning opportunities students were exposed to, or their practice. At the same time, field instructors in direct practice settings found they rarely could provide learning assignments or field instruction for students that would help them master the competencies needed for organization and community practice. Therefore, in this first study only students in field settings where they were learning direct practice were examined. Scores from the evaluation reports of 249 students in the two-year Master's of Social Work program from 1992 to1998 were analysed on five dimensions: practice in a professional context, assessment, planning, intervention, and evaluation. These five dimensions consisted of 80 skill indicators or items. Scores included field instructors' ratings for these students in Year 1 and in Year 2. Statistical procedures are described in Bogo, Regehr, Hughes, and colleagues (2002). Results demonstrated a consistent factor structure with excellent consistency along the following dimensions: values and ethics; differential use of self; empathy and alliance; assessment; intervention planning and implementation; report writing; and presentation skills. A revised evaluation tool, entitled the Competency-Based Evaluation (CBE)

Tool, was developed and can be found in Appendix A. This revised tool was then adopted for use in the master's program, with competencies for organizational and community contexts added along with supplementary competencies for second-year specializations. This CBE Tool may serve as a useful template for educators who are redesigning evaluation tools.

Along with strong internal consistency in the factors on the tool, the study found that student scores on the field evaluation were significantly associated with academic grades. Students with better academic scores also had better field scores. This finding may mean that there is a relationship between academic and field performance. This may, however, not be the case. Since field instructors generally evaluate students based on their communication about practice, rather than observing practice, better communication skills may be associated with better grades. This explanation was offered by Reid and colleagues (1996) in their critical review of the consistent linkage found in the literature between measures of academic ability and field performance. They proposed that students who excel in written and oral skills may give an impression of their work which favorably impresses evaluators.

A troubling finding when testing the CBE Tool was that there was poor consistency between ratings of individual students in their first and second years. The tool could reliably identify students in difficulty in the first year of the program. In the second year, however, the tool did not reliably identify students in difficulty or those who were performing extremely poorly. This suggests that students are not being rated consistently by different field instructors. Since the second year is the final gatekeeping year, more research needs to be conducted on field evaluation for graduating students, to understand possible reasons for this and to develop more discriminating tools. Some questions to be addressed in the next study were: Was the problem with the tool? Are there process issues experienced in field evaluation which interfere with instructors' ability to identify poorly performing students in the second year? Is it some interaction between these two factors? Related is whether there is a need for competency evaluations that do not rely totally on field instructors as evaluators.

Before concluding this section on testing the reliability and validity of tools, it is strongly recommended that all programs undertake systematic testing and review of their evaluation tools. This data is routinely collected by field practicum offices and could quite easily yield important information for building the profession's knowledge base for field education, and for providing more effective tools for field instructors to administer.

Tapping Implicit Criteria and Language Used by Field Instructors

The literature on professional practice discussed at length in chapters 2 and 3 supports a view that goes beyond the performance of clinical or technical procedures and includes the use of tacit knowledge. To briefly recap, the most influential scholar, Schon (1983), argued that professional practice is more than the application of knowledge and techniques to situations confronted by practitioners. Rather, professional practice involves confronting uncertain and complex situations where application of knowledge must be supplemented. Expert practitioners use practice wisdom and highly developed intuition, often while in the situation, to address the contingencies presented by each unique circumstance. This rich reservoir of knowledge is constructed from the experience of interacting with numerous complex cases over time. In social work this tacit or implicit knowledge has been referred to as practice wisdom or the 'art' of social work. This view stands in contrast to a behaviouristic perspective of professional practice as consisting of numerous discrete elements which can be described in a concrete and specific manner.

A more fluid understanding of professional practice may require an evaluation approach, which is more consistent with this view. However, traditionally, practice wisdom has been more difficult to define and elucidate, and hence to evaluate. When practitioners who were becoming field instructors were asked directly about the theory or approaches they use, they were taken aback and often responded that their practice is eclectic or intuitive (Bogo & Vayda, 1998). However, through a structured dialogue they were able to recall and reflect on their practice and articulate some of the implicit components that affect their actions in an interview. Similarly, Kenyon (2002) interviewed field instructors to understand how they teach social work students to integrate theory and practice. Respondents did not separate theory from practice in the way that university-based educators do; they did not clearly identify the theories they used, nor did they describe a systematic application of concepts in practice. Instead, they described a process where they were making meaning of the information they received and from their observations. These understandings were described in everyday language, and revealed that these social workers were continuously engaged in building a theory about the case. When pressed by the research interviewer, they could describe how they work. In these descriptions formal theories were obvious, although not labelled as such. However, they were integrated into their 'talk' about their practice. These findings are compatible with those of Eraut (2002), who observed that many professionals 'provide very limited accounts of their knowledge, practice and learning' (p. 2), with the result that research about what professionals know and how they come to know it is difficult to conduct.

Given this theoretical perspective on professional practice, the goal of the second study was to tap into this reservoir of tacit knowledge or practice wisdom and discover the underlying ideas or constructs used by field instructors to arrive at global assessments of students (Bogo, Regehr, Power et al., 2004). The aim was to elicit descriptions of the real-life experiences and reflections of these experienced practitioners about practice, student performance, and evaluation. A series of in-depth interviews was first conducted with 19 experienced field instructors who had provided numerous student practicums in child protection, health, and mental health settings (Bogo, Regehr, Woodford, Hughes et al., 2006). They were asked to describe students they considered to be exemplary, problematic, and average. They were also asked to describe student performance along each of the seven core practice dimensions which were identified from the previous study as having theoretical and practice coherence. These dimensions are: values and ethics; differential use of self; empathy and alliance; assessment; intervention planning and implementation; report writing; and presentation skills. Fifty-seven descriptions of students resulted from these interviews. Through data abstraction and aggregation, 20 iconic representative student vignettes were developed which represented the range of student behaviour and performance. Each vignette was written in a similar manner, with descriptions of student performance and competencies and examples of students' interactions with clients and colleagues (see Appendix B).

The next step consisted of having 10 experienced field instructors, none of whom had been involved in the earlier study, independently sort the 20 vignettes into as many categories as they felt necessary to reflect various levels of student performance (Bogo et al., 2004). Each instructor then placed the vignettes on a continuum relative to each other, from high to low, and assigned numbers to them. Instructors were then placed into two groups, discussed and compared their individual rankings with each other, and were asked to achieve consensus in constructing and naming a new set of rankings. Results from individual and group categorization were highly consistent: the inter-rater reliability for placement of vignettes into categories was 0.77; for overall ranking of students, 0.83; and for agreement on categorizations between the two different groups of instructors, 0.99. The categories generated by the instructors were: (5) exemplary, (4) ready to practice, (3) on the cusp, (2) needs more training, and (1) unsuitable for practice. The researchers concluded that experienced field instructors were remarkably consistent in their ability to differentiate between levels of student competence when they were evaluating students based on descriptions of student performance. Their written and verbal comments and group discussion during the ranking process revealed the importance they gave to students' motivation, self-confidence, relational capacity, and integrity. The discussion of students' concrete skills was subsumed under the discussion of these broader qualities and abilities. These global judgments appeared to emanate from shared practice wisdom about what constitutes student competence, and are indicative of implicit concepts that lie behind or under evaluation activities. These concepts are congruent with the qualities and meta-competencies discussed earlier in this text in the chapter on conceptualizing competence.

Constructing Scales

The research team now believed that the earlier phases of the project had provided an empirical foundation to move forward in constructing a new scale which would make use of the underlying, implicit constructs and practice wisdom used by field instructors when conducting student evaluations. With behavioural descriptors for students at five levels of performance, gleaned from the ranked vignettes, it appeared that a scale could be developed using instructors' conceptualizations of competence and the language they used to describe performance. The new scale was called the Practice-Based Evaluation (PBE) Tool. It consists of six dimensions of practice, deemed important by instructors, incorporating meta-competencies and procedural competencies. The dimensions are: learning and growth, behaviour in the organization, clinical relationships, conceptualizing practice, assessment and intervention, and professional communication. Each dimension is anchored with detailed descriptions of student performance for each of five levels. The resulting scale is a six-item measure with five levels for each item (see Appendix C).

The new tool was tested by asking 43 field instructors to recall their most recent student and to evaluate that student with the current competency-based tool used by the program at that time. When this evaluation was completed the instructors were asked to evaluate that student again using the new six-item Practice-Based Evaluation (PBE) Tool (Regehr, Bogo et al., 2007). Since all studies received approval from the Research Ethics Board, no identifying data about the instructors or the students they were evaluating was collected. Despite the care taken to design this new tool, it was not able to produce greater discrimination by field instructors of students' performance than the usual tool. The new tool produced only slightly higher variance in student scores and failed to identify students at or below the midpoint in the scale. As noted 'the new tool failed to eliminate a ceiling effect in scoring, failed to differentiate students more effectively on the basis of skill, and failed to identify students with serious performance deficits' (p. 332). The instructors experienced the tool as more 'user-friendly,' and some participants preferred the more global descriptions of students. However, other instructors preferred the older competency-based tool, as it provided a greater number of specific behaviours to evaluate.

Given the failure to produce a better tool, the research team came to question whether the problem was not with the nature of the specific tools but rather with the very nature of scales. It was noted that scales for evaluation require field instructors to engage in a number of steps, which progressively may lead them to become more distant from the actual student performance they are evaluating. First, field instructors in their teaching role interact with and may observe students in a wide range of situations; they also receive information about students' practice in written or oral form. Through these interactions over time, they form a general impression of that student. Second, they are presented with a rating scale which requires them to engage in an abstract process of making meaning of the description of discrete items, as they might appear in their setting. Third, they must then deconstruct their impression of the student's performance along the parameters presented in the school's rating scales, either as abstracted dimensions (as in the PBE scale) or as discrete behaviours (as in the CBE scale). And fourth, they must further abstract that performance and rate those dimensions or behaviours on a scale, becoming familiar with the criteria of each level of the rating scale. This cognitive process appears to take the instructor away from their experience with the student and the holistic impression they may have developed. To further test out this speculation, the researchers developed another study that would use more global or holistic descriptive impressions of student performance in a matching process.

Evaluation without Scales

In this study in this program of research another set of instructors were given the same 20 student vignettes described above, and these vignettes were provided in a random manner (Regehr, Bogo et al., 2007). The performance level of each hypothetical student had been established in the earlier study, but the participants were not made aware of these rankings. Twenty-eight experienced field instructors were asked to read all the vignettes and select those 'similar' to their student, and to then further select one or two vignettes that were 'most similar' to their student. This procedure was carried out a few weeks after instructors had evaluated students in the final year of the program using the competency-based evaluation scale, so that they had recent recall of the student. Participants were also asked to use the PBE and CBE scales to rate the same student. In a comparison of the ratings, the matching method was far superior to the other two in producing greater variability in student evaluation. Field instructors were more likely to place students at both ends of the continuum in the matching process; that is, more students were rated as performing poorly or as performing in an exceptional way in the matching method than in the other two scales. An additional interesting finding was that field instructors' choices of 'most similar' vignettes were most often in the same performance level or within one performance level of each other. Instructors were not randomly choosing vignettes across the range of performance levels. Rather, their selection of vignettes was from vignettes located close to each other in the rankings. This further reinforces the finding from the previous study that there appears to be a common practice wisdom about student performance which field instructors draw upon when evaluating students in this global manner (Bogo et al., 2004).

The vignette matching tool and method of evaluating competence is not suggested as a new method for schools of social work. This study was conducted in an artificial setting and not within the typical student-field instructor dyad where field evaluation takes place. The matching method is offered as an alternative way of conceptualizing evaluation, and may stimulate the creation of other innovative approaches to assessing students' field performance. The researchers expressed the hope that this work would be replicated to provide greater understanding of the cognitive and social processes involved when field instructors are asked to evaluate their students (Regehr, Bogo et al., 2007). The same study is currently underway with social work practitioners in community, administrative, and policy practice. Colleagues in medical education research are also replicating the study with graduate medical residents in internal medicine (Ginsburg, McIlroy et al., 2010). In a study aimed at identifying personality factors predictive of MSW students' field performance, Sowbel (2009) used the Vignette Matching Evaluation (VME) Tool (see Appendix B) as the measure of field performance of foundation-year students. Of interest to this discussion is Sowbel's (2009) finding that 52 per cent of the 154 instructors matched their students with exceptional vignettes at the end of the foundation year and 21 per cent as ready for practice, providing further support for the concern about inflation of ratings in field education. There was, however, greater variance in overall scores than is typically found in evaluations, with 13 per cent of instructors matching students with vignettes in the 'on the cusp' range, 12 per cent in the 'needs more training' range, and 2 per cent unsuitable. The researcher cautions that the sample may not fully represent the population, based on anecdotal evidence that the students who might have been 'rated least favorably may have been underrepresented; that is, the 'problem' students may have been less likely to be rated than other students' (p. 105).

Another Attempt at a Tool

A new model of practicum, a rotational model, was developed where students rotate through two to three shorter settings with a different field instructor in each rotation. The competency-based evaluation tool was considered too extensive and cumbersome to administer in these shorter rotations. As a result the Practice-Based Evaluation Tool described above was adapted for use by the field instructors and students in the rotation format. This provided an opportunity to pilot the use of a new tool.

In the Practice-Based Evaluation Tool, six dimensions are evaluated: learning and growth, behaviour in the organization, clinical relationships, conceptualizing practice, assessment and intervention, and professional communication. Each dimension is anchored with detailed descriptions of student performance for each of five levels. However, in this version, rather than present the dimensions visually along a continuum with rankings from 1 to 5, detailed descriptions for each dimension are provided, arranged alphabetically. The numerical value for each statement is known to the researchers but is not provided for the field instructor or student. To conduct the evaluation, each field instructor and student select four to six descriptors within each dimension that best describe the student. The tool is only available in a password-protected online format and is programmed to automatically assign a rating from 1 to 5 for each dimension based on the original levels assigned to each descriptor. The final score is the average score of all six dimensions.

The pilot study involved 14 field instructors and 14 students in five field sites, and qualitative feedback indicated positive reactions: the ease of use, the descriptors of dimensions, and, from field instructors, that they filled the form out independently without the need to negotiate grades. After the field instructor and student completed the evaluation, they met to compare their assessments. There were many opportunities in the online form for narrative comments from each. The Practice-Based Evaluation Tool appeared to provide greater variation in scores than the traditional Competency-Based Evaluation Tool. Accordingly, the new format was adopted for use with all students in the following year, and 120 students and their field instructors gave informed consent for the researchers to analyse the scores they attained on the tool (Regehr, Bogo, & Regehr, in review). The study found internal consistency for the total scale. Of importance to this discussion is that the new tool provided better discrimination between student field performance than the previous Competency-Based Evaluation Tool, with a significantly lower mean (4.46 vs. 4.70, $p<.0001$), with the difference in means representing an effect size of approximately 0.76 standard deviations. Further testing of the tool on larger numbers of students and further development of an online program is underway. Other schools could use this process to develop their own tool for assessing student competence.

Interpersonal Dynamics in Field Evaluation

Through this program of research it became obvious that in any effort to build a better tool the social context of administering the tool needs to be considered. Field evaluations completed by a field instructor are based on the recognition that the field instructor is an expert practitioner, by virtue of her knowledge and experience. Field instructors' approach to evaluation, however, is not only influenced by their expertise. Schools of social work, and hence their graduates, practitioners in the community who are field instructors, are influenced by educational and practice approaches. For example, schools of social work use principles of adult education (Knowles, Halston, & Swanson, 2005) and strengths-based practice models (Saleeby, 2002) which emphasize empowerment (Gutierrez et al., 1998). Active learning, collaboration, and mutual participation of the student and field instructor in all aspects of the practicum are evident in the role the student plays in most schools, in choosing and negotiating the practicum, in contracting for learning, and in the mutuality expected in the relationship between students and instructors. These themes and the related literature have been presented throughout this text.

When the field instructor and student approach periodic and final evaluations, these theoretical and philosophical stances are complicated by the differential positions of teacher and learner. Since students are expected to be actively involved in all aspects of their learning, completion of the final ratings of student performance on the evaluation form likely involves some consultation and perhaps negotiation between student and field instructor. The collegiality in the partnership is now subject to the nuances of the power dynamic inherent in the instructor's role as evaluator. A competency-based approach expects field instructors, from their position of greater knowledge and authority, to grade and rate the student.

Giving Feedback

The question of evaluation of students is related closely to the process of providing corrective feedback, and the way in which the student receives and uses this information through the course of the practicum. Students who are active and open learners, who are committed to their own development, will welcome and use feedback from field instructors, even if they may feel temporarily disappointed that their performance is not more advanced. In turn, field instructors report that it is rewarding to teach and prepare the next generation of social workers (Bogo & Power, 1992; Globerman & Bogo, 2003).

What are the links between giving feedback and evaluation? Earlier studies have suggested that field instructors are uncomfortable with the power and authority in their role and do not like conducting evaluations (Gitterman & Gitterman, 1979; Kadushin, 1985). Through the various studies in the Toronto program of research on evaluation, instructors spoke spontaneously and in response to questions asked in focus groups about feedback and evaluation. They talked about what makes it hard to evaluate students' performance: what happens in the student-instructor relationship when the student does not use the feedback offered and is not able to develop the competencies, and/or displays many deficits in their practice, and how they respond to these situations when the responsibility of evaluation and gatekeeping begins to supersede the pleasure derived from teaching. Using qualitative analytic methods, the responses from 100 field instructors were examined, revealing useful information for understanding the dilemmas and difficulties instructors face in their role as evaluators. These findings have implications for training initiatives and support mechanisms for field instructors.

Instructors clearly recognized that evaluation of student performance was important, but noted it was difficult to carry out. They spoke about dilemmas they experienced 'when values collide' (Bogo, Regehr, Power, & Regehr, 2007, p. 99). On the one hand, as social workers they are strongly committed to values such as being nonjudgmental, searching for and promoting strengths, understanding and prizing the uniqueness of individuals, and interpreting behaviours in context. These values guide their practice and are brought to their teaching role as well. They also recognize and appreciate that schools of social work must protect the public through graduating students who are ready to practice. However, when confronted with evaluation tools and criteria which described students' behaviour or performance in negative terms they felt caught between the need to be accountable for accurate evaluation and their commitment to social work values. Although they acknowledged that negative behaviours on students' part do occur, they were critical of tools which used terminology they perceived as negative (for example, describing student practice as unfocused, authoritarian with clients, inflexible in intervention planning). Despite their descriptions of the crucial role of personal qualities (for example, self-directed, open, responsible) (Bogo, Regehr, Woodford, Hughes et al., 2006), they disliked tools which included reference to these qualities. For example, phrases such as, 'does not take initiative in seeking out learning opportunities, is passive in team meetings, does not display warmth or sensitivity to clients,' were seen negatively. When asked to rate, grade, or categorize students, they felt such rankings interfered with their social work values, of individualizing the person/student in the unique situation/practice context. Rating led them to feel they were acting in a judgmental manner. And, if they had to rate students' negatively, they felt they were not focusing enough on strengths.

Instructors spoke about giving both positive and negative feedback as an integral part of their usual social work practice as well as their teaching role. They expected students to respond in a variety of ways, not necessarily to simply accept all that the instructor offers. Some students will accept the feedback and use it in the next interaction with the client. Some students will not accept the feedback, may struggle with it, and may ultimately use only some aspects of what was offered. The difficulty occurs when a student is utterly rejecting of the feedback, argues strenuously, adopts a defensive position, or verbally attacks the instructor. Students who experience critical feedback as a blow to their personal self, and withdraw and avoid the instructor thereafter, were also described as difficult to teach and to evaluate.

Instructors identified three situations where critical feedback did not appear to be understood or integrated. The first situation occurred with students who are not able to understand the nature of social work and the role of the social worker in a particular context in a real and grounded manner. These students might be able to pass their academic courses and even to discuss social work concepts at a theoretical level. However, they are not able to integrate theory and practice, and this is evident in their inability to carry out a social work role or use practice principles and professional values in their work with clients. Since they are not able to understand the essential nature of social work practice, such students do not have the ability to assess their own practice or their progress in learning with any degree of accuracy.

The second situation where students had difficulty accepting feedback occurred with some students who had previous social work experience. Many students with undergraduate social work degrees enrol in graduate studies eager, motivated, and highly committed to advance their knowledge and skill or to study a new specialization. Drawing on their past social work experience, these students are often among those most valued by field instructors. Some students who have worked in social work, however, may experience feedback as challenging their self-image as a competent and experienced worker. Field instructors described such students, who reacted to critical feedback as if the instructor was attacking their personal sense of self and core identity. Some students became aggressive or so distraught that they withdrew from the program.

The third situation described was one in which a student's personality style was such that the usual way of presenting self and related behaviours was a pervasive aspect of his or her interactions with clients and staff members. For example, a student who stated that in his own life he could not keep to a schedule, was generally late or inconsistent in attending scheduled interviews with clients or team meetings, and rarely completed agency reporting requirements as expected. Feedback from the instructor about these matters had no effect in bringing about change. The student somehow managed the consequences of this characteristic in his personal life but could not change to meet professional standards.

The Impact on the Instructional Relationship

The importance of the student and field instructor relationship as the key factor in students' perception of the quality of their field practicum has been a consistent theme throughout this text based on the numerous studies reviewed (Alperin, 1996; Bogo, 2005; Fortune, McCarthy, & Abramson, 2001; Knight, 2001). This intensive dyadic tutorial model is also valued by field instructors for the teaching, mutual learning, and mentoring opportunities it provides (Globerman & Bogo, 2003). Instructors in the evaluation study emphasized the importance of building a strong relationship as the necessary context within which feedback is given to both clients and students (Bogo et al., 2007). Consistent with their values, feedback is given which is positive, balanced, examines other ways of behaving, and encourages joint review and brainstorming about improved performance.

When critical feedback and negative evaluation are given, a disjuncture can occur in the relationship, one that is not easily repaired. One instructor commented, while others in the focus group nodded in agreement: 'giving negative feedback to the student is so difficult … it feels so personal' (Bogo et al., 2007, p.108). This is so especially when the student does not agree with the evaluation, feels unfairly judged, or experiences the comments as a personal attack. The relationship can deteriorate, interactions become tense and acrimonious, and learning and growth is compromised or halted. Field instructors described that their attempts at continuing to help the student learn became emotionally exhausting. The field liaison is usually involved at this point, and, while perceived as helpful and supportive, the focus increasingly becomes concerned with following policies and procedures required for supporting a failing grade (Koerin & Miller, 1995).

Participants commented on the inordinate amounts of time involved in these situations. Extra time was needed for the process of working with the student with a poor evaluation – to document evidence of poor performance; to inform and meet with all relevant parties; to plan, undertake, and review the remedial steps taken. Frequently there were numerous consultations and meetings with the faculty. When staff in the setting were also involved this required additional time for either documenting their concerns or managing repercussions from the student's behaviour.

Contextual Factors

Social work field education takes place in organizations, many of which are secondary settings for social workers. Social workers discussed the hard work involved in establishing positive perceptions of the value and competence of the social worker. Students represent the profession and reflect the field instructor to some extent. The participants in the study reflected that problematic student behaviour could be experienced by the instructor as a source of professional and personal humiliation in the team. They were concerned about the impact of the student's behaviour on the general perception of social workers.

Instructors reported second-guessing whether contextual factors – teams with poor relationships, highly complex and challenging client situations, or limited learning opportunities – accounted for the student's lack of progress. They were troubled by the thought that perhaps in another setting, in a more supportive team, in a setting with 'easier' clients, the student would have been able to learn.

Another important contextual factor was the university social work program. In some instances field instructors were concerned about whether the school would support their evaluations, or whether a poor student evaluation would reflect negatively on the instructor's ability to teach and provide a positive learning experience for the student. It was not unusual to hear participants express anger at the school regarding the admissions criteria. They also felt it unfair that the responsibility to identify problematic student behaviours rests largely with field instructors rather than instructors in courses. They were critical of the lack of university-based, final overarching assessment processes that evaluated students' practice competence, as is done in related health professions.

Impact on the Field Instructor

For those participants who had worked closely with students who had difficulty accepting feedback, or displayed problematic behaviours warranting a failing grade, the experience was emotionally taxing and difficult. Clearly their decision to alert the school and their recommendation of a failing grade was not taken lightly. Influenced by their deep commitment to social work values, they questioned their own judgment, were concerned whether they were too harsh or not fair, and questioned whether they had done all they could to help the student learn and progress. They reported feeling drained and exhausted, and generally refrained from offering a student practicum for a number of years.

It appears that the university's responsibility for accountability that students are competent to practice is, in some large measure, burdensome for field instructors. Social workers are motivated to voluntarily provide learning opportunities for students; they are not necessarily expecting that they will become the de facto gatekeeper for the profession (Bogo et al., 2007). The structural issues discussed earlier contribute to this tension; faculty members are not closely involved with students' practice unless the field instructor signals that there is a problem. In the short term, schools can provide support and training for field instructors in the evaluation component of their roles, especially when circumstances become more difficult than anticipated. It is useful to talk about the tension inherent between facilitating and supporting students and also evaluating them. Open communication, transparent and clear processes, and the ability to discuss concerns in an emotionally contained way are useful (Carroll, 2009). As well, new approaches to evaluation should be developed and tested to determine whether there are ways to more effectively address these evaluation issues.

It is likely that the development of more reliable and valid evaluation tools will always be limited due to the interpersonal dynamics described above. With the new emphasis on assessing competence, schools will likely institute systems of evaluation that include a variety of approaches and measures. Evaluation of day-to-day practice in real-life settings and situations will always form an important part of such a system, as it provides the most authentic picture of student competence. There is, however, the need for multiple measures and the opportunity for creative development and testing of a range of procedures.

9 Towards Multiple Approaches to Evaluation of Competence

Comprehensive evaluations of performance in a practice setting are improved when there are opportunities to evaluate students in a range of social work roles and activities: for example, with a range of individual clients; with clients and their families or significant relationship partners; with colleagues and staff from other professions; and, where possible, with community members. Involving more raters, beyond the sole reliance on the field instructor, is useful for a number of reasons. It relieves the field instructor of the burden of bearing primary responsibility for evaluation. Through systematically using the opinions of a number of raters, more data and a greater number of perspectives about the individual's competence is gained. Raters can be drawn from staff in the setting and from faculty members unfamiliar with the context. Since resource implications will affect the scope of assessment systems, any choice of approaches must consider its feasibility and practicality.

At the beginning of the twenty-first century a new approach to assessing competence was introduced by the Accreditation Council of Graduate Medical Education (ACGME, 2000). Educational programs are expected to develop an assessment system (the term 'assessment' is generally used in these documents) to provide a thorough evaluation of each resident's competence. Multiple assessment methods and multiple raters provide broader input about the resident's competence. Rather than sole reliance on one clinical evaluator, numerous assessments are made based on performance in multiple situations and conditions. All these assessments then provide data for a comprehensive evaluation of a resident's competence at the end of a rotation. The rationale for this approach is that multiple evaluators and multiple observations can improve the reliability of the evaluation. Suggestions are made about matching appropriate evaluation approaches to particular competencies; differentiating between competencies such as patient care, medical procedural knowledge, interpersonal and communication skills, professionalism, and so on; and these will also vary by specialization (Swick, Hall, & Beresin, 2006). In constructing an assessment system, programs are advised to consider the following: (1) using a range of tools that together will provide a picture of the resident's entire performance, (2) identifying who the evaluators will be, (3) specifying what aspect of performance will be evaluated, and (4) stipulating how frequently assessment occurs. Some or all of the recommended evaluation methods could be adapted and used to create more comprehensive evaluation systems in social work, and are presented here. The initiative of the accrediting body has stimulated the development and testing of evaluation methods (for a systematic review of the current research, see Lurie et al., 2009).

Global Evaluation in the Clinical Setting

Similar to the traditional field evaluation completed by the field instructor, a global clinical performance rating is one of the recommended methods (ACGME, 2000). The specialty training programs define educational outcome objectives as competencies, and develop a rating scale with behavioural descriptors along a continuum. Faculty evaluators use these rating scales on a monthly basis during a rotation, which may take place over a number of months or one year. A second recommended method is a focused observation method, which entails direct observation of an encounter with a patient. Observations of the resident conducting a specific procedure may also be observed, based on the nature of the specialty. This real-life encounter is evaluated by a designated rater using a rating instrument designed specifically for this observation. This instrument is also used to provide feedback to the resident. The observation can be live or videotaped. The first approach provides global impressions based on observations and interactions over time. The second approach provides specific feedback on actual behaviour immediately after the performance. (This approach bears some similarity to using a simulated patient, as discussed in the following section.) Both approaches can usefully supplement each other.

A third approach is a 360-degree global rating where the opinions of nurses, peers, and allied health personnel are obtained regarding the resident's interpersonal and communication skills and professionalism. In addition, patients are asked to provide their perceptions along a number of dimensions. A self-evaluation is also completed and compared with the results of the other evaluators. This method provides multiple perspectives about the resident's performance, and also helps her or him see whether one's own self-assessment is accurate in relation to patients and colleagues.

Portfolios

The remaining recommended approaches for graduate medical education use written documentation for evaluation. These methods are similar to written methods used in social work, and include case logs that describe in some detail the type of practice situations the student has been involved with, and their interventions and accomplishments. One such approach is a portfolio where the student collects materials that represent learning activities, progress, and performance. Social work educators are using portfolios as they enable students to reflect on their learning and select samples of their practice that demonstrate their current level of competence (Alvarez & Moxley, 2004). Through written presentations and accompanying recordings, students can show how they link theory and practice through providing their rationale for the specific actions they took in an interview or in planning for an entire intervention. Portfolios are especially useful for students who are involved in community, advocacy, and organizational practice, where it may be more representative of their practice to use written reports, letters, briefs, and presentations to evaluate competence. Programs provide guidelines for portfolios, including the learning objectives to be achieved, the type of materials to be submitted, and the criteria that will be used to evaluate the materials. Following the emphasis on directly observing students' practice throughout the discussion of competence in this book, the portfolio must include samples of observable practice to meet the criteria for authentic evaluation. Controversy about the usefulness of portfolios is also expressed by educators of elementary and secondary school teachers as potentially requiring a lot of time to exhibit work which may be trivial, not worthy of reflection, not a true picture of competence, and subject to questionable scoring practices (Shulman,1998, as quoted in Lombardi, 2008).

An Innovative Approach:
The Objective Structured Clinical Examination (OSCE)

The approaches discussed above include clinical evaluations produced by clinical instructors (as in social work field evaluation), as well as approaches which can supplement such evaluations. In these examples field experiences are evaluated by clinical or field instructors, faculty, or others in the setting. Given the findings about the difficulties in field evaluation, the Toronto research team began to examine the potential to develop and test an evaluation method used in related fields, such as nursing, pharmacy, and medicine. A new project is underway to adapt and test the Objective Structured Clinical Examination (OSCE), originally developed for medical education, for use in social work. In this adaptation both student performance and reflection on that performance is evaluated. This approach is intended to evaluate the various dimensions of competence as presented earlier in this book: higher-order, over-arching meta-competencies and students' procedural or operational competencies.

The OSCE was developed to assess medical students' clinical competence through a procedure that involves observing and evaluating student's actual performance (Harden & Gleeson, 1979; Hodges, Hanson, McNaughton, & Regehr, 2002; van der Vleuten & Swanson, 1990). A simulated client is trained to enact a practice situation that might typically be seen by a practitioner. The student is provided with identifying information and then directed to conduct an interview that is rated on a number of competencies by a faculty member or clinical instructor following guidelines. Through the use of standardized simulated patients (played by trained actors), the nature of the problem and level of difficulty is the same for all students. While the OSCE methodology originated in medicine (Harden, Stevenson, Downie, & Wilson, 1975), it has been used in assessing educational outcomes for a range of health professionals, such as nurses, pharmacists, physical therapists, chiropractors, and dentists.

The view of professional competence underlying the OSCE is consistent with the behaviourist framework discussed earlier: that complex professional practice can be defined in discrete, concrete, observable behaviours. The conceptualization of competence presented in this book is one in which competence is seen as holistic and a range of competencies are integrated, including meta-competencies, which are not necessarily observable. Hence, an examination for social work must include a process for assessing both the crucial meta-competencies and actual procedural competencies. An integrated examination has been developed and field tested for use with undergraduate and graduate social work students (Bogo, Regehr et al., in press; Rawlings & Bogo, 2009).

The examination consists of two components. First is a 15-minute interview with a simulated client portraying a situation that a social worker could be expected to confront; the researchers worked with experienced social workers to develop scenarios similar to actual client situations. Written descriptions are used to train and rehearse professional actors so that they can play the scenario described in an authentic manner. Rating scales were developed which identify the key competencies to be evaluated, and raters are trained to use these scales. Raters are field instructors, field liaisons, and faculty members who teach practice courses.

In the second component of the examination the student engages in a post-interview, reflective dialogue with an interviewer. This dialogue aims to tap into and elicit the student's conceptualization of the interview, the way in which the student integrates social work concepts and values, and how the student understands her intentional use of self. The reflective dialogues are videotaped and analysed to identify and assess the more elusive aspects of professional practice. The drawback in an examination where the student is observed and evaluated arises from the artificial nature of the setting. While some students may become anxious about being observed, and this could affect their performance, students in this pilot study reported that they quickly forgot about the observer-evaluator and were able to engage 'as if' the actor were a real client.

The research team developed five scenarios (also referred to as 'stations' in the medical literature) to portray authentic social work situations. Scenario development involved an intensive process of pilot testing with students, experienced social workers, and well-trained actors. An iterative process ensued, including the *refinement* of scenarios; of rating scales to capture the dimensions, constructs, and practice behaviours for assessment; and of efficient examination procedures. An OSCE was conducted to begin the process of testing the tools and methods. Participants included current MSW students, recent graduates, and experienced social workers. The study demonstrated promising reliability for the method and the rating tools developed. Correlations between performance and reflection scores demonstrated that they are related, yet different aspects of competence, and are seen differently in the evaluators' rating process. The method demonstrated construct validity, in that the five stations or scenarios were able to clearly differentiate between social workers in training and experienced workers. There was, however, little variation in the scores of the second-year students and the recent graduates. The researchers recommend more testing of the approach, with greater numbers of students and the use of more scenarios. The need for more scenarios or stations arises from the finding that the inter-station alpha values in the study suggest that the level of correlation for scores generated on any two randomly selected scenarios or stations would be sufficiently low as to emphasize the 'context specificity' of social work skills. For example, a student might perform well when interacting with an adolescent who is struggling with issues of sexual identity, but this same student might not be able to perform as well when interacting with a recently immigrated woman who is feeling isolated and burdened since the birth of her first child. To obtain a clear overall sense of a student's general performance as a social worker, it is necessary to obtain a greater number of samples of behaviour addressing a variety of social work practice situations. The use of only one or two scenarios or stations might provide valuable information about the student's performance, but the scores generated by such a small number of interactions are not sufficiently generalizable for educators to have confidence in high-stakes decisions such as passing or failing. Further experimentation with OSCE with more than five stations or scenarios is recommended.

The approach appears very promising to use as a method in conjunction with field evaluations and other methods in a comprehensive assessment system. In a review of studies on the use of standardized client simulations in social work education, the researchers found high rates of student satisfaction with this approach to learning social work practice (Bogo, Logie, Regehr, & Regehr, in review). This finding was the same for all participants in the Toronto study; they viewed the experience of interviewing and reflecting on five simulated clients as contributing to their learning, and recommended more such opportunities be included in the program. The articles reviewed did not, however, report data on the effectiveness of the standardized client simulation on evaluating student learning and practice competence. In conclusion, there appears to be some history with and interest in using standardized client simulations, or variations of the OSCE adapted for social work. More empirical work is needed to establish the reliability and validity of this method, and to determine the number and types of scenarios that will most accurately capture the expected dimensions of social work practice competence.

Student Self-Assessment

Finally, student self-assessment of practice competence has been suggested as a way to build skills for lifelong learning. The findings from a number of studies lead to more caution about their use beyond that of a teaching and learning tool. In a study comparing independent student self-assessment and field instructor assessments of student competence, Regehr and colleagues (2002) found relative consistency in the assessments of certain tasks, such as interviewing skills, group work skills, and community knowledge. Less concrete skills, however, were assessed very differently. A difference was noted between students' and field instructors' rankings in domains that were more related to personality characteristics or personal values. For example, students ranked their skills on dealing with relationship issues of resistance, ambivalence, or conflict; ability to function on the team; and adherence to social work ethics higher than did their field instructors. In other contexts it has been demonstrated that individuals may hold overly favourable views of their competence in a range of social and intellectual domains (Kruger & Dunning, 1999). These researchers conclude that people who lack competence in a particular area may also lack the metacognitive ability to realize it. The result may be not only poor performance, but also the inability to recognize that one's performance is poor. This phenomenon was found in a study of family medicine residents' competence in interviewing skills. The self-assessments of those residents in the highest-performing group were more accurate after they viewed benchmark videos; however, while some in the lowest group also could correct their initial assessments, some individuals actually further increased their already inflated self-assessments after viewing the benchmarks (Hodges, Regehr, & Martin, 2001). This study led the researchers to question the assumption that learners can accurately evaluate their own performance, and identify and remedy gaps in their knowledge and skills. These findings shed further light on the difficulties field instructors encounter with some students who do not agree with the instructor's rating of the student's competence.

In this final section of the book the topic of evaluation of competence has been reviewed, including lessons learned from a several-year program of research. The literature and experience of related health professions has been reviewed, revealing more varied and comprehensive evaluation systems and approaches. These approaches provide some possibilities for social work educators for further development of evaluation systems. New approaches should be tested before adopted for entire programs so that their effectiveness can be established. Given the complex nature of professional practice, and the many challenges in evaluating competence, it is likely that such research and development will help social workers to better clarify and understand the concept; however, as Kane (1992) commented, it is unrealistic to think we can eliminate the difficulties in trying to evaluate it.

Concluding Thoughts and Further Developments for Field Education

As noted throughout this book, field education is a long and valued educational component of social work education. It is based on the assumption that becoming a professional practitioner must entail authentic experiences of practicing the profession, where students learn to think, to act as, and to be social workers – 'to serve others responsibly and with integrity' (Shulman, 2005b, p. 3). Learning comes from observing and experiencing the role of the social worker with structured and systematic ways of reflecting on practice. An ideal type of model has evolved where the vision includes prized processes such as individual field instruction for each student, offered by experienced, effective social workers who are also well trained as field instructors. The ideal type of field setting is a learning organization where students are welcomed and taught by all staff members, one that is seen as providing enrichment for staff through interaction with students and the fresh ideas, energy, and inquisitive attitudes they bring. Faculty members are committed to quality field learning, and make every effort in their teaching and their research to bridge the academic work occurring in the university and professional practice and the knowledge-generation occurring in the field. The current designation by the Council on Social Work Education (EPAS, 2008) of field education as the signature pedagogy of social work recognizes this tradition, and hopefully will provide the impetus and momentum for increased scholarship, research, and educational innovation.

As noted in this book, the context within which field education occurs has become far more complicated and resource challenged over time. Related health and human service professions are able to continue to provide quality field or clinical experiences due to the structural relationships they have with university-affiliated teaching hospitals and university-based counselling centres. Social work has not developed similar institutional arrangements, resulting in partnerships which may become unstable when field settings are faced with competing resource demands. It is timely for national and local leadership to explore, develop, and study alternate inter-organizational relationships for more enduring field structures if graduates are to achieve competence through field education.

The adoption of a competence framework by the Council on Social Work Education is consistent with trends in many professions and jurisdictions worldwide. A useful critique of the competence movement from professions and countries using this approach should be taken into account. Based on lessons learned, North American social work educators can productively adopt a competency framework that includes the internal intellectual-cognitive processes of self-reflection, reasoning, and judgment that underlie the actions practitioners decide to take, as well as their competence in the use of a range of skills and interventions. At this point in the development of social work education, it appears that the benefits of a competence approach are significant: specifically, that it requires clear articulation of and attention to outcomes – to determine whether educators are achieving the goals they strive towards, and whether they can support the claims they make. In this regard, competence and outcomes assessment are inextricably linked, and social work educators will need to focus considerable energy on the design of reliable and valid assessment methods. As reviewed in this book, traditional evaluation systems are largely inadequate for this task. The search for better ways of assessing learning and performance, however, will not be easy, and will require financial resources as well as commitment, creativity, and willingness to try new models. Consistent with new approaches is the need for rigorous evaluation of these assessment methods to ensure that they are an improvement over what has traditionally been used. Social work programs will need education scholars and researchers who are able to lead these innovations.

Education for professional practice is increasingly recognized as a legitimate field of scholarship and research beyond the traditional domain of educational theorists. Related to this development is a burgeoning interest in the very nature of professional practice, which in turn stimulates more creative thinking about education for professional practice. As a result, the knowledge base for field education has been greatly expanded, with contributions from educational theorists working in higher education and education for related professional disciplines, as well as from scholars in social work education. There is much to learn and to offer through interprofessional collaboration and interchanges.

Knowledge about field education has developed beyond strongly held notional convictions, moving the field towards developing empirically supported pedagogical principles, approaches, and evaluation methodologies. Such knowledge is the result of years of reflection on field instructors' teaching experiences and study about the nature of student learning and the optimal ways to facilitate that learning. Field education is about learning how to offer a service and how to use the knowledge, values, and skills of the profession in collaboration with clients, communities, and colleagues. However, practice involves much more. Social work is an activity which engages our personal, subjective, and emotional self and this dynamics process can be both exhilarating and unnerving. With increasing understanding and attention to cultural competence and issues of diversity, oppression, and power in social work, field instruction now incorporates an expanded view of how the personal and professional domains of the self are present in learning and in practice. This overall theme of personal and professional has been explored in this book, as it is likely that it is in field education where students can find the best opportunities to experience and work through struggles related to the self as they develop into professional social workers.

The implications for supporting, facilitating, and encouraging growth and helping students achieve competence were examined through a range of educational approaches, methods, and formats. Attesting to the creativity in field education, a variety of formats have developed over time, although the individual student and individual field instructor tutorial dyad appears to remain the most prevalent. Numerous pedagogical approaches also exist. The issue for field instructors is how to balance a number of dimensions: (1) creating and maintaining a productive and collaborative relationship while comfortable with the evaluation component in this role; (2) teaching the necessary practice skills and competencies through opportunities for observation of experienced practitioners, and observations of students' practice with accompanying feedback: (3) providing opportunities for reflection, and linking practice decisions to the relevant theoretical and empirical knowledge related to a situation, role, and population; (4) drawing connections to the service context, including the role of the social worker and the nature of the interprofessional team; and (5) assisting students with integration of the personal and professional. Frequent and multiple sequences of practice/action subjected to reflection, critical thinking, analysis, and conceptualization of practice – with observation and feedback about students' practice, and further opportunities for practice – appear necessary for students to develop a holistic competence of conceptual, professional, and practice capabilities and skills.

Some studies have added to our understanding of pedagogical processes in the field; however, more consistent programs of research are needed to more fully advance our knowledge base for social work field education. Furthermore, how field instructors can provide this rich array of educational interventions in agency and service settings that provide little formal recognition of the time needed for education remains a structural issue. As noted above and throughout this book, and at the risk of being repetitious, new inter-organizational relationships for more enduring field structures are needed if graduates are to achieve competence through field education.

National and international social work education associations can advance the educational mission of social work through innovative programs to develop, sustain, and recognize education researchers. Through this book, a number of themes for future research have been identified. Social work education researchers are crucial, so that the profession can develop knowledge that schools can use to provide the best learning opportunities for their students. The quality of service delivery to clients, consumers, and organizations is highly dependent on the quality of the educational programs that prepare practitioners to meet the needs of the community.

Appendix A: Competency-Based Evaluation (CBE) Tool*

SOCIAL WORK PRACTICUM EVALUATION OF SOCIAL WORK
PRACTICE COMPETENCY ELEMENTS –
MICRO INSTRUCTIONS FOR RATING

For each skill, instructors are asked to assign a rating from 1 to 5 by circling one of the numbers as follows:

1 Unacceptable: The student can demonstrate little understanding of what the skill means or of its purposes.
2 The student understands the skill, but there is limited evidence of the skill in practice.
3 The student understands the skill and offers evidence of tentative appropriate attempts to put it into practice. More practice is needed.
4 The student has demonstrated effective use of the skill.
5 The student uses this skill regularly and appropriately, as part of his/her interpersonal style.

The ratings are intended to identify stages in skill acquisition, starting with understanding and ending with behavioural integration.

PLEASE CIRCLE ONLY THE HIGHEST APPROPRIATE NUMBER

---

* Bogo, M., Regehr, C., & Power, R. (2002). Toronto: Factor-Inwentash Faculty of Social Work, University of Toronto. Research Institute for Evidence Based Practice, Competency for Professional Practice. http://www.socialwork.utoronto.ca/Assets/Research/Competency/CBE+Tool.pdf

This Competency-Based Evaluation (CBE) Tool consists of 7 domains or sub-scales with associated items expressed as behavioural skills. The overall score is calculated by averaging across all 57 items. The sub-scores are calculated by averaging across items listed under each domain. An average value of less than 3.5 for a particular student implies a student in potential difficulty, in general or in a particular domain.

Social Work Practice Competency Elements

A   Values and Ethics
1   Demonstrate congruence between one's activities
and professional values and ethics.   1 2 3 4 5
2   Take into account all value systems, including one's
own, that impinge on the practice situation.   1 2 3 4 5
3   Demonstrate respectful behaviour for various cultural norms, value systems, ethics, and moral beliefs
in interaction with colleagues and client groups.   1 2 3 4 5
4   Be accountable to the client system, the agency, and
the profession.   1 2 3 4 5
5   Describe behaviour in non-judgmental terms.   1 2 3 4 5

B   Differential Use of Self
1   Identify and deal with personal, interpersonal, and
structural/institutional barriers to change.   1 2 3 4 5
2   Use a range of techniques and roles to achieve planned outcomes.   1 2 3 4 5
3   Use the organization's policies and procedures
flexibly.   1 2 3 4 5
4   Accurately assess interaction between self and others.   1 2 3 4 5
5   Use an awareness of culture and diversity to accurately assess the verbal and non-verbal interaction
between self and others.   1 2 3 4 5
6   Establish purposeful, culturally competent interpersonal relationships with clients and other
professionals.   1 2 3 4 5
7   Use oneself differentially with client or colleagues as
required.   1 2 3 4 5
8   Probe for significant information, reactions, sensiti-
vities, and feelings relevant to the situation but not
verbalized by the client.   1 2 3 4 5

9   Advocate on behalf of the client/organization/com-
    munity to facilitate service delivery.   1 2 3 4 5
10 Understand, explain, and implement the agency's
    social work roles.   1 2 3 4 5
11 Identify the social, institutional, cultural, and ethno-
    specific contexts within which the problem is pre-
    sented and how these impact on the problem.   1 2 3 4 5
12 Respond to field instructor request for feedback
    about his/her instructional style/method so that
    optimal learning can take place.   1 2 3 4 5

C   Empathy and Alliance
1   Express warmth non-verbally.   1 2 3 4 5
2   Express warmth verbally.   1 2 3 4 5
3   Express acceptance verbally.   1 2 3 4 5
4   Reflect information about positives about the client
    or the situation.   1 2 3 4 5
5   Provide support through use of realistic reassurance.   1 2 3 4 5
6   Reflect affective information skillfully.   1 2 3 4 5
7   Reflect cognitive (beliefs, meanings) information
    skillfully.   1 2 3 4 5

D   Assessment
1   Collect relevant data from primary and secondary
    sources.   1 2 3 4 5
2   Observe behaviour in relation to the context in which
    it occurs.   1 2 3 4 5
3   Define the problem from the perspective of all
    involved.   1 2 3 4 5
4   Consult with appropriate informal and formal
    resources.   1 2 3 4 5
5   Use theoretical concepts to analyse data and formu-
    late an assessment.   1 2 3 4 5
6   Identify the resources necessary to solve the problem.   1 2 3 4 5
7   Reformulate the problem as new or revised data are
    obtained.   1 2 3 4 5
8   Articulate the desired goals and particular outcomes
    to be achieved.   1 2 3 4 5

E   *Intervention – Planning and Implementation*
1   Seek and use evidence and best practices to provide
    a rationale for planned interventions.   1 2 3 4 5
2   Express warmth non-verbally.   1 2 3 4 5
3   Identify clients' attempts to cope with or change the
    situation.   1 2 3 4 5
3   Identify potential obstacles.   1 2 3 4 5
4   Break complex or overwhelming problems into
    manageable parts.   1 2 3 4 5
5   Develop a mutual agreement (contract) between those
    involved in the problem definition and resolution.   1 2 3 4 5
6   Develop and use an appropriate time frame in the
    implementation process.   1 2 3 4 5
7   Prioritize the activities of the helping strategy ac-
    cording to importance and feasibility.   1 2 3 4 5
8   Identify and confront a reluctance to recognize viable
    options.   1 2 3 4 5
9   Appropriately challenge the client system when
    required.   1 2 3 4 5
10 Give feedback on above in a manner which conveys
    respect and understanding.   1 2 3 4 5
11 Give information, or correct misinformation, to help
    clients/systems develop new perspectives on their
    problems.   1 2 3 4 5
12 Respond effectively to inappropriate client behaviour. 1 2 3 4 5
13 Recognize and accept a diverse range of behaviours.   1 2 3 4 5
14 Anticipate external resistance to client system change. 1 2 3 4 5

F   **Report Writing**
1   Write clear, organized, and succinct reports, asses-
    sments, and notes.   1 2 3 4 5
2   Use agency guidelines accurately to write reports,
    assessments, and notes.   1 2 3 4 5
3   Organize and present data in a comprehensive and
    well-written assessment.   1 2 3 4 5
4   Submit written material on time.   1 2 3 4 5

G   **Presentation Skills**
1   Prioritize information to be delivered.   1 2 3 4 5
2   Focus on relevant information.   1 2 3 4 5

3   Pace the presentation skillfully.   1 2 3 4 5
4   Select the most effective method to communicate in-
    formation while taking into account who the
    audience is and how the information will be used.   1 2 3 4 5
5   Make use of appropriate non-verbal communication.   1 2 3 4 5
6   Respond to questions effectively (by accurate listen-
    ing, responding with confidence, clarity, acknowl-
    edging validity of questions).   1 2 3 4 5
7   Use the skill of persuasion appropriately.   1 2 3 4 5

Appendix B:
Vignette Matching Evaluation (VME) Tool*

Use and Scoring of the VME Tool

To use the VME, a field instructor should be asked to get an image of the student to be evaluated in her head, then read through a randomly ordered set of the vignettes and pull out all vignettes that seem like her student (with no limit on the number of vignettes selected). The instructor should then be asked to review the subset of 'similar' vignettes and identify the one or two that are 'most like' the student. The 'score' for the student is then calculated as a weighted average of scores represented by all the 'similar' vignettes (given a weight of 0.5) and the 'most similar' vignettes (given a value of 1.0). For example if an instructor identifies vignettes C and D as similar and vignettes T and K as most similar, then the student's score would be calculated as:

$$[(4*0.5) + (3*0.5) + (5*1.0) + (4*1.0)] / [0.5 + 0.5 + 1.0 + 1.0] = 12.5 / 3.0$$
$$= 4.17$$

* Bogo, M., Regehr, C., Hughes, J., Woodford, M., Power, R., & Regehr, C. (2006). Toronto: Factor-Inwentash Faculty of Social Work, University of Toronto. Research Institute of Evidence Based Practice, Competency for Professional Practice. http://www.socialwork.utoronto.ca/Assets/Research/Competency/VME+Tool.pdf

Vignette	Rank	Category Descriptor	Score Value
F	1	**'Exemplary'** Clearly exceptional More colleagues than students	5
P	2		5
J	3		5
T	4		5
L	5		5
C	6	**'Ready to practice'** Clearly passable from the program	**4**
K	7		4
Q	8		4
R	9		4
N	10	**'On the cusp'** May or may not be ready for practice	3
O	11		3
D	12		3
S	13	**'Needs more training' &/or supervision** May be in year 1 of 2-year program	2
E	14		2
A	15		2
G	16		2
M	17	**'Unsuitable for practice'**	1
V	18		1
B	19		1
H	20		1

MENTAL HEALTH   A

A presents as very pleasant and is well liked by clients and other workers in your agency, yet he/she only seems to do the bare minimum. That is, he/she arrives on time, sees clients, finishes reports, and generally does what needs to be done. A performs adequately, but really does not progress past this level or display any motivation to excel. In his/her relationships with other team members, A is present but not well connected. In supervision, A brings few issues and concerns for discussion and continually appears to give little thought to the placement. A tells you that this placement is not his/her first choice. Further, A works part-time at another agency where he/she is more comfortable and where he/she will begin working at the end of the school year.

A's assessment skills are basically fine, although limited. A's assessments are comprehensive and well-developed when clients' situations and concerns mirror what A understands. Beyond this, A lacks knowledge about the practice setting and the issues and difficulties faced by clients. A's intervention skills are broad, ranging from practical issues, such as developing a discharge plan, to process issues, such as slowing down and listening to clients in sessions.

A's report writing skills are adequate, but some of his/her assessments and the resulting written reports are superficial and seem rushed. Ethically, you have no concerns about A's professional behaviour.

MENTAL HEALTH   B

For the first week of the placement, B arrives habitually late and consistently avoids supervision. When you ask specifically about this behaviour, B becomes aggressive and defensive with you. You wonder about B's interest or personal motivation to become a social worker when he/she avoids you and clients and is not attentive in group sessions.

At the beginning of the placement, B had difficulty engaging, displaying warmth, and joining with clients. With some clients, B is hostile and openly shows dislike. For you as the field instructor, B requires much help as he/she appears to struggle to learn everything and consistently has to learn and relearn the same or similar practice skills or organizational procedures. You spend a great deal of time helping B to improve his/her relationship-building skills. These skills improve only slightly to where B is able to move beyond displays of hostility to learn to be non-judgmental towards clients; however B is never able to really convey warmth to clients.

Assessment is similarly difficult for B as he/she has continual difficulty getting beyond just simply understanding the immediate facts of clients' situations. B demonstrates little to no evidence of using him/herself differentially with clients. Because B takes everything extremely literally and concretely, you spend a great deal of time to help B make the necessary connections. You think that B lacks the necessary ability to go beyond what is literally being said by clients to make deeper connections between the various aspects of the clients' situations or presenting problems. This lack of ability in critically analysing clients' situations is also demonstrated in B's written reports. These reports contain only basic information about what clients literally have said during interviews. B never progresses to the point where he/she has the opportunity to present at a team meeting or a formal presentation for other students and colleagues.

MENTAL HEALTH   C

C presents to you as very friendly, open, warm, and comfortable with clients. In the beginning of the placement, however, C appears to be intimidated by colleagues, especially those from other professions. C does the required readings for the placement and spends a lot of time at the beginning of the placement observing the field instructor and other colleagues to learn how to assess and intervene in this practice setting.

As C begins to work with clients, he/she demonstrates excellent assessment and intervention skills. C works with a variety of different client groups and uses his/her own lived experience to join with and engage clients. In working with clients who are extremely angry or resistant, C uses innovative and unique strategies to establish trust. For example, C engages a resistant client by asking the client if he likes food or music and then uses these interests to join with the client. In working with clients with intellectual limitations, C is non-judgmental, patient, and spends time breaking down large concepts and ideas so that these can be easily understood by these clients.

At the beginning of the placement, C's report writing and presentation skills were weak as C lacked confidence in his/her abilities in both of these areas. Over the course of the placement, you worked closely with C to ensure that written reports become more concise and less subjective. Through this work, you notice that C becomes more confident in these abilities. Near the end of the placement, C makes a formal presentation to other students and colleagues in which C is well prepared and appears quite comfortable.

HOSPITAL   D

D comes to your agency with considerable personal maturity and life experiences. This combination helps D to be reflective and attuned to his/her personal reactions, but this also makes D somewhat nervous and hesitant about the possibility of making mistakes. Consequently, D acts constrained and avoids taking risks, which slows the learning process. D accesses various learning opportunities (for example, co-leading a group); however, these are low risk activities. D checks in with you and the team a lot for reassurance. You sense a feeling of trust from the team toward D – they really like D. In field instruction, D is comfortable in raising personal issues, including describing practice events that trigger traumatic memories for D.

In clinical work, D presents as a very caring and genuine individual, which communicates to others as warmth and genuine concern. D also has a good sense of boundaries and is comfortable with casual conversations with clients. D has good listening skills and uses questioning effectively. D has a good differential use of self in that he/she is able to adapt his/her use of self to different clients. You notice, however, his/her struggle with power issues in the client/worker relationship. D seems to work more intuitively as opposed to being directed by theory. Also, D is more likely to focus on affect and not contain client emotions. Yet, D is able to move beyond the beginning level of intervention and link affect, behaviour, and cognition. As per agency practices, D works in the here and now with clients. However, after a certain point, D tends to get stuck. That is, D is able to assess clients psychologically and socially, but then is not sure what to do next as there is a lack of depth in D's intervention skills.

D's understanding of ethics is very good and he/she raises significant philosophical issues in supervision and D is committed to working through them. D is comfortable with agency policies and procedures and ensures that clients are following them. D's report writing skills are satisfactory. Initially, D's reports were more like stories containing lots of information, some of which were not clinically relevant.

Although some reports are late, time-sensitive ones submitted efficiently. Presentations are satisfactory structurally. In group meetings with the team and clients, D effectively communicates the team's feedback to the client, but finds it difficult to respond to anxious comments from clients.

HOSPITAL   E

E is pleasant, personable, easy to connect with, and forthcoming in sharing information. E has some experience working in human services, but not in a social work capacity. Despite E's verbal skills and personality, he/she struggles to build equitable relationships with other team members, especially with the medical staff as they view E primarily as a student. E has clear learning goals, but requires help focusing on the social work aspects of the setting as E seems to identify more with the medical role than with the social work role. For instance, E spends time learning medical definitions that are not useful in his/her role as a social worker. You believe E sees the placement as an opportunity to explore career goals which are not necessarily related to social work. In supervision, you help E to focus on the social work perspective. E is open to and responsive to feedback and is able to integrate new information effectively. E reads situations realistically and raises relevant information in field instruction.

E's verbal skills and personality enable him/her to connect with clients and other team members. He/she is able to identify factors that clients bring to the social work relationship (e.g., age, gender, socio-economic status) and tries to relate to clients in an appropriate manner (e.g., addressing older clients as Mr., Mrs., or Ms.). However, E tends to talk down to clients and does not share power with them. Over the course of the placement, this changes. E approaches assessment as a means to collect client information, but E lacks boundaries around what information is relevant and not relevant. Further, for E information is to be collected quickly and he/she does not consider the client's experiences in the process. You sense that E collects as much information as possible and later formulates an assessment, as opposed to doing the two simultaneously. Moreover, the information E collects is more factual than psychosocial. Therefore, E's intervention plans are incomplete and not sensitive to clients' instrumental needs, as E does not obtain a full picture of the client's situation and needs.

Initially, E's reports resemble academic papers, but with time and support E makes the adjustment to more fact-based reports; however, you have concerns regarding the legibility of the reports. Verbal reports are somewhat verbose, but improve given time and direction from you. You have no concerns about the ethics of E's work. He/she is very comfortable in assuming an advocacy role with clients.

MENTAL HEALTH   F

To prepare for the placement, F called and asked for recommended readings, performed literature searches, and read books and articles. Upon arriving at your agency, F clearly identifies and articulates what he/she wants to accomplish during the placement. When these aims are reached, F sets new goals. Initially, F observes you in practice and asks a lot of questions, however, early in the placement, F learns to take appropriate action with clients and seek necessary clarification from you and other colleagues. B is excellent in terms of soliciting and receiving feedback from you and clients; however, you notice that F can at times be too critical about his/her own work.

F exudes warmth and compassion. F is able to be him/herself effectively with clients, to be genuine, use humour, and admit when he/she makes mistakes. Although F uses him/herself and his/her personal experiences with clients or groups of clients, F balances this effectively with the need to be professional. F has awareness of personal and professional boundaries with clients. F is able to work with a broad range of clients and use him/herself differently with various client groups and apply a variety of theoretical models as well. This includes working with people with intellectual difficulties and other clients who can be difficult and require a more directive approach. In group work, F demonstrates that he/she can understand group dynamics, assess concerns articulated by individual group members and the group as a whole, discuss these concerns, and negotiate a resolution.

In the beginning of the placement, F's reports were thorough, but they lacked conciseness and objectivity. You spend time working with F to ensure that reports became more concise and crisper. F arrives at team meetings well prepared to discuss clients' situations. F is assertive in presenting his/her assessment of client situations and his/her intervention goals and plans, without being aggressive with other team members at meetings.

MENTAL HEALTH   G

In practice, G is not confident and does not act or think independently. G is not assertive with other team members in that information is provided only when directly requested, and, consequently, G is not viewed as a team member but rather as a student. You sense that for G, this practicum is a means to obtaining a graduate degree and securing future employment. G has outside priorities (i.e., planning a wedding) that cause you to conclude he/she is not an enthused learner, even though G's work and skills are satisfactory. All of G's interventions and interactions are ethical and G is able to present as professional with satisfactory and timely performance of duties. However, overall, G appears to invest little in the placement experience.

In interactions with clients and agency staff, G comes across as somewhat irritable, hesitant, and lacking warmth. G is able to provide feedback concerning client input, but his/her clinical interventions are not well directed or goal oriented, thus some issues go unexplored unless you specifically take the time to prompt G to consider these issues. The same level of prompting is required throughout the placement period. You notice that G approaches meetings with clients as informal discussions rather than focused clinical interviews.

G possesses strong writing skills, although reports tend to be descriptive and lack sufficient information to enable the reader to fully understand clients' situations and clinical interventions. Consequently, you need to support G in report preparation throughout the placement period. Verbally G presents well, yet is uncomfortable with public speaking due to not being well prepared.

CHILD WELFARE   H

When H first came to the practicum, he/she presented as bright, energetic, and skilled as a social worker. Early in the placement, however, it is obvious to you that H has come to this practice setting with very definite ideas about how your agency should operate and he/she tries to implement these views. This behaviour creates difficulties for H in his/her interactions with other team members, with you in supervision, and in his/her interactions with clients. H makes no attempts to integrate with other colleagues and to work as part of the team. In H's first team meeting, he/she was argumentative with other workers and was asked to leave the meeting by your supervisor. This behaviour continues throughout the placement as H argues with other colleagues in the office. H also argues with you in supervision and ignores your suggestions for improvements to his/her practice. H also brings very personal issues to supervision. Although young clients like H, his/her relationships violate professional/personal boundaries. As examples, H takes clients to his/her apartment during lunch, tells young clients that they do not have to go to school if they did not want to go, and also tells young clients that it is okay to run away from foster homes.

Although H understands conceptually how to do an assessment, H starts with his/her personal view of clients' situations and then tries to find information that supports his/her own view. Because H is unwilling to take the time to really listen to clients, H is unable to form adequate assessments and develop logical, meaningful, and practical intervention plans.

H struggles with ethical professional behaviour by continually becoming over involved with clients. H does not respect the confidentiality of clients by bringing clients to his/her home to meet his/her partner and sharing clients' confidential information, including clients' names with his/her university classmates. H has no opportunity to do written reports, and, because of his/her argumentative behaviour in team meetings, he/she also has no opportunity to present during meetings.

HOSPITAL J

J is personally mature (although young in age), motivated, has a thirst for knowledge, and is clear regarding his/her learning goals. J arrives at the agency inexperienced, but J works hard throughout the practicum. J takes advantage of learning opportunities, effectively integrates new competencies into his/her practice, welcomes challenges, and is willing to take risks by trying new approaches and skills in order to grow professionally. For example, J frequently volunteers to assist other team members in order to maximize learning opportunities. Throughout the placement, J builds good, respectful relationships with you, the team, and referring consultants. The field instructor-student relationship is a positive, well-managed one. J comes to supervision prepared for discussion and is open and willing to expose him/herself and solicit feedback from you. J has a good sense of the areas he/she knows and does not know. J is able to find many opportunities to engage with colleagues and J works well with other team members and also seeks and uses their feedback. Moreover, J offers assistance when needed, but remains humble and respects the organizational hierarchy. J avoids getting involved in workplace politics and is able to find a good place within the organizational culture. J does not allow the agency culture and work dynamics to interfere with clinical practice or the learning process.

Clinically, J is able to establish and maintain positive relationships with clients. J has good listening skills, is able to attend to what is being said and not said, and is good at partializing. Further, J feels comfortable with silences and appropriately uses humour. As per the nature of the agency's work, J focuses on the here and now with clients. Initially in the therapeutic process, J focuses on surface/concrete issues in working with clients, but over time J learns to do in-depth work and becomes competent at putting together many layers of clients' situations. During in-take assessments, J at first followed established agency forms (i.e., asked one question after the other). With experience, J learns to conduct assessments in a freer flowing manner that is sensitive to the particular client, while still obtaining information required by the agency. J demonstrates empathy and works effectively with affect, but is also able to conduct an in-take interview at an appropriate pace so that clients do not feel uncomfortable or vulnerable. J's assessments are conclusive and help J to develop comprehensive intervention plans. During the intervention phase, when needed, J is able to facilitate the client exploring affect in more detail. In doing so, clients are helped to make connections among various aspects of their lives. Overall J is focused when working with clients. Initially, J admits to some uneasiness with personal disclosure, but with increased confidence J becomes better at using him/herself and his/her personal experiences. J, however, does have difficulty dealing with conflict and setting limits with clients.

J demonstrates a good understanding of ethical issues and is able to consider these issues in the context of ethical principles. J also has a good sense of professional responsibility. Report writing is a particularly strong skill for J. They are well written and concise, contain relevant information, and are submitted on time. Further, J provides you and your agency with a suggestion to improve agency record keeping procedures by expanding the current record to include additional information about an area not currently recorded (although highly relevant). As for presentation skills, J is well organized for case rounds and consistently presents information following established agency processes. In group meetings (i.e., clients and team), J is able to provide feedback to the client effectively, and, with time, is able to respond comfortably and suitably to clients' remarks.

MENTAL HEALTH   K

K is bright, very skilled, and has a balanced sense of self-confidence when working with clients and interacting with agency staff. K is very personable and engaging and combines this enthusiasm with a sense of professionalism by completing work in a timely and well-organized fashion. Within the work environment, K is seen as part of the team as opposed to being in the student role.

In clinical intervention, assessments are analytical and reflect a systems-eclectic approach. Communication with clients involves feedback in which K ensures accuracy of understanding. Because K is analytical, he/she is able to provide a lot of insight into clients' situations. Although K has this insight and shares this information with clients, you worry that K does not always share information at a pace that is respectful of clients' readiness for such awareness. While you observe that K is too exuberant, you do not observe any significant impacts on clients. K's ability to look beyond present, individual pathology serves as a reminder to you and your colleagues to also consider other systems and systemic issues in your assessments.

K's verbal and written communication skills are strong. Presentations to the team are clear and follow a logical flow. Writing competencies are excellent as reports are well organized, articulate, and enable the reader to understand the clinical situation. No concerns regarding ethics or differential use of self are noted.

HOSPITAL   L

L is very energetic, insightful, and clear about what he/she wants to learn from the placement. In addition, L has a lot of initiative. For instance, L identifies a gap in the agency's literature and takes it upon him/herself to develop a much-needed patient booklet. L is punctual, reliable, and communicates with you, other team members, and clients with ease. L worked in a hospital previously, although not in a social work capacity. Therefore, L has a lot to discover about social work, but is eager and open to do so. Because of this past exposure to the hospital setting, he/she builds rapport easily with the team and understands and interacts in the hospital setting quite well. L's social skills are very good, and help in this regard. In addition, L's appearance is always appropriate for the workplace. In supervision, L has the ability to be critical of his/her own work and to be very honest and straightforward about his/her competencies and limitations. But when needed, L reaches out for help. At the end of placement, L identifies an area of interest for the second-year practicum, which he/she pursues. L is very clear on his/her educational and practice goals.

From the outset, L connects well with patients, and these skills continue to grow. He/she is able to empathize and perceive client needs. In the therapeutic context, L discloses appropriately while respecting professional boundaries. L has a good sense of humour and uses it effectively to build relationships. Initially, L's energy, eagerness, and insight are problematic in working with clients as L finds it challenging to be patient and listen. L interrupts frequently and puts words in the client's mouth. With time in the placement L learns to control this tendency and then improves to become a better listener. In the therapeutic context, L does not present him/herself as an expert, but acknowledges with clients that he/she does not have all the answers. L is aware of the power dynamics traditionally found in a hospital setting, and attempts to ensure that the patient has power in the social work relationship. For instance, L always knocks before entering patients' rooms and asks patients how they would like to be addressed. In addition, L attempts to be culturally aware, takes time to become informed about client's respective cultural norms and observances, and then L attempts to work with clients based on this understanding. In doing so, L looks for commonalties between him/herself and the client in order to engage.

L's reports are well written in terms of writing style and content, and he/she is able to differentiate between what should be included in and excluded from the file. Reports meet the agency's expectations. When presenting information orally, L is articulate, concise, focuses on facts, and is open to feedback based on a sense of mutuality between L and the team. L raises ethical concerns about some of the gray areas of practice and maintains good boundaries between work and personal life.

HOSPITAL   M

M arrives at the agency with high expectations and wants to develop his/her clinical skills. However, M quickly becomes interested in and involved in the organization's politics. This not only detracts from M's learning, but your energies are continually focused on managing M in the political realm. Consequently, there is little opportunity for M to practice clinical skills. Despite these challenges, M does seem to learn through his/her experiences.

M struggles in building relationships. You think that M is anxious talking socially with clients and when it comes to responding to negative comments from clients in group work, M is uncomfortable. In team meetings with colleagues, M considers and presents him/herself as more knowledgeable than he/she actually is, and challenges his/her place in the organization's hierarchy. M asks questions that other team members find disrespectful. This makes M's interactions with the team problematic and you have to intervene quite frequently. You and others find M difficult to read. In field instruction, you also observe that M cannot take feedback, even when you raise issues and invite M to discuss them with you. Fundamentally, you see M as being well intended, but you question if M should be a social worker.

In terms of clinical skills, M follows the established assessment questionnaire and elicits the information required. However, M's empathy and attunement skills are not well developed. M needs help in reading between the lines, as it appears that M focuses too much on concrete information and avoids exploring affect. Nevertheless, M does possess enough basic intervention skills to be able to plan appropriate interventions. Also, M is comfortable in using the agency's therapeutic model, but cannot individualize the model to each client. Consequently, clients' situations are made to fit the therapeutic model and M does not work at a reasonable pace for clients. M struggles with authenticity, as M is one-dimensional in his/her use of self and does not seem able to understand that different clients have different needs.

M thinks about and processes ethical issues; however, M cannot translate ethical principles and standards into practice. For example, B is not able to look at his/her own use of power. M is able to think about ethics in the abstract form, but not from a practical stance. In rounds and group meetings with all staff and team members, M articulates the facts of clients' situations well and summarizes client information in written form.

CHILD WELFARE   N

N is eager to learn and very bright; however, he/she lacks self-confidence. Although this lack of self-confidence somewhat hampers N's ability to develop relationships with colleagues and clients, N is well liked and respected by other workers. N has a difficult time interacting with clients, as he/she appears nervous and uncomfortable. Overall, N comes to the placement with some skills and works very hard to develop others.

Initially, N has difficulties with doing assessments because he/she seems to lack basic assessment skills. Both you and your supervisor spend time working with N going through case studies and client scenarios to help N develop these skills. Eventually, N learns how to determine what information needs to be gathered, how to process this information, and who needs to be contacted to obtain crucial information. By the end of the placement, N's assessment skills improve and N is able to produce strong, focused assessments. N's intervention skills are also affected by his/her lack of self-confidence. N has great ideas and can develop intervention plans, but he/she is afraid to express these plans to clients. Before intervening, N continually consults with you.

Ethically, N has clear boundaries and is very respectful with other staff. N's report writing skills improve along with his/her assessment skills. N does not have the opportunity to present at a team meeting.

CHILD WELFARE   O

O is organized, knows what information to collect from clients, follows up on contacts, and links with other agencies. O has a good sense of him/herself and is able to keep issues in O's private life separate from professional work. O is well liked by the other members of the team, as he/she works well with other colleagues and agencies and clearly understands the agency's mandate and purpose.

In interviews, O does not attend to the emotional aspects of clients' situations. O remains task-focused and concentrates on families' practical needs. For instance, instead of spending time with clients who are in emotional distress, O notes this as a concern and then refers them for counselling. O seems to lack skills in developing longer-term, more intensive relationships. In supervision, you spend time with O trying to get him/her to move beyond just the surface issues and concrete needs of clients and to help O develop in-depth clinical skills.

O's reports are organized and finished on time. However, you need to help and support O to develop in-depth psycho-social reports. Ethically, you have no concerns about O, as he/she is quite clear about what is appropriate and what is not appropriate. He/she has good boundaries with clients, colleagues, and other staff. O is a very good presenter, as he/she is confident.

CHILD WELFARE   P

From the beginning of the practicum, P presents as resilient, versatile, and energetic. Although young in age, he/she displays maturity. P has the ability to use his/her life experiences to go beyond simple understanding of clients' situations on a purely clinical or theoretical level. P's sense of maturity and confidence is evident in his/her work with clients and his/her ability to adapt to a difficult and challenging work environment. For example, P is able to present a calm exterior when confronted with a hostile client, and P is also able to speak to a large group in a credible, professional, and confident manner. In supervision, P is able to critically and effectively reflect on his/her work.

P's client relationship-building skills are well developed. With non-voluntary clients who are angry and hostile, P is able to be forthright, clear, and concise, yet compassionate and sensitive. You observe that P has a personal style in his/her interactions with clients that engenders their trust. P is also able to use him/herself differently in knowing when to be directive and when to sit back and say nothing.

P's assessments are very comprehensive and demonstrate his/her understanding of the families and the environment, and past and present influences on clients' lives. P is also able to transfer his/her thoughts to paper, which is absolutely critical in this setting. P entered the placement with previous work experience that helps P in preparing assessments, but P learns from colleagues how to specifically write an assessment/report for this agency. P's reports are strong, clear, concise, and delivered on time. P understands and respects professional standards and ethics, yet P does not rigidly adhere to them. For example, P demonstrates respect for diversity. P does not struggle when clients are from different cultures and races, or in work with clients whose sexual orientation and gender differ from P's.

MENTAL HEALTH   Q

Q enters placement very keen and motivated. He/she is outgoing, very comfortable meeting others, and engages well with team members. Q is mature and has a lot of previous work experience in another setting, which helps Q fit in and feel comfortable and confident. However, this particular practice setting is difficult for Q in that the setting, the practice of social work, and clients are very different from Q's experience. Yet, Q is quite motivated and enthusiastic to learn more about the practice setting and he/she takes advantage of the many learning opportunities that are available. You spend time orienting Q to this new practice environment and helping Q develop an understanding of the practice theories and models used in your agency. Supervision sessions with Q are quite rich, as Q is very motivated and eager to learn and soaks up everything like a sponge.

Clinically, Q has no difficulty engaging and joining with clients. Because the setting and the clients are so different for Q, he/she must work to understand the issues and struggles faced by these clients and to develop appropriate interventions and treatment goals. Q also has difficulty in accepting, because of the overwhelming difficulties and challenges faced by this group of clients, that client change resulting from his/her interventions are limited. You work closely with Q to help him/her to recognize these limitations, and Q works hard to become familiar with the setting and these accompanying limitations. With time, Q's assessments and intervention plans improve greatly.

You have no concerns about Q's ethical or professional behaviour. Because of his/her past work experience, Q understands the social work role.

MENTAL HEALTH   R

R is a mature learner (mid-30s) and has the ability to integrate professional knowledge with life experience. This ability is particularly useful with clients, as R uses his/her life experiences to relate to clients as part of the engagement-therapy process. This combination of maturity/life experience and professional/academic knowledge also helps colleagues view R as a co-worker from whom they can learn, rather than an inexperienced student. R arrives at your agency with clearly defined learning goals that are specific to the practice area. However,

R has a number of other responsibilities and time commitments outside of the placement that create struggles for him/her in devoting time and energy to the placement and really feeling as though he/she is part of the team. Nevertheless, other team members and clients see R as an experienced worker. Team members look to R to learn new information based on R's non-academic knowledge and life experiences. R always behaves ethically and professionally.

Clinically, R enters the placement well versed in family of origin and psychodynamic perspectives, and thus works from these theories. Although R has an appreciation for other therapeutic frameworks, R prefers to work within family of origin and psychodynamic perspectives. Assessment skills related to these theories are strong; however, R needs additional practice with intervention skills. Despite this focus on one particular theoretical framework, R effectively uses her/his own life experiences to inform his/her practice, which reflects a positive use of self.

Report writing skills overall are fine, with some room for improvement in the finer points of grammar. R speaks English as a second language, thus he/she is not secure when making formal presentations but is confident in other interactions, with clients and with team members and in other settings such as case conferences and team meetings.

HOSPITAL   S

S is eager to learn and would like to do well, but is not clear about his/her learning goals. Further, he/she is not a risk taker and is unsure, therefore repeatedly asks the same questions. You and other team members are very directive and detailed with S, but he/she struggles to accomplish tasks. S requires a lot of your time. In supervision, S is somewhat cautious. That is, he/she shares information learned from clients, but not his/her responses to them. In terms of relationships with team members, S requires much time and support and therefore relationships become stressed. For you or the team to get information from S, direct questions are asked as opposed to S voluntarily sharing information during rounds. S has to be encouraged to present at rounds. Although there are many struggles with S, you perceive growth by the end of the placement.

Clients see S as being patient, mild mannered, and calming. He/she is able to recognize the individuality of each client and uses commonalties shared with the client as a means of building a relationship. S makes clients feel comfortable, as S is unthreatening. Working with clients, S has good listening skills and effectively elicits information, yet is unsure how to use the information and struggles with intervention planning. As the practicum progresses, S's assessment skills improve and he/she is able to identify client needs and develop an effective plan.

S uses self-disclosure to encourage clients to go deeper in terms of opening up. There is a tendency, however, for S to over identify with clients because of S's past medical experiences, which he/she does not disclose to you until part way through the placement. S has a medical background that is similar to that of the clients at your agency. While this background helps S to identify with clients, there is a tendency to over identify. This becomes a recurrent issue throughout the practicum. Despite this concern, S respects some boundaries and overall his/her work is ethical.

Initially, S's reports resemble academic assignments. Reducing things to the facts is a problem for S, but he/she is eventually able to do so. With time, S learns to differentiate what information should be included in a report and what is unnecessary.

CHILD WELFARE   T

T is very eager to learn, asks a lot of questions, and takes the initiative to adapt to the agency environment. For example, T always attends supervision with you equipped with examples, questions, and a lot of ideas, which he/she brings into practice with clients. T's relationship-building skills are excellent and he/she presents as a very warm individual, which immediately makes others feel comfortable with him/her. T does not take an expert role with clients, but assumes a position of wanting to learn. T is able to engage involuntary clients and develop effective working relationships by being very respectful of these clients and beginning where clients are at. As a reflective listener, T conveys to clients that they have been heard and that their emotions and feelings are understood. He/she is very clear in setting respectful boundaries with clients. T adapts well to the agency setting as he/she always works as part of the team. Overall, T is talented, confident, and completes required tasks.

T arrived at your agency with very good assessment skills. His/her assessments are thorough, as T is able to gather needed information from a variety of relevant sources and use this information to develop assessments that are meaningful and build on clients' strengths. T is very creative in applying theory in practical terms and translating these ideas into positive interventions, which creates meaningful interventions and agreements with clients.

Ethically, you have no concerns about T. He/she understands his/her role as a student and does not become involved in office politics. Although initially T's written reports are completed on time, the reports are too long. When you explain to T the need to write more concise case notes and records, he/she immediately begins to shorten his/her reports and notes so that these contain only relevant information. In presenting to groups, T has good communication skills, is organized, and appears confident.

CHILD WELFARE   V

V presents as very intelligent, sincere, gentle, and rather quiet. V is very religious and conservative and seems to have very limited to no life experience out of the home, school, and community. Although V displays strong compassion for others, he/she also has very strong and inflexible ideas about what is right and wrong. This inflexibility combined with anxiousness hinders V's client work and satisfaction with the practicum.

Clinically, V is clearly uncomfortable with many of the issues in clients' lives. For example, V cannot understand how parents can harm their children, and as a result V is judgmental and condescending towards clients. Rather than engaging clients with understanding and empathy, V takes a lecturing approach causing some clients to become defensive and hostile. Because V puts much forethought and analysis into preparing for interviews, V becomes preoccupied and anxious with doing it right. During the actual interview, he/she has no ability to be natural and spontaneous and at times becomes incapacitated.

V has a very strong textbook, theoretical understanding of the various aspects of comprehensive assessment. In supervision, V articulates the various aspects and dimensions of an assessment and demonstrates that he/she knows what to observe during a client interview. However, V's completed assessments lack depth. V's basic relationship skills are not sufficient to engage clients in order to gather the information needed to complete a comprehensive assessment.

V takes a long time to complete reports because of his/her need for these reports to be perfect. Although V believes that his/her reports are complete, there is something lacking. V takes a checklist approach to filling in required agency forms, but does not go beyond this level to offer a truly comprehensive and dynamic assessment of clients' situations. In team meetings, V is given opportunities to interact with colleagues and to present cases. V requires a great deal of preparation to present these cases. In presenting, V is articulate and intelligent but is unable to engage team members in discussion. It is the substance and content of the presentation that is lacking, not V's presentation skills.

Appendix C:
Practice-Based Evaluation (PBE) Tool*

Use and Scoring of the PBE Tool (paper version)

In the original study, field instructors were asked to read one of the dimensions and the descriptors under each level of performance (Regehr, Bogo et al., 2007). The field instructor is then to highlight the level of the dimension that best describes the student. For example, the first dimension in Learning and Growth. After reading all of the levels and descriptors, the field instructor is to choose one from the following: exemplary, ready to practice, on the cusp, more training, unsuitable.

Use and Scoring of the PBE Tool (online version)

The online tool can be constructed as follows (Regehr, C., Bogo, M., & Regehr, G., in review): For each dimension, all descriptive phrases under all the levels (exemplary, ready to practice, on the cusp, more training, unsuitable) are arranged alphabetically, with the dimension serving as the heading. For example, for the first dimension, Learning and Growth, when all descriptive phrases are arranged alphabetically there are 26 descriptors. The numeric weighting of each phrase is not indicated in the online tool.

---

* Bogo, M., Regehr, C., Hughes, J., Woodford, M., Power, R., & Regehr, G. (2006). Toronto: Factor-Inwentash Faculty of Social Work, University of Toronto. Research Institute for Evidence Based Practice, Competency for Professional Practice. http://www.socialwork.utoronto.ca/Assets/Research/Competency/PBE+Tool.pdf

To conduct the evaluation, the field instructor and student independently select, from the list of descriptive phrases for each dimension, 4 to 6 phrases that best describe the student using a pull-down menu. To create an overall score for the student, once all relevant phrases are selected for each dimension and the evaluation is submitted online, a numerical value of 1 to 5 is assigned to each selected phrase based on level of performance at which the phrase was an anchor in the original PBE tool. A mean score is derived for each dimension and a final score is calculated as the unweighted average of the 6 dimensional scores. Students and instructors both complete the form independently and then review the ratings of the other only after they have submitted their own assessment online. A space for narrative comments is available on the online tool for each dimension and at the end.

Your Number: _____   Year 1   Year 2   Year 2 BSW

Practice-Based Evaluation (PBE) Tool
Learning & Growth

Exemplary	Ready to Practice	On the Cusp	More Training	Unsuitable
• Possess appropriate learning objectives from the outset of the placement and demonstrate initiative, energy, and motivation in achieving these goals. • Strong capacity to learn. • Self-identify her/his skills needing improvement (e.g., dealing with conflict, setting limits, report writing) and use placement opportunities to address these. • Demonstrate confidence in taking risks and challenging her/himself (e.g., to work with clients early in the placement, work with challenging client situations, or assume more challenging roles, such as group leader). • Transfer learning from field instruction to clinical practice.	• Eager to learn and can establish clear learning objectives. • Somewhat hesitant to take risks to meet chosen goals. • Confidence develops through field instruction and learning opportunities in the placement. • Demonstrate strong capacity to learn and grow when given feedback.	• Are eager to learn and establish learning objectives, but nervousness interferes with learning. • Consult with you frequently as she/he is not confident in her/his skills and abilities. • Demonstrate some strengths and capacity for growth and learning, but show little progress in moving beyond the basic level. • Improvements are needed.	• Enter the placement with some general, unfocused learning goals. • Invest little in the learning process and do not make the placement a priority. • Are cautious and avoid taking risks, such as seeking out new learning opportunities. • Ask a lot of direct questions in order to understand basic information, such as policies, procedures, and the worker role. • Possess the capacity to hear and integrate feedback, but minimal improvements are observed. • Some struggle with understanding the basic functions of social work at the end of placement. • Significant areas for improvement are identified at the end of placement.	• Lack clear learning objectives as the student is uncertain about her/his desired learning outcomes. • Do not demonstrate much interest in the placement or the clients. • Do not seek out or maximize learning opportunities available in the agency. • Do not seek out or integrate constructive feedback. • Difficulty in integrating new information and skills from field instruction to their clinical work. • Demonstrate a general lack of improvement.

Behaviour in the Organization

Exemplary	Ready to Practice	On the Cusp	More Training	Unsuitable
• Work in a responsible and experienced manner within the agency.	• Relate to agency staff with humility and respect.	• Follow agency procedures and are accepted by the team.	• Experience difficulty in building relationships with organizational staff.	• Lack appreciation of the student role and self-awareness about interactions with organizational staff.
• Show respect to other staff and work well within the agency's culture.	• Viewed as co-workers by other members of the team.	• Tend to work well in the student role.	• Struggles with the student role, as she/he wants more clients and responsibility, but does not possess or demonstrate the needed skills and abilities to take on this extra responsibility.	• No respect for the agency and its procedures.
• Understand the student role and maintain professional boundaries with other team members.	• Work well with colleagues, but can be intimidated by members of other professions.	• Regarded as a student/learner by other members of the team.	• Viewed primarily as a student.	• Experience difficulty in fitting into the agency and engage in problematic behaviours, such as being highly critical of and argumentative with other staff and the field instructor, and/or becoming involved in agency politics.
• Respected and valued by agency staff. Other staff regard her/him as a valued colleague.				• Demonstrate an overall inflexibility in the workplace.
• Highly flexible and adaptable.				

Clinical Relationships

Exemplary	Ready to Practice	On the Cusp	More Training	Unsuitable
• Establish and sustain effective relationships with a broad array of clients by drawing on the ability to be genuine, respectful, and client-focused; and to use oneself appropriately and differentially. • Demonstrate a good use of self. • Use creativity in connecting with difficult to reach clients. • Are responsible and respectful with clients. • Begin where the client is and pace the interview to meet the needs of the client. • Understand their own personal experiences and draw on these life experiences to understand clients and their life situations.	• Personable and engaging. • Establish meaningful relationships and work well with an array of clients. • Demonstrate some creativity and innovation in connecting with clients. • Possess some very strong skills, but, at times, can experience difficulty in applying these with clients, such as moving too quickly in client interviews or struggling to understand client situations and issues. • With feedback and through supervision, skills improve during the placement.	• Possess good basic skills, such as listening, questioning, and differential use of self. • Maintain professional boundaries with clients. • Can build relationships, but struggle with establishing deeper, more therapeutic connections. • Attention is given primarily to tasks and meeting the practical needs of clients, not to exploring deeper emotional issues. • Areas for improvement are identified.	• Act with clients in a friendly manner, like a student/volunteer, rather than a student/worker, as interactions with clients tend to resemble informal discussions, rather than therapeutic interviews. • Struggle with establishing therapeutic relationships and interventions, as she/he is unfocused in her/his interactions with clients or she/he struggles with being genuine or non-judgmental. • Compassion and empathy for clients is lacking or slow to develop. • Does not use professional power appropriately, as interactions with clients can be intrusive and authoritarian.	• Tend to be judgmental, condescending, overly anxious, inflexible, not genuine, one-dimensional, and can become frustrated with some clients' inability to change. • Lack basic skills, such as affect and warmth, and these do not develop during the placement. • Lack of self-awareness, as she/he tends to confuse her/his own personal experiences with those of clients'. • Try to form inappropriately close and friendly relationships with clients and other staff, rather than worker-client or worker-worker relationships.

Conceptualizing Practice

Exemplary	Ready to Practice	On the Cusp	More Training	Unsuitable
• Think about and understand practice on multiple levels from instrumental tasks to deeper, therapeutic interventions. • Possess strong critical thinking skills. • Competent in using numerous theories in practice, and apply them in a flexible manner. • Understand and carry out the mandate of the organization, while remaining sensitive to clients' situations and needs. • Maintain an ethical practice, but are not rigid or inflexible.	• View practice on multiple levels, but in some cases this develops only with field instruction. • Knowledgeable about theory and are capable of applying it to practice. Some students, however tend to know one approach very well and work primarily from that framework. • Understand and maintain professional, ethical practice. • Some ability to think critically.	• View practice as simply the process of collecting factual or affective information and demonstrate only a limited ability to link affect, behaviour, and cognition. • Experience difficulty integrating theory, but some growth is observed. • Understand and maintain an ethical practice.	• Give attention primarily to the concrete aspects of clients' situations. • Tend to think in the here and now and experience difficulties in making deeper connections. Able to identify and discuss ethical matters. • Work well within established frameworks, but demonstrate inflexibility in using different practice approaches. • Struggle with understanding the difference between personal relationships and worker-client relationships.	• View practice at a concrete level only and experience extreme difficulty in going beyond this level. • Have difficulty applying theoretical understanding to practice situations. • Do not understand ethical practice and client-worker boundaries. Some students have the potential to be harmful to clients. • Demonstrate rigidity in her/his thinking and belief systems. • Struggle in understanding social work values. • Personal issues and difficulties are not kept out of her/his work and practice.

Assessment and Intervention

Exemplary	Ready to Practice	On the Cusp	More Training	Unsuitable
• Perform comprehensive assessments and use these for goal-directed interventions. • Capable of clear, concise, and comprehensive assessments. • Use theory flexibly to fit clients' situations, instead of trying to make client situations fit to theoretical models. • Assessment and intervention skills become more differentiated and complex throughout the placement.	• Complete focused and relevant assessments, but with some struggle in knowing what information to include and being concise. • Able to intervene effectively. • Developments are made with field instruction.	• There is a lack of depth as there is a tendency to focus on identifying and addressing instrumental needs. • Mainly focus on offering practical assistance to clients. • Interventions are often not goal directed. • Attempt to make client situations fit and conform to theory. • Through field instruction, improvements are seen.	• Assessments focus on basic and factual information. • Assessments are conducted at a pace that is not respectful of the client or client-centred. • Weak critical analysis of collected information. • Struggle with understanding the purpose of intervening and interventions are often unfocussed. • Experience difficulty in constructing good intervention plans with clients. • Considerable assistance is needed to understand the basics of a good assessment and intervention plan.	• Assessments and intervention plans tend to be factual and one-dimensional. • Assessments are not founded on the clients' situation, but are based more on the students' assumptions and perceptions. • When applied, therapeutic models are used very rigidly and are not individualized to the client situation.

Professional Communication

Exemplary	Ready to Practice	On the Cusp	More Training	Unsuitable
• Possess comprehensive written and verbal skills. • Capable of producing well-developed reports. • Effective and confident in case conferences and team meetings. • Deliver clearly organized and effective presentations.	• Reports are well organized, but can be unfocused and contain too much information. • Experience some struggles in meeting agency expectations or being too academic in her/his reports. • Presentations are clear and well organized.	• Reports lack focus and depth. • Presentations tend to be satisfactory. • In case conferences or team meetings, students lack self-confidence and may not speak unless required or asked.	• Reports tend to be superficial and too descriptive. For some, reports read like academic assignments.	• Reports tend to be a reiteration of the actual interview with the client and lack clinical analysis.

References

Abbott, A.A., & Lyter, S.C. (1998). The use of constructive criticism in field supervision. *The Clinical Supervisor, 17*(2), 43–57.

Abels, P. (1977). Group supervision of students and staff. In F.W. Kaslow (Ed.), *Supervision, consultation, and staff training in the helping professions* (pp. 175–98). San Francisco: Jossey-Bass.

Abram, F.Y., Hartung, M.R., & Wernet, S.P. (2000). The Non-MSW task supervisor, MSW field instructor, and the practicum student: A triad for high quality field education. *Journal of Teaching in Social Work, 20*(1, 2), 171–85.

ACGME. (2000). ACGME Outcome Project [electronic version]. Chicago: Accreditation Council of Graduate Medical Education.

Adams, K.B., LeCroy, C.W., & Matto, H.C. (2009). Limitations of evidence-based practice for social work education: Unpacking the complexity. *Journal of Social Work Education, 45*(2), 165–86.

Alper, S. (2005). Enhancing your effectiveness through mindfulness. Washington, DC: Psychotherapy Networker.

Alperin, D.E. (1996). Empirical research on student assessment in field education: What have we learned? *The Clinical Supervisor, 14*(1), 149–61.

Alperin, D.E. (1998). Factors related to student satisfaction with child welfare field placements. *Journal of Social Work Education, 34*(1), 43–54.

Alvarez, A.R., & Moxley, D.P. (2004). The student portfolio in social work education. *Journal of Teaching in Social Work, 24*(1, 2), 87–103.

Arkava, M.L., & Brennan, E.C. (Eds.). (1976). *Competency-based education for social work: Evaluation and curriculum issues.* New York: Council on Social Work Education.

Armour, M.P., Bain, B., & Rubio, R. (2004). An evaluation study of diversity training for field instructors: A collaborative approach to enhancing cultural competence. *Journal of Social Work Education, 40*(1), 27–38.

Baer, B.L., & Frederico, R. (1978). *Educating the baccalaureate social worker.* Cambridge, MA: Ballinger.

Barlow, C.A. (2007). In the third space: A case study of Canadian students in a social work practicum in India. *International Social Work, 50*(2), 242–54.

Barlow, C., & Hall, B.L. (2007). 'What about feelings?' A study of emotion and tension in social work field education. *Social Work Education, 26*(4), 399–413.

Barlow, C., Rogers, G., & Coleman, H. (2003). Peer collaboration: A model for field instructor development and support. *The Clinical Supervisor, 22*(2), 173–90.

Barretti, M.A. (2009). Ranking desirable field instructor characteristics: Viewing student preferences in context with field and class experience. *The Clinical Supervisor, 28*(1), 47–71.

Barth, R., & Gambrill, E. (1984). Learning to interveiw: The quality of training opportunities. *The Clinical Supervisor, 2*(1), 3–14.

Barton, H., Bell, K., & Bowles, W. (2005). Help or hindrance? Outcomes of social work student placements. *Australian Social Work, 58*(3), 301–12.

Beals, H. (2003). *The need for a social work profile to regulate and promote the profession in Nova Scotia.* Halifax: Nova Scotia Association of Social Workers.

Benavides III, E., Lynch, M.M., & Valasquez, J.S. (1980). Toward a culturally relevant field work model: The community learning centre project. *Journal of Education for Social Work, 16*(2), 55–62.

Bennett, S., Mohr, J., Szoc, K.B., & Saks, L.V. (2008). General and supervision-specific attachment styles: Relations to student perceptions of field supervisors. *Journal of Social Work Education, 44*(2), 75–94.

Bennett, S., & Saks, L.V. (2006). A conceptual application of attachment theory and research to the social work student-field instructor supervisory relationship. *Journal of Social Work Education, 42*(3), 669–82.

Bernard, J.M., & Goodyear, R.K. (2008). *Fundamentals of clinical supervision* (4th ed.). Boston, MA: Allyn and Bacon.

Birkenmaier, J., & Berg-Weger, M. (2006). *The practicum companion for social work: Integrating class and field work* (2d ed.). Boston: Allyn and Bacon.

Birkenmaier, J., Wernet, S.P., Berg-Weger, M., Wilson, R.J., Banks, R., Olliges, R., et al. (2005). Weaving a web: The use of internet technology in field education. *Journal of Teaching in Social Work, 25*(1, 2), 3–19.

Black, J.E., Maki, M.T., & Nunn, J.A. (1997). Does race affect the social work student-field instructor relationship? *The Clinical Supervisor, 16*(1), 39–54.

Black, P.N., & Feld, A. (2006). Process recording revisited: A learning-oriented thematic approach integrating field education and classroom curriculum. *Journal of Teaching in Social Work, 26*(3,4), 137–53.

Bocage, M., Homonoff, E., & Riley, P. (1995). Measuring the impact of the current state and national fiscal crises on human service agencies and social work training. *Social Work, 40*(5), 701–5.

Bogo, M. (1993). The student/field instructor relationship: The critical factor in field education. *The Clinical Supervisor, 11*(2), 23–36.

Bogo, M. (2005a). Field instruction in social work: A review of the research literature 1999-2005. *The Clinical Supervisor, 24*(1, 2), 163–93.

Bogo, M. (2005b). Practicum. In F. Turner (Ed.), *Canadian Encyclopaedia of Social Work* (pp. 290–1). Kitchener, ON: Wilfrid Laurier Press.

Bogo, M. (2006). *Social work practice: Concepts, processes, and interviewing.* New York: Columbia University Press.

Bogo, M., & Globerman, J. (1995). Creating effective university-field partnerships: An analysis of two inter-organization models. *Journal of Teaching in Social Work, 11*(1, 2), 177–92.

Bogo, M., & Globerman, J. (1999). Inter-organizational relationships between schools of social work and field agencies: Testing a framework for analysis. *Journal of Social Work Education, 35*(2), 265–74.

Bogo, M., Globerman, J., & Sussman, T. (2004a). The field instructor as group worker: Managing trust and competition in group supervision. *Journal of Social Work Education, 40*(1), 13–26.

Bogo, M., Globerman, J., & Sussman, T. (2004b). Field instructor competence in group supervision: Students' views. *Journal of Teaching in Social Work, 24*(1, 2), 199–216.

Bogo, M., Logie, C., Regehr, C., & Regehr, G. (in review). The use of standardized client simulations in social work education: A systematic review.

Bogo, M., & McKnight, K. (2005). Clinical supervision in social work: A review of the research literature. *The Clinical Supervisor, 24*(1, 2), 49–67.

Bogo, M., & Power, R. (1992). New field instructors' perceptions of institutional supports for their roles. *Journal of Social Work Education, 28*(2), 178–89.

Bogo, M., & Power, R. (1994). Educational methodologies and group elements in field instructor training. *The Clinical Supervisor, 12*(2), 9–25.

Bogo, M., Regehr, C., Hughes, J., Power, R., & Globerman, J. (2002). Evaluating a measure of student field performance in direct service: Testing reliability and validity of explicit criteria. *Journal of Social Work Education, 38*(3), 385–401.

Bogo, M., Regehr, C., Logie, C., Katz, E., Mylopoulos, M., & Regehr, G. (in press). Adapting objective structured clinical examinations to assess social work students' performance and reflections. *Journal of Social Work Education.*

Bogo, M., Regehr, C., Power, R., Hughes, J., Woodford, M., & Regehr, G.

(2004). Toward new approaches for evaluating student field performance: Tapping the implicit criteria used by experienced field instructors. *Journal of Social Work Education, 40*(3), 417–26.

Bogo, M., Regehr, C., Power, R., & Regehr, G. (2007). When values collide: Providing feedback and evaluating competence in social work. *The Clinical Supervisor, 26*(1, 2), 99–117.

Bogo, M., Regehr, C., Woodford, M., Hughes, J., Power, R., & Regehr, G. (2006). Beyond competencies: Field instructors' descriptions of student performance. *Journal of Social Work Education, 42*(3), 191–205.

Bogo, M., & Vayda, E. (1987). *The practice of field instruction in social work: Theory and process.* Toronto and New York: University of Toronto Press.

Bogo, M., & Vayda, E. (1998). *The practice of field instruction in social work: Theory and process.* 2d ed. Toronto: University of Toronto Press and Columbia University Press.

Boitel, C. (2002). *Development of a scale to measure learning in field education.* PhD diss., Case Western Reserve University, Cleveland, OH.

Bordin, E. (1983). A working alliance based model of supervision. *The Counseling Psychologist, 11*, 35–42.

Boud, D. (1999). Avoiding the traps: Seeking good practice in the use of self assessment and reflection in professional courses. *Social Work Education, 18*(2), 121–32.

Boud, D., & Walker, D. (1998). Promoting reflection in professional courses: The challenge of context. *Studies in Higher Education, 23*(2), 191–206.

Bowlby, J. (1988). *A secure base.* New York: Basic Books.

Brandell, J.R. (2004). *Psychodynamic social work.* New York: Columbia University Press.

Bronstein, L.R., & Kelly, T.B. (1998). Field education units: Fostering mutual aid in multicultural settings. *Arete, 22*(2), 54–62.

Brookfield, S. (1998). Critically reflective practice. *The Journal of Continuing Education in the Health Professions, 18*, 197–205.

Bruce, A., & Davies, B. (2005). Mindfulness in hospice care: Practicing meditation-in-action. *Qualitative Health Research, 15*, 1329–44.

Burke, S.G., Condon, S., & Wickell, B. (1999). The field liaison role in schools of social work: A break with the past. *The Clinical Supervisor, 18*(1), 203–10.

Caragata, L., & Sanchez, M. (2002). Globalization and global need: The new imperatives for expanding international social work education in North America. *International Social Work, 45*(2), 217–38.

Carraccio, C., Wolfsthal, S.D., Englander, R., Ferentz, K., & Martin, C. (2002). Shifting paradigms: From Flexner to competencies. *Academic Medicine, 77*(5), 361–7.

Carroll, M. (2009). Supervision: Critical reflection for transformational learning. Keynote address at Fifth International Conference on Clinical Supervision, Buffalo, NY. June.

Caspi, J., & Reid, W.J. (2002). *Educational supervision in social work*. New York: Columbia University Press.

Chapman, M.V., Oppenheim, S., Shibusawa, T., & Jackson, H.M. (2003). What we bring to practice: Teaching students about professional use of self. *Journal of Teaching in Social Work, 23*(3, 4), 3–14.

Cheetham, G., & Chivers, G. (1996). Towards a holistic model of professional competence. *Journal of European Industrial Training, 20*(5), 20–30.

Cheetham, G., & Chivers, G. (1998). The reflective (and competent) practitioner: A model of professional competence which seeks to harmonize the reflective practitioner and competence-based approaches. *Journal of European Industrial Training, 22*(7), 267–76.

Cheetham, G., & Chivers, G. (2005). *Professions, competence and informal learning*. Cheltenham, UK: Edward Elgar.

Choy, B.K., Leung, A.Y., Tam, T.S.K., & Chu, C.H. (1998). Roles and tasks of field instructors as perceived by Chinese social work students. *Journal of Teaching in Social Work, 16*(1, 2), 115–32.

Clark, F., & Arkava, M. (1979). *The pursuit of competence in social work*. San Francisco: Jossey-Bass.

Clark, S. (2003). The California collaboration: A competency-based child welfare curriculum project for master's social workers. *Journal of Human Behavior in the Social Environment, 7*(1), 135–57.

COCEI (2007). *Rationale and guiding principles used to draft EPAS*. Alexandria, VI: Council on Social Work Education.

Collins, P. (1993). The interpersonal vicissitudes of mentorship: An exploratory study of the field supervisor-student relationship. *The Clinical Supervisor, 11*(1), 121–35.

Collins-Camargo, C. (2006). *Testing structured approaches to clinical casework supervision in child welfare*. Paper presented at the Southern Regional Quality Improvement Center for Child Protection, Lexington, KY. September.

Cooper, L. (2007). Backing Australia's future: Teaching and learning in social work. *Australian Social Work, 60*(1), 94–106.

Coulton, P., & Krimmer, L. (2005). Co-supervision of social work students: A model for meeting the future needs of the profession. *Australian Social Work, 58*(2), 154–66.

Cowan, B., Dastyk, R., & Wickham, E.R. (1972). Group supervision as a teaching/learning modality in social work. *The Social Worker/Le Travailleur Social, 40*(4), 256–61.

Crisp, B.R., & Lister, P.G. (2002). Assessment methods in social work education: A review of the literature. *Social Work Education, 21*(2), 259–69.

Cuzzi, L., Holden, G., Chernack, P., Rutter, S., & Rosenberg, G. (1997). Evaluating social work field instruction: Rotations versus year-long placements. *Research on Social Work Practice, 7*(3), 402–14.

Cuzzi, L., Holden, G., Rutter, S., Rosenberg, G., & Chernack, P. (1996). A pilot study of fieldwork rotations vs. year long placments for social work students in a public hospital. *Social Work in Health Care, 24*(1), 73–91.

Dalgleish, K.B., Kane, R.B., & McNamara, J.J. (1976). Rotating social work students within a medical center. *Health and Social Work, 1*(2), 166–71.

Damasio, A. (2003). *Looking for Spinoza: Joy, sorrow and the feeling brain.* Orlando, FL: Harcourt.

Damron-Rodriguez, J., Lawrance, F.P., Barnett, D., & Simmons, J. (2006). Developing geriatric social work competencies for field education. *Journal of Gerontological Social Work, 48*(1, 2), 139–60.

Davis, D.A., Mazmanian, P.E., Fordis, M., Harrison, R.V., Thoerpe, K.E., & Perrier, L. (2006). Accuracy of physician self-assessment compared with observed measures of competence: A systematic review. *Journal of the American Medical Association, 296*(9), 1094–1102.

Deal, K.H. (2000). The usefulness of developmental stage models for clinical social work students: An exploratory study. *The Clinical Supervisor, 19*(1), 1–19.

Deal, K.H. (2002). Modifying field instructors' supervisory approach using stage models of student development. *Journal of Teaching in Social Work, 22*(3, 4), 121–37.

Deal, K.H., Hopkins, K.M., Fisher, L., & Hartin, J. (2007). Field practicum experience of macro-oriented graduate students: Are we doing them justice? *Administration in Social Work, 31*(4), 41–58.

Dean, R. (2001). The myth of cross-cultural competence. *Families in Society, 82*(6), 623–30.

Detlaff, A.J. (2003). *From mission to evaluation: A field instructor training program.* Alexandria, VI: Council on Social Work Education.

Detlaff, A.J., & Dietz, T.J. (2004). Making training relevant: Identifying field instructors' perceived needs. *The Clinical Supervisor, 23*(1), 15–32.

Dettlaff, A.J., & Wallace, G. (2002). Promoting integration of theory and practice in field education: An instructional tool for field instructors and field educators. *The Clinical Supervisor, 21*(2), 145–60.

Dewey, J. (1933). *How we think.* Boston: D.C.Heath.

Donner, S. (1996). Field work crisis: Dilemmas, dangers, and opportunities. *Smith College Studies in Social Work, 66*, 317–31.

Downie, R.S. (1990). Professions and professionalism. *Journal of Philosophy of Education, 24*(2), 147–55.

Drake, B. (1994). Relationship competencies in child welfare services. *Social Work, 39*(5), 595–602.

Dreyfus, H.L., & Dreyfus, S.E. (1986). *Mind over machine: The power of human intuition and expertise in the era of the computer.* Oxford: Basil Blackwell.

Edmond, T., Megivern, D., Williams, C., Rochman, E., & Howar, M. (2006). Integrating evidence-based practice and social work field education. *Journal of Social Work Education, 42*(2), 377–96.

Edwards, J.K., & Bess, J.M. (1998). Developing effectiveness in the therapeutic use of self. *Clinical Social Work Journal, 26*(1), 89–105.

Ellis, M.V. (2009). *Bridging the science and practice of clinical supervision: Some discoveries, some misconceptions.* Paper presented at the the Fifth International Interdisciplinary Conference on Clinical Supervision, Buffalo, NY. June.

Ellison, M.L. (1994). Critical field instructor behaviors: Student and field instructor views. *Arete, 18*(2), 12–20.

England, H. (1986). *Social work as art.* London: Allen and Unwin.

EPAS. (2004). *Educational Policy and Accreditation Standards.* Alexandria, VI: Council on Social Work Education.

EPAS. (2008). *Educational Policy and Accreditation Standards.* Alexandria, VI: Council on Social Work Education.

Epstein, R.M., & Hundert, E.M. (2002). Defining and assessing professional competence. *Journal of the American Medical Association, 287*(2), 226–35.

Epstein, R.M., Siegel, D.J., & Silberman, J. (2008). Self-monitoring in clinical practice: A challenge for medical educators. *Journal of Continuing Education in the Health Professions, 28*(1), 5–13.

Eraut, M. (1994). *Developing professional knowledge and competence.* London: Falmer Press.

Eraut, M. (2002). Editorial. *Learning in Health and Social Care, 1*(1), 1–5.

Eraut, M. (2003). Editorial. *Learning in Health and Social Care, 2*(3), 117–22.

Eraut, M. (2004). Editorial: The practice of reflection. *Learning in Health and Social Care, 3*(2), 47–52.

Ericsson, K.A., Krampe, R., & Tesch-Romer, C. (1993). The role of deliberate practice in the acquisition of expert performance. *Psychological Review, 100*(3), 363–406.

Fleming, D. (1991). The concept of meta-competence. *Competence and Assessment, 16*, 9–12.

Fook, J. (2004). Critical reflection and transformative possibilities. In L. Davis & P. Leonard (Eds.), *Social work in a corporate era: Practices of power and resistance.* Ashgate, UK: Aldershot.

Fortune, A.E. (1994). Field education. In F.J. Reamer (Ed.), *The foundations of social work knowledge* (pp. 15194). New York: Columbia University Press.

Fortune, A.E. (2001). Initial impressions and performance in field practica: Predictors of skills attainment and satisfaction among graduate students. *The Clinical Supervisor, 20*(2), 43–54.

Fortune, A.E., & Abramson, J. S. (1993). Predictors of satisfaction with field practicum among social work students. *The Clinical Supervisor, 11*(1), 95–110.

Fortune, A.E., Feathers, C.E., Rook, S.R., Scrimenti, R.M., Smollen, P., Stemerman, P., et al. (1985). Student satisfaction with field placement. *Journal of Social Work Education, 21*(3), 92–104.

Fortune, A.E., Lee, M., & Cavazos, A. (2007). Does practice make perfect? Practicing professional skills and outcomes in social work field education. *The Clinical Supervisor, 26*(1, 2), 239–63.

Fortune, A.E., McCarthy, M., & Abramson, J.S. (2001). Student learning processes in field education: Relationship of learning activities to quality of field instruction, satisfaction, and performance among MSW students. *Journal of Social Work Education, 37*(1), 111–24.

Fortune, A.E., Miller, J., Rosenblum, A.F., Sanchez, B.M., Smith, C., & Reid, W.J. (1995). Further explorations of the liaison role: A view from the field. In G. Rogers (Ed.), *Social work field education: Views and visions*. Dubuque, IA: Kendall/Hunt.

Foster, R.P. (1998). The clinician's cultural countertransference: The psychodynamics of culturally competent practice. *Clinical Social Work Journal, 26*(3), 253–70.

Fox, R., & Zischka, P.C. (1989). The field instruction contract: A paradigm for effective learning. *Journal of Teaching in Social Work, 3*(1), 103–16.

Fraser, S.W., & Greenhalgh, T. (2001). Coping with complexity: Educating for capability. *British Medical Journal, 323*(7316), 799–803.

Freeman, E. (1985). The importance of feedback in clinical supervision: Implications for direct practice. *The Clinical Supervisor, 3*(1), 5–26.

Friedlander, M., & Ward, L. (1984). Development and validation of the supervisory styles inventory. *Journal of Counseling Psychology, 4*, 541–57.

Frumkin, M. (1980). Social work education and the professional commitment fallacy: A practical guide to field-school relations. *Journal of Education for Social Work, 16*(2), 91–9.

Furness, S., & Gilligan, P. (2004). Fit for purpose: Issues from practice placements, practice teaching and the assessment of students' practice. *Social Work Education, 23*(4), 465–79.

Gambrill, E. (1999). Evidence-based practice: An alternative to authority-based practice. *Familes in Society, 80*, 341–50.

Geller, C. (1994). Group supervision as a vehicle for teaching group work to students: Field instruction in a senior center. *The Clinical Supervisor, 12*(1), 199–214.

Gelman, C.R. (2004). Anxiety experienced by foundation-year MSW students entering field placement: Implications for admissions, curriculum, and field education. *Journal of Social Work Education, 40*(1), 39–54.

Gergen, K.J., & Davis, K.E. (1985). *The social construction of the person*. New York: Springer-Verlag.

Gibbs, L. (2002). *Evidence-based practice for social workers*. Pacific Grove, CA: Brooks/Cole.

Giddings, M.M., Vodde, R., & Cleveland, P. (2003). Examining student-field instructor problems in practicum: Beyond student satisfaction measures. *The Clinical Supervisor, 22*(2), 191–214.

Gilbert, C. (2009). Editorial. *The Clinical Supervisor, 28*(1), 1–2.

Gingerich, W.J., Kaye, K.M., & Bailey, D. (1999). Assessing quality in social work education: Focus on diversity. *Assessment and Evaluation in Higher Education, 24*(2), 119–29.

Ginsburg, S., McIlroy, J., Oulanova, O., Eva, K.W., & Regehr, G. (2010). Towards authentic clinical evaluation: Pitfalls in the pursuit of competency. *Academic Medicine, 85*(5), 780–6.

Ginsburg, S., Regehr, G., & Mylopoulos, M. (2009). From behaviors to attributions: Further concerns regarding the evaluation of professionalism. *Medical Education, 43*(5), 414–25.

Gitterman, A., & Gitterman, N. (1979). Social work student evaluation: Format and method. *Journal of Education for Social Work, 15*(3), 103–8.

Gladstein, M., & Mailick, M. (1986). An affirmative approach to ethnic diversity in field work. *Journal of Social Work Education, 22*(1), 41–9.

Gladwell, M. (2008). *Outliers: The story of success*. New York: Little, Brown.

Globerman, J., & Bogo, M. (2002). The impact of hospital restructuring on social work field education. *Health and Social Work, 27*(1), 7–16.

Globerman, J., & Bogo, M. (2003). Changing times: Understanding social workers motivation to be field instructors. *Social Work, 48*(1), 65–73.

Graybeal, C., & Ruff, E. (1995). Process recording: It's more than you think. *Journal of Social Work Education, 31*(2), 169–81.

Gross, G.M. (1981). Instructional design: Bridge to competence. *Journal of Education for Social Work, 17*(3), 66–74.

Grossman, B., Levine-Jordano, N., & Shearer, P. (1990). Working with students' emotional reactions in the field: An educational framework. *The Clinical Supervisor, 8*(1), 23–39.

Gutierrez, L.M., Parsons, R.J., & Cox, E.O. (1998). *Empowerment in social work practice*. Pacific Grove, CA: Brooks/Cole.

Haber, R., Marshall, D., Cowan, K., Vanlandingham, A., Gerson, M., & Fitch, J.C. (2009). 'Live' supervision of supervision: 'Perpendicular' interventions in parallel processes. *The Clinical Supervisor, 28*(1), 72–90.

Hackett, S. (2001). Educating for competency and reflective practice: Fostering a conjoint approach in education and training. *Journal of Workplace Learning, 13*(3), 103–12.

Hall, D.T. (1986). *Career development in organisations*. San Francisco: Jossey-Bass.

Hamilton, G. (1954). Self-awareness in professional education. *Social Casework, 35*(9), 371–9.

Hammond, K.R. (1980). *Human judgment and decision making*. New York: Hemisphere.

Harden, R.M., Crosby, J.R., Davis, M.H., & Friedman, M. (1999). AMEE Guide No. 14: Outcome-based education: Part 5, From competency to meta-competency: A model for specification of learning outcomes. *Medical Teacher, 21*(6), 546–52.

Harden, R.M., & Gleeson, F.A. (1979). Assessment of clinical competence using an observed structured clinical examination. *Medical Education, 13*, 41–7.

Harden, R.M., Stevenson, M., Downie, W.W., & Wilson, G.M. (1975). Assessment of clinical competence using objective structured examination. *British Medical Journal, 1*(5955), 447–51.

Hatcher, R.L., & Lassiter, K.D. (2007). Initial training in professional psychology: The practicum competencies outline. *Training and Education in Professional Psychology, 1*, 49–63.

Haynes, R.B., Devereaux, P.J., & Guyatt, G.H. (2002). Editorial: Clinical expertise in the era of evidence based medicine and patient choice. *APC Journal Club, 136*, A11–14.

Hendricks, C.O., Finch, J.B., & Franks, C. (2005). *Learning to teach: Teaching to learn*. Washington, DC: CSWE.

Hensley, P.H. (2002). The value of supervision. *The Clinical Supervisor, 21*(1), 97–110.

Ho, D. (1995). Internalized culture, culturocentrism, and transcendence. *The Counseling Psychologist, 23*(1), 4–24.

Hodges, B., Hanson, M., McNaughton, N., & Regehr, G. (2002). Creating, monitoring, and improving a psychiatry OSCE. *Academic Psychiatry, 26*(3), 134–61.

Hodges, B., Regehr, G., & Martin, D. (2001). Difficulties in recognizing one's own incompetence: Novice physicians who are unskilled and unaware of it. *Academic Medicine, 76*(10), S87–9.

Holley, L.C., & Steiner, C. (2005). Safe space: Student perspectives on classroom environment. *Journal of Social Work Education, 41*(1), 49–64.

Hollis, F. (1964). *Casework: A psycho-social therapy.* New York: Random House.

Holman, S.L., & Freed, P. (1987). Learning social work practice: A taxonomy. *The Clinical Supervisor, 5*(1), 321.

Hopkins, K.M., Bloom, J.D., & Deal, K.H. (2005). Moving away from tradition: Exploring the field experiences of part-time, older, and employment-based students. *Journal of Social Work Education, 41*(3), 573–85.

Hyland, T. (1995). Behaviorism and the meaning of competence. In P. Hodkinson & M. Issitt (Eds.), *The challenge of competence: Professionalism through vocational education and training* (pp. 44–57). London: Cassell.

Ivry, J., Lawrance, F.R., Damron-Rodriguez, J., & Robbins, V.C. (2005). Fieldwork rotation: A model for educating social work students for geriatric social work practice. *Journal of Social Work Education, 41*(3), 407–25.

Jarman-Rohde, L., McFall, J., Kolar, P., & Strom, G. (1997). The changing context of social work practice: Implications and recommendations for social work educators. *Journal of Social Work Education, 33*(1), 29–46.

Johns, C. (2005). Expanding the gates of perception. In C. Johns & D. Freshwater (Eds.), *Transforming nursing through reflective practice* (2d ed., pp. 1–12). London: Blackwell Science.

Kabat-Zinn, J. (1990). *Full catastrophe living: Using the wisdom of your body and mind to face stress, pain and illness.* New York: Delacorte.

Kabat-Zinn, J. (2003). Mindfulness-based interventions in context: Past, present, and future. *Clinical Psychology: Science and Practice, 10*(2), 144–56.

Kadushin, A. (1974). Supervisor-supervisee: A survey. *Social Work, 19*(3), 289–97.

Kadushin, A. (1985). *Supervision in social work.* New York: Columbia University Press.

Kadushin, A.E. (1991). Introduction. In D. Schneck, B. Grossman, & U. Glassman (Eds.), *Field education in social work: Contemporary issues and trends* (pp. 11-12). Dubuque, IA: Kendall/Hunt.

Kane, M.T. (1992). The assessment of professional competence. *Evaluation in the Health Professions, 15*(2), 163–82.

Kaplan, T. (1991). Reducing student anxiety in field work: Exploratory research and implications. *The Clinical Supervisor, 9*(2), 105–17.

Kaslow, N.J., Borden, K.A., Collins Jr., F.L., Forrest, L., Illfelder-Kaye, J., Nelson, P.D., et al. (2004). Competencies conference: Future directions in education and credentialing in professional psychology. *Journal of Clinical Psychology, 60*(7), 699–712.

Kelly, J., & Horder,W. (2001). The how and why: Competences and holistic practice. *Social Work Education, 20*(6), 689–99.

Kenyon, G.L. (2000). No magic: The role of theory in field education. In G.L. Kenyon & R. Power (Eds.), *No magic: Readings in social work field education* (pp. 3–23). Toronto: Canadian Scholars Press.

Kilpatrick, A.C., Turner, J., & Holland, T.P. (1994). Quality control in field education: Monitoring students' performance. *Journal of Teaching in Social Work, 9*(1, 2), 107–20.

Knight, C. (2000). Engaging the student in the field instruction relationship: BSW and MSW students' views. *Journal of Teaching in Social Work, 20*(3, 4), 173–201.

Knight, C. (2001). The process of field instruction: BSW and MSW students' views of effective field supervision. *Journal of Social Work Education, 37*(2), 357–79.

Knowles, M.S. (1972). Innovations in teaching styles and approaches based upon adult learning. *Journal of Education for Social Work, 8*(2), 32–9.

Knowles, M.S. (1980). *The modern practice of adult education.* Chicago: Association Press/Follett.

Knowles, M.S., Halston, E.F., & Swanson, R.A. (2005). *The adult learner: The definitive classic in adult education and human resource development.* (6th ed.). Boston: Elsevier.

Koerin, B., & Miller, J. (1995). Gatekeeping policies: Terminating students for nonacademic reasons. *Journal of Social Work Education, 31*, 247–60.

Kolb, D.A. (1984). *Experiential learning: Experience as the source of learning and development.* Englewood Cliffs, NJ: Prentice Hall.

Koroloff, N.M., & Rhyne, C. (1989). Assessing student performance in field instruction. *Journal of Teaching in Social Work, 3*, 3–16.

Kruger, J., & Dunning, D. (1999). Unskilled and unaware of it: How difficulties in recognizing one's own incompetence lead to inflated self-assessments. *Journal of Personality and Social Psychology, 77*(6), 1121–34.

Lacerte, J., Ray, J., & Irwin, L. (1989). Recognizing the educational contributions of field instructors. *Journal of Teaching in Social Work, 3*(2), 99–113.

Lager, P.B., & Robbins, V.C. (2004). Field education: Exploring the future, expanding the vision. *Journal of Social Work Education, 40*(1), 3–11.

Langer, E.J. (1989). *Mindfulness.* Reading, MA: Addison-Wesley.

Leach, D. (2006). Six competencies, and the importance of dialogue with the community [electronic version]. *ACGME e-Bulletin,* 3.

Leung, W.C. (2002). Competency based medical training: Review. *British Journal of Medicine, 325*, 693–5.

Levitin, D.J. (2006). *This is your brain on music: The science of a human obsession.* New York: Dutton.

Lewin, K. (1951). *Field theory in social sciences.* New York: Harper and Row.

Lindsay, T. (2005). Group learning on social work placements. *Groupwork, 15*(1), 61–89.

Linehan, M.M. (1993). *Cognitive-behavioral treatment of borderline personality disorder.* New York: Guilford Press.

Lister, P.G., Dutton, K., & Crisp, B.R. (2005). Assessment practices in Scottish social work education: A practice audit of Scottish universities providing qualifying social work courses. *Social Work Education, 24*(6), 693–711.

Litvack, A., Bogo, M., & Mishna, F. (2010). Understanding the emotional impact of field experiences on MSW students. *Journal of Social Work Education, 46*(2), 227–43.

Lombardi, J. (2008). To portfolio or not to portfolio: Helpful or hyped? *College Teaching, 56*(1), 7–10.

Lough, B.J. (2009). Principles of effective practice in international social work field placements. *Journal of Social Work Education, 45*(3), 467–80.

Lurie, S.J., Mooney, C.J., & Lyness, J.M. (2009). Measurement of the general competencies of the accreditation council for graduate medical education: A systematic review. *Academic Medicine, 84*(3), 301–9.

MacKeracher, D. (1996). *Making sense of adult learning.* Toronto: Culture Concepts.

Mackey, R., & Mackey, E. (1994). Personal psychotherapy and the development of a professional self. *Families in Society, 75*(8), 490–8.

Mackey, R., Mackey, E., & O'Brien, B. (1993). Personal treatment and the social work student. *Journal of Teaching in Social Work, 7*(2), 129–46.

Maidment, J. (2000). Methods used to teach social work students in the field: A research report from New Zealand. *Social Work Education, 19*(2), 145–54.

Marshack, E.F., Hendricks, C.O., & Gladstein, M. (1994). The commonality of difference: Teaching about diversity in field instruction. *Journal of Multicultural Social Work, 3*(1), 77–89.

Marsick, V.J. (1990). Action learning and reflection in the workplace. In J. Mezirow & Associates (Eds.), *Fostering critical reflection in the workplace* (pp. 23–46). San Francisco: Jossey-Bass.

Matorin, S., Monaco, G., & Kerson, T.S. (1994). Field instruction in a psychiatric setting. *The Clinical Supervisor, 12*(1), 159–80.

Mauzey, E., Harris, M.B., & Trusty, J. (2000). Comparing the effects of live supervision phone-ins: A phenomenological inquiry. *The Clinical Supervisor,* *19*(2), 109–22.

Mayers, F. (1970). Differential use of group teaching in first year field work. *Social Service Review, 44*(1), 63–70.

McCollum, E.E., & Wetchler, J.L. (1995). In defense of case consultation: Maybe 'dead' supervision isn't dead after all. *Journal of Marital and Family Therapy, 21*(2), 155–66.

McRoy, R.G., Freeman, E.M., Logan, S.L., & Blackmon, B. (1986). Cross-cultural field supervision: Implications for social work education. *Journal of Social Work Education, 22*(1), 50–6.

Merriam, S. (2001). Andragogy and self-directed learning: Pillars of adult learning theory. *New Directions for Adult and Continuing Education, 89*(spring), 3–13.

Mertz, L.K.P., Fortune, A.E., & Zendell, A.L. (2007). Promoting leadership skills in field education: A university-community partnership to bring macro and micro together in gerontological field placements. *Journal of Gerontological Social Work, 50*(1, 2), 173–86.

Messinger, L. (2004). Out in the field: Gay and lesbian social work students' experiences in field placement. *Journal of Social Work Education, 40*(2), 187–204.

Messinger, L. (2007). Supervision of lesbian, gay, and bisexual social work students by heterosexual field instructors: A qualitative dyad analysis. *The Clinical Supervisor, 26*(1, 2), 195–222.

Messinger, L., & Topal, M. (1997). 'Are you married?' Two sexual-minority students' perspectives on field placements. *Affilia, 12*(1), 106–13.

Mezirow, J.M., & Associates. (1990). *Fostering critical reflection in adulthood: A guide to transformative and emancipatory learning.* San Francisco: Jossey-Bass.

Miller, J., Hyde, C.A., & Ruth, B.J. (2004). Teaching about race and racism in social work: Challenges for white educators. *Smith College Studies in Social Work, 74*(2), 409–26.

Mishna, F., & Bogo, M. (2007). Reflective practice in contemporary social work classrooms. *Journal of Social Work Education, 43*(3), 529–41.

Mishna, F., & Rasmussen, B. (2001). The learning relationship: Working through disjunctions in the classroom. *Clinical Social work Journal, 29*(4), 386–99.

MorBarak, M.E., Travis, D.J., Pyun, H., & Xie, B. (2009). The impact of supervision on worker outcomes: A meta-analysis. *Social Service Review, 83*(1), 3–32.

Mullen, E.J., Shlonsky, A., Bledsoe, S.E., & Bellamy, J.L. (2005). From concept to implementation: Challenges facing evidence-based social work. *Evidence & Policy, 1*(1), 61–84.

Mumm, A.M. (2006). Teaching social work students practice skills. *Journal of Teaching in Social Work, 26*, 71–89.

Netting, F.E., Hash, K., & Miller, J. (2002). Challenges in developing geriatric field education in social work. *Journal of Gerontological Social Work, 37*(1), 89–110.

Newman, P., Bogo, M., & Daley, A. (2008). Self-disclosure of sexual orientation in social work field education: Field instructor and lesbian/gay student perspectives. *The Clinical Supervisor, 27*(2), 215–37.

Newman, P., Bogo, M., & Daley, A. (2009). Breaking the silence: Sexual orientation in social work field education. *Journal of Social Work Education, 45*(1), 7–27.

Norcross, J.C. (Ed.). (2002). *Psychotherapy relationships that work: Therapist contributions and responsiveness to patients*. Washington, DC: American Psychological Association.

O'Hare, T., Collins, P., & Walsh, T. (1998). Validation of the practice skills inventory with experienced clinical social workers. *Research on Social Work Practice, 8*, 552–63.

Panos, P.T. (2005). A model for using videoconferencing technology to support international social work field practicum students. *International Social Work, 48*(6), 834–41.

Panos, P.T., Pettys, G.L., Cox, S.E., & Jones, E. (2004). Full survey of international field practicum placements of accredited schools of social work. *Journal of Social Work Education, 40*(3), 467–78.

Papell, C.P., & Skolnik, L. (1992). The reflective practitioner: A contemporary paradigm's relevance for social work education. *Journal of Social Work Education, 28*(1), 18–26.

Parker, J. (2007). Developing effective practice learning for tomorrow's social workers. *Social Work Education, 26*(8), 763–79.

Peebles-Wilkins, W., & Shank, B.W. (2003). A response to Charles Cowger: Shaping the future of social work as an institutional response to standards. *Journal of Social Work Education, 39*(1), 49–56.

Phan, P., Vugia, H., Wright, P., Woods, D.R., Chu, M., & Jones, T. (2009). A social work program's experience in teaching about race in the curriculum. *Journal of Social Work Education, 45*(2), 325–33.

Poe, N.T., & Hunter, C.A. (2009). A curious curriculum component: The non-mandated 'given' of field seminar. *The Journal of Baccalaureate Social Work, 14*(2), 31–47.

Poulin, J., Silver, P., & Kauffman, S. (2006). Serving the community and training social workers: Service outputs and student outcomes. *Journal of Social Work Education, 42*(1), 171–84.

Power, R., & Bogo, M. (2002). Educating field instructors and students to deal with challenges in their teaching relationships. *The Clinical Supervisor, 21*(1), 39–58.

Proctor, B. (2000). *Group supervision: A guide to creative practice.* London: Sage.

Raphael, F.B., & Rosenblum, A.F. (1987). An operational guide to the faculty field liaison role. *Social Casework, 68*(3), 156–63.

Raskin, M. (1983). A Delphi study in field instruction: Identification of issues and research priorities by experts. *Arete, 8*(2), 38–48.

Raskin, M. (1989). Factors associated with student satisfaction in undergraduate social work field placements. In M. Raskin (Ed.), *Empirical studies in field instruction* (pp. 321–35). New York: The Haworth Press.

Raskin, M. (1994). The delphi study in field instruction revisited: Expert consensus on issues and research priorities. *Journal of Social Work Education, 30*(1), 75–88.

Raskin, M., & Bloome, W.W. (1998). The impact of managed care on field instruction. *Journal of Social work Education, 34*(3), 365–75.

Raskin, M., Wayne, J., & Bogo, M. (2008). Revisiting field education standards. *Journal of Social Work Education, 44*(2), 173–88.

Rawlings, M., & Bogo, M. (2009). Designing objective structured clinical examinations (OSCE) to assess social work student competencies. Workshop presentation. Faculty Development Institute. Council on Social Work Education, APM. San Antonio, TX.

Reamer, F.G. (Ed.). (1994). *The foundations of social work knowledge.* New York: Columbia University Press.

Regehr, C., Bogo, M., & Regehr, G. (in review). The development of an online practice-based evaluation tool.

Regehr, C., Bogo, M., Regehr, C., & Power, R. (2007). Can we build a better mousetrap? Improving measures of social work practice performance in the field. *Journal of Social Work Education, 43*(2), 327–43.

Regehr, C., Regehr, G., Leeson, J., & Fusko, L. (2002). Setting priorities for learning in the field practicum: A comparative study of students and field instructors. *Journal of Social Work Education, 38*(1), 55–65.

Reid, W.J., Bailey-Dempsey, C., & Viggiana, P. (1996). Evaluating student field education: An empirical study. *Journal of Social Work Education, 32*(1), 45–52.

Reid, W.J., & Fortune, A.E. (2003). Empirical foundations for practice guidelines in current social work knowledge. In A. Rosen & E.K. Proctor (Eds.), *Developing practice guidelines for social work intervention: Issues, methods, and research agenda* (pp. 59–79). New York: Columbia University Press.

Reisch, M., & Jarman-Rohde, L. (2000). The future of social work in the

United States: Implications for field education. *Journal of Social Work Education, 36,* 201–14.

Reynolds, M., & Snell, R. (1988). *Contribution to development of management competence.* Sheffield, UK: Manpower Services Commission.

Roberts-DeGennaro, M., Brown, C., Min, J.W., & Siegel, M. (2005). Using an online support site to extend the learning to a graduate field practicum in the United States. *Social Work Education, 24*(3), 327–42.

Rogers, G., & McDonald, P.L. (1995). Expedience over education: Teaching methods used by field instructors. *The Clinical Supervisor, 13*(2), 41–65.

Rogers, R.R. (2001). Reflection in higher education: A concept analysis. *Innovative Higher Education, 26*(1), 37–57.

Rolfe, G. (2001). Reflective practice: Where now? *Nurse Education in Practice,* 2, 21–9.

Rompf, E.L., Royse, D., & Shooper, S.S. (1993). Anxiety preceding field work: What students worry about. *Journal of Teaching in Social Work, 7*(2), 81–95.

Rosen, A., Proctor, E.K., & Staudt, M.M. (1999). Social work research and the quest for effective practice. *Social Work Research, 23*(1), 4–14.

Rosen, A.L., Zlotnik, J.L., Curl, A.L., & Green, R.G. (2000). *The CSWE/SAGE-SW National Aging Competencies Survey Report.* Alexandria, VI: Council on Social Work Education.

Rosenblatt, A., & Mayer, J.E. (1975). Objectionable supervisory styles: Students' views. *Social Work, 20*(3), 184–9.

Rosenblum, A.F., & Raphael, F.B. (1983). The role and function of the faculty field liaison. *Journal of Education for Social Work, 19*(1), 67–73.

Rosenthal Gelman, C. (2004). Anxiety experienced by foundation-year MSW students entering field placement: Implications for admissions, curriculum, and field education. *Journal of Social Work Education, 40*(1), 39–54.

Rosenthal Gelman, C., & Lloyd, C.M. (2008). Field notes-pre-placement anxiety among foundation-year MSW students: A follow-up study. *Journal of Social Work Education, 44*(1), 173–83.

Rossiter, A. (2002). The social work sector study: A response. *Canadian Social Work Review, 19*(2), 341–8.

Ruch, G. (2002). From triangle to spiral: Reflective practice in social work education, practice and research. *Social Work Education, 21*(2), 199–216.

Ruffolo, M.C., & Miller, P. (1994). An advocacy/empowerment model of organizing: Developing university-agency partnerships. *Journal of Social Work Education, 30*(3), 310–16.

Ruth-Sahd, L.A. (2003). Reflective practice: A critical analysis of data-based studies and implications for nursing education. *Journal of Nursing Education, 42*(11), 488–97.

Saari, C. (1989). The process of learning in clinical social work. *Smith College Studies in Social Work, 60*, 35–49.

Saleeby, D. (2002). *The strengths perspective in social work practice* (3d ed.). Boston: Allyn and Bacon.

Scharlach, A., Damron-Rodriguez, J., Robinson, B., & Feldman, R. (2000). Educating social workers for an aging society: A vision for the twenty-first century. *Journal of Social Work Education, 36*, 521–38.

Scharlach, A.E., & Robinson, B.K. (2005). The consortium for social work training in aging: Schools of social work in partnership with county departments of adult and aging services. *Journal of Social Work Education, 41*(3), 427–40.

Schiller, L.Y. (1995). Stages of development in women's groups: A relational model. In R. Kurland & R. Salmon (Eds.), *Group work practice in a troubled society: Problems and opportunities* (pp. 117–38). New York: The Haworth Press.

Schiller, L.Y. (1997). Rethinking stages of development in women's groups: Implications for practice. *Social Work with Groups, 20*(3), 3–19.

Schon, D. (1983). *The reflective practitioner: How professionals think in action.* London: Temple Smith.

Schon, D. (1987). *Educating the reflective practitioner.* San Francisco: Jossey-Bass.

Segal, Z., Williams, M., & Teasdale, J. (2002). *Mindfulness-based cognitive therapy for depression: A new approach to preventing relapse.* New York: Guilford Press.

Shapiro, S.L., Schwartz, G.E., & Bonner, G. (1998). Effects of mindfulness-based stress reduction on medical and premedical students. *Journal of Behavioral Medicine, 21*, 581–99.

Sheafor, B.W., & Jenkins, L.E. (Eds.). (1982). *Quality field instruction in social work.* New York: Longman.

Shulman, L. (1993). *Interactional supervision.* Washington, DC: NASW Press.

Shulman, L. S. (2005a). Signature pedagogies in the profession. *Daedalus, 134*(3), 52–9.

Shulman, L. (2005b). The signature pedagogies of the professions of law, medicine, engineering, and the clergy: Potential lessons for the education of teachers. Speech at the National Research Council Center for Education, Irvine, CA.

Siegel, D.J. (2007). *The mindful brain: Reflection and attunement in the cultivation of well-being.* New York: W.W. Norton.

Singer, C.B., & Wells, L.M. (1981). The impact of student units on services and structural change in homes for the aged. *Canadian Journal of Social Work Education, 7*(3), 11–27.

Siporin, M. (1982). The process of field instruction. In B.W. Sheafor & L.E. Jenkins (Eds.), *Quality field instruction in social work: Program development and maintenance* (pp. 175–97). New York: Longman.

Skinner, K., & Whyte, B. (2004). Going beyond training: Theory and practice in managing learning. *Social Work Education, 23*(4), 365–81.

Slater, P. (2007). The passing of the practice teaching award: History, legacy, prospects. *Social Work Education, 26*(8), 749–62.

Sousa, D.A. (2006). *How the brain learns* (3d ed.). Thousand Oaks, CA: Corwin Press, Sage.

Sowbel, L.R. (2009). *Personality traits predictive of field performance for foundation year MSW students: An exploratory study.* Baltimore, MD: University of Maryland Baltimore.

Spitzer, W., Holden, G., Cuzzi, L., Rutter, S., Chernack, P., & Rosenberg, G. (2001). Edith Abbott was right: Designing fieldwork experiences for contemporary health care practice. *Journal of Social Work Education, 37*(1), 79–90.

Stephanson, M., Rondeau, J.C., Michaud, J., & Fiddler, S. (2001). *In critical demand: Social work in Canada.* Toronto: Grant Thornton.

Stoltenberg, C.D. (2005). Enhancing professional competence through developmental approaches to supervision. *American Psychologist, 60*(8), 857–64.

Stoltenberg, C.D. (2008). *Applying evidence-based practice (EBP) principles to the process of clinical supervision.* Paper presented at the Fourth International Clinical Supervision Conference, Buffalo, NY. June.

Stoltenberg, C., & Delworth, U. (1987). *Supervising counselors and therapists: A developmental approach.* San Francisco: Jossey-Bass.

Stoltenberg, C.D., McNeill, B.W., & Delworth, U. (1998). *IDM supervison: An integrated developmental model for supervising counselors and therapists.* San Francisco: Jossey-Bass.

Strozier, A.L., Barnett-Queen, T., & Bennett, C.K. (2000). Supervision: Critical process and outcome variables. *The Clinical Supervisor, 19*(1), 21–39.

Strozier, A.L., & Stacey, L. (2001). The relevance of personal therapy in the education of MSW students. *Clinical Social Work Journal, 29*(2), 181–95.

Sun, A. (1999). Issues BSW interns experience in their first semester's practicum. *The Clinical Supervisor, 18*(1), 105–23.

Sussman, T., Bogo, M., & Globerman, J. (2007). Field instructor perceptions in group supervision: Establishing trust through managing group dynamics. *The Clinical Supervisor, 26*(1, 2), 61–80.

Swick, S., Hall, S., & Beresin, E. (2006). Assessing the ACGME competencies in psychiatry training programs. *Academic Psychiatry, 30*(4), 330–51.

Talbot, M. (2004). Monkey see, monkey do: A critique of the competency model in graduate medical education. *Medical Education, 38*(6), 587–92.

Tebb, S., Manning, D.W., & Klaumann, T.K. (1996). A renaissance of group supervision. *The Clinical Supervisor, 14*(2), 39–51.

Teigiser, K.S. (2009). New approaches to generalist field education. *Journal of Social Work Education, 45*(1), 139–46.

Thyer, B.A., & Myers, L.L. (1998). Supporting the client's right to effective treatment: Touching a raw nerve? *Social Work, 43*(1), 87–91.

Thyer, B.A., Sower-Hoag, K., & Love, J.P. (1987). The influence of field instructor and student gender combinations on student perceptions of field instruction quality. *Arete, 11*(2), 25–30.

Tolson, E.R., & Kopp, J. (1988). The practicum: Clients, problems, interventions and influences on student practice. *Journal of Social Work Education, 24*(2), 123–34.

Towle, C. (1954). *The learner in education for the professions.* Chicago: University of Chicago Press.

Tsang, A.K.T., Bogo, M., & Lee, E. (in press). Engagement in cross-cultural clinical practice: Narrative analysis of first sessions. *Clinical Social Work Journal.* Available at www.springerlink.com/content/606625215m418041/.

Urbanowski, M., & Dwyer, M. (1988). *Learning through field instruction: A guide for teachers and students.* Milwaukee, WI: Family Service Association.

van der Vleuten, C.P.M., & Swanson, S. (1990). Assessment of clinical skills with standardized patients: State of the art. *Teaching and Learning in Medicine, 2,* 58–76.

van Manen, J. (1977). Linking ways of knowing with ways of being practical. *Curriculum Inquiry, 6,* 205–8.

van Soest, D., Garcia, B., & Graff, D. (2001). Sensitivity to racism and social work professors' responsiveness to critical classroom events. *Journal of Teaching in Social Work, 21*(1, 2), 39–58.

Vayda, E., & Bogo, M. (1991). A teaching model to unite classroom and field. *Journal of Social Work Education, 27*(3), 271–8.

Vonk, M.E., Zucrow, E., & Thyer, B.A. (1996). Female MSW students' satisfaction with practicum supervision: The effect of supervisor gender. *Journal of Social Work Education, 32*(3), 415–19.

Vourlekis, B., Bambry, J., Hall, G., & Rosenblum, P. (1996). Testing the reliability and validity of an interviewing skills evaluation tool for use in practicum. *Research on Social Work Practice, 6,* 492–503.

Walter, C.A., & Young, T.M. (1999). Combining individual and group supervision in educating for the social work profession. *The Clinical Supervisor, 18*(2), 73–89.

Wampold, B.E. (2001). *The great psychotherapy debate: Models, methods, and findings.* Mahwah, NJ: Lawrence Elbaum Associates.

Wayne, J., Bogo, M., & Raskin, M. (2006). The need for radical change in field education. *Journal of Social Work Education, 42*(1), 161–9.

Wayne, J., Bogo, M., & Raskin, M. (in press). Field education as the signature pedagogy of social work education: Congruence and disparity. *Journal of Social Work Education.*

Wayne, J., & Cohen, C. (2001). *Group work education in the field.* Alexandria, VI: Council on Social Work Education.

Weinert, F.E. (2001). Concept of competence: A conceptual clarification. In D.S. Rychen & L.H. Salganik (Eds.), *Defining and selecting key competencies* (pp. 45–66). Seattle, WA: Hogrefe & Huber.

Wenger, E. (1998). *Communities of practice: Learning, meaning and identity.* New York: Cambridge University Press.

Westhues, A. (2002). The social work sector study: Reflections on process and issues of concern. *Canadian Social Work Review, 19*(2), 329–48.

Wheeler, B.R., & Gibbons, W.E. (1992). Social work in academia: Learning from the past and acting on the present. *Journal of Social Work Education, 28*(3), 300–11.

Whitcomb, M.E. (2002). Competency-based graduate medical education: Of course But how should competency be assessed? *Academic Medicine, 77*(5), 359–60.

Whitcomb, M.E. (2007). Redirecting the assessment of clinical competence. *Academic Medicine, 82*(6), 527–8.

Wijnberg, M.H., & Schwartz, M.C. (1977). Models of student supervision: The apprenticeship, growth, and role systems models. *Journal of Education for Social Work, 13*(3), 107–13.

Wilson, S.J. (1981). *Field instruction: Techniques for supervision.* New York: Macmillan.

Witkin, S. (1998). The right to effective treatment and the effective treatment of rights: Rhetorical empiricism and the politics of research. *Social Work, 43*(1), 75–80.

Wodarski, J.S., Feit, M.D., & Green, K. (1995). Graduate social work education: A review of two decades of empirical research and considerations for the future. *Social Service Review, 69*(1), 108–30.

Wolfson, G.K., Magnuson, C.W., & Marsom, G. (2005). Changing the nature of the discourse: Teaching field seminars online. *Journal of Social Work Education, 41*(2), 355–61.

Woods, M.E., & Hollis, F. (2000). *Casework: A psychosocial therapy* (5th ed.). Boston: McGraw-Hill.

Yager, J., & Kay, J. (2003). Assessing psychotherapy competence in psychiatric residents: Getting real. *Harvard Review of Psychiatry, 11*, 109–12.

Younghusband, E. (1967). The teacher in education for social work. *Social Service Review, 41*(4), 359–70.

Zayas, L.H., Gonzalez, M.J., & Hanson, M. (2003). 'What do I do now?' On teaching evidence-based interventions in social work practice. *Journal of Teaching in Social Work, 23*(3/4), 59–72.

Zeira, A., & Schiff, M. (2010). Testing group supervision in fieldwork training for social work students. *Research on Social Work Practice, 20,* 427–34

Zendell, A.L., Fortune, A., Mertz, L.K.P., & Koelewyn, N. (2007). University-community partnerships in gerontological social work: Building consensus around student learning. *Journal of Gerontological Social Work, 50*(1, 2), 155–72.

Zosky, D.L., Unger, J.M., White, K., & Mills, S.J. (2003). Non-traditional and traditional social work students: Perceptions of field instructors. *Journal of Teaching in Social Work, 23*(3, 4), 185–201.

Index

Abbott, A.A., and S.C. Lyter, 143, 159

Abels, P., 154

Abram, F.Y., M.R. Hartung, and S.P. Wernet, 161, 162

Abramson, J.S., 29, 104, 106, 143, 150, 159, 195

Accreditation Council of Graduate Medical Education (ACGME), 199, 200

active learning, 87– 8, 148, 192

Adams, K.B., C.W. LeCroy, and H.C. Matto, 38, 132, 133

adult learning theory, 6, 30–1, 43, 76, 79–88, 107, 108–9, 121, 152; active learning, 87– 8, 148, 192; critiques of, 79, 82; learners' self-concept, 80–3; principles of adult education used in social work schools, 90, 192; readiness to learn, 87; role of learners' experience, 83– 6; self-directed learning, 79, 82–3; term 'andragogy,' 79. *See also* student learning

agencies. *See* organizations, 12, 19–20, 24–30; settings, 13, 19, 24–7, 66, 102, 110, 128–9, 137–9,

150, 151, 155, 160, 168–70, 180–1, 196–7, 206

Alper, S., 49, 130

Alperin, D.E., 29, 176, 195

Alvarez, A.R., and D.P. Moxley, 201

American Association for Graduate Medical Education, 60

American Psychological Association, 60

Arkava, M., 57

Armour, M.P., B. Bain, and R. Rubio, 94

attachment theory, 106–7

Australia: critiques of competency approaches in, 59; field instructors in (study), 28–9; status of field learning in, 12

Baer, B.L., and R. Frederico, 57

Bailey-Dempsey, C., 181

Barlow, C., 31, 102, 118–19, 152, 169, 170

Barnett, D., 61

Barnett-Queen, T., 105

Barretti, M.A., 105

Barth, R., and E. Gambrill, 139

Barton, H., K. Bell, and W. Bowles, 28–9
Beals, H., 58
Benavides III, E., M.M. Lynch, and J.S. Valesquez, 164
Bennett, C.K., 105
Bennett, S., 106, 107
Berg-Weger, M., 151
Bernard, J.M., and R.K. Goodyear, 149, 157
Birkenmaier, J., 151, 171
Black, J.E., M.T. Maki, and J.A. Nunn, 94
Black, P.N., and A. Feld, 145– 6
Bloom, J.D., 34
Bloome, W.W., 32
Bocage, M., E. Homonoff, and P. Riley, 32
Bogo, M., 12, 14, 17, 20, 23, 24–30, 30–1, 43, 48–9, 61, 78, 92, 96, 97, 104, 115, 122, 128, 135, 137, 140, 142, 144, 147, 150, 152, 164, 168, 171, 175, 176, 185, 192, 195, 203; on the essence of field education, 13; on the instructor-student relationship, 113, 114; on interviewing skills, 143; on the personal self of the social worker, 77; on student satisfaction, 102. See also Integration of Theory and Practice (ITP) Loop Model; University of Toronto: group supervision study; University of Toronto: program of research concerning evaluation of competence
Boitel, C., 57
Boud, D., 128
Bowlby, J., 106
Brandell, J.R., 61, 131
Brennan, E.C., 57

Bronstein, L.R., and T.B. Kelly, 165
Brookfield, S., 128
Bruce, A., and B. Davies, 50
Burke, S.G., S. Condon, and B. Wickell, 33

California Social Work Education Center (CalSWEC), 63
Canadian Association of Schools of Social Work, 58
Caragata, L., and M. Sanchez, 169
Carnegie Foundation for the Advancement of Teaching, 16; Preparation for the Professions Program, 4
Carraccio, C., S.D. Wolfsthal, R. Englander, K. Ferentz, and C. Martin, 56
Carroll, M., 103, 121, 197
Caspi, J., and W.J. Reid: Task-Centered Model for Field Instruction and Staff Development, 149
Cavazos, A., 136, 150
Chapman, M.V., S. Oppenheim, T. Shibusawa, and H.M. Jackson, 90
Cheetham, G., and G. Chivers, 16, 35, 36, 47, 51–3, 56, 60, 70, 71, 73, 128; proposal concerning modified epistemology of practice, 53, 125
child welfare competencies, 63, 72
Choy, B.K., A.Y. Leung, T.S.K. Tam, and C.H. Chu, 106, 132, 134
Clark, F., 57
Clark, S., 63
class (social), 39, 78, 89–90, 93, 116, 170. See also social identity
classroom learning: coordination of classroom and field learning (integration of theory and practice),

13–14, 16, 17, 18–21, 22, 23, 40, 42, 54, 57, 68, 86, 101, 126–7, 132, 135, 136, 141, 142, 143, 148 (*see also* Integration of Theory and Practice (ITP) Loop Model); evaluation of classroom vs. field learning, 175–6

Cohen C., 150

Coleman, H., 31

Collins, P., 92

Collins-Camargo, C., 175

Commission on Curriculum and Educational Innovation: working principles of, 58–9

competence (professional), 55–75; Canadian study on national competencies for social work, 58; child welfare competencies, 63, 72; competencies for practice with the elderly, 19, 60–1, 63–4, 72; competency-based education (defined), 56–7, 64; competency models and social work education, 57–9, 65–75, 207; concept of, 5, 20, 59–62, 124; cognitive/conceptual, 71, 74, 74 table 3.1, 75, 124; as consisting of observable behaviours and cognitive processes, 61–2; critiques and limitations of competency approaches, 59–60, 65–6; and curriculum planning, 21–2, 55–7, 58–9, 65, 74–5; defining competence in social work, 58, 61, 62–75; as distinguished from expert status, 62; as goal or learning outcome of social work education, 5, 21–3, 55, 75, 125; hierarchy of, 71– 3; holistic, 124–5, 148, 179, 202, 209; interpersonal/relational, 71, 74, 74 table 3.1, 75, 124; meta-

competencies, 70–2, 74, 74 table 3.1, 75, 124–5, 202–3; personal/professional, 71, 74, 74 table 3.1, 75, 124; procedural, 71, 72, 74, 74 table 3.1, 75, 124–5, 134–48; relationship between how competence is defined and constructions of professional practice, 61; ten core competencies for social work (EPAS, 2008), 64–5; University of Toronto program of research concerning, 6–7, 20, 66–73, 104, 105, 134, 177, 182–5, 186–91, 193, 195, 197, 204, 206; University of Toronto social work competency model (1970s), 65–6. *See also* conceptualizing practice; evaluation; medicine; psychology; student learning

Competency-Based Evaluation (CBE) Tool, 182, 183–5, 189, 190, 191, 211–15

conceptualizing practice: and student learning, 19, 69–70, 73; as professional competency, 70, 72, 74 table 3.1, 124

Cooper, L., 12

Coulton, P., and L. Krimmer, 161

Council on Social Work Education: adoption of competency-based framework, 177, 207; Commission on Accreditation, 17, 58; designation of field education as 'signature pedagogy' of social work, 3, 12, 17, 86, 168, 178, 206; *Educational Policy and Accreditation Standards* (EPAS, 2008), 3, 12, 17–18, 21, 55–6, 58–9, 64, 86, 168, 172, 176, 182; field education value statement, 17–18; Strengthening

Aging and Gerontological Education in Social Work (CSWE/SAGE-SW), 63–4; ten core competencies for social work identified by, 64–5; working principles of the Commission on Curriculum and Educational Innovation, 58–9

Cowan, B., R. Dastyk, and E.R. Wickham, 154

Cox, S.E., 168, 169

Crisp, B.R., 175–6

critical thinking: as cognitive meta-competency, 71; as component of competence in social work, 61, 64, 69; as component of reflective practice, 42, 127; fostered in social work students, 13, 139, 146

Crosby, J.R., 67

Curl, A.L., 64

curriculum content (of social work programs): competency-based approach to, 21–2, 55–7, 58–9, 65, 74–5; and field education, 17, 21–4; as reflection of current faculty and stakeholders' views, 23; role of adjunct faculty in development and implementation of, 14; and tension between specific and general knowledge, 22–3; working principles of the Commission on Curriculum and Educational Innovation, 58–9

Cuzzi, L., G. Holden, P. Chernack, S. Rutter, and G. Rosenberg, 162, 163

Daley, A., 96

Dalgleish, K.B., R.B. Kane, and J.J. McNamara, 162

Damasio, A., 88

Damron-Rodriguez, J., 19, 61, 64, 163

Davis, M.H., 67, 87

Deal, K.H., 34, 82, 92, 110, 111, 112, 138

Dean, R., 131

Delworth, U. 111–12

Dettlaff, A.J., 30–1, 141, 146

Dewey, J., 43, 84

Dietz, T.J., 30–1

diversity (social), 39–40, 55, 64, 78, 89–90, 93–8, 108, 117, 208. See also social identity

Donner, S., 32

Downie, R.S., 35

Downie, W.W., 202

Drake, B., 63

Dreyfus, H.L., and S.E. Dreyfus, 53

Dutton, K., 175

Edmond, T., D. Megivern, C. Williams, E. Rochman, and M. Howar, 41, 133

Educational Policy and Accreditation Standards. See under Council on Social Work Education

educators (social work): challenges confronted by, 18–19, 58, 197; faculty field liaison, 4, 4–5, 7, 14, 27, 31, 33, 115, 119, 122, 166, 167, 170, 171, 176, 180, 196, 203; field instructor as educator and therapist, 92, 93; field instructor as key component in field education, 29; field instructor training, 30–31, 94; impact of negative evaluations on field instructors, 197–8; implicit criteria used by field instructors, 185–7; importance of communication between faculty members

and field instructors, 23, 197;
instructor-student relationship, 6,
26–7, 92–8, 101–23, 127–9, 149–54,
195–6; instructor-student relationship, power dynamics in, 34, 93,
101–2, 103, 113, 115–23, 124, 192,
193 (*see also* evaluation: interpersonal dynamics); key issues for
field instructors, 208–9; roles and
responsibilities of field instructors, 15, 31, 77, 92, 93, 96, 98, 107,
108–9, 113, 116, 118, 120, 151,
159–60, 161, 194, 197, 208–9;
student perceptions of field
instructors and instruction, 11,
26–7, 102–3, 104, 105–6, 110–11,
118–19, 121, 132, 134–5, 151, 154,
195; tenure stream vs. adjunct
faculty members, 14, 18, 33. *See
also* teaching methods
Edwards, J.K., and J.M. Bess, 88–9
elderly: competencies for practice
with, 19, 60–1, 63–4, 72. *See also*
Hartford Practicum Partnership
Projects
Ellis, M.V., 141
Ellison, M.L., 105
Epstein, R.M., 21, 49–50, 56, 60, 61,
62, 129
Eraut, M., 16, 22, 43, 47, 59, 60, 73,
139–40, 177, 180–1, 186
Ericsson, K.A., R. Krampe, and C.
Tesch-Romer, 137
ethics and values: as component of
professional competency, 72–3, 74
table 3.1
evaluation (of student learning and
competence in social work): 6–7,
57, 109, 175–206, 207, 209; challenges associated with, 57, 58,
65–6, 75, 104–5, 134, 176–7,
178–80; classroom vs. field
practicum, 175–6; Competency-
Based Evaluation (CBE) Tool, 182,
183–5, 189, 190, 191, 211–15; contextual factors, 196–7; global evaluation in clinical setting, 200–1;
impact on field instructor, 197–8;
implicit criteria used by field
instructors, 185–7;
instruments/tools, 134, 176,
178–85 (*see also* individual evaluation tools, 211–43); interpersonal
dynamics in, 134, 191–8, 205;
methods, 177–8; Objective Structured Clinical Examination
(OSCE), 202–5; observation as
evaluative method, 176, 177, 178,
201; Practice-Based Evaluation
(PBE) tool, 187–9, 190–1, 236–43;
Practice-Based Evaluation (PBE)
tool (online version), 171, 191; in
professions related to social work,
7 (*see also* medicine); scales, 178–9,
187–9; self-evaluation, 201, 205–6;
University of Toronto program of
research concerning, 6–7, 20,
66–73, 104, 105, 134, 177, 182–5,
186–91, 193, 195, 197, 204, 206; use
of portfolios in, 201; Vignette
Matching Evaluation (VME) Tool,
190, 216–35; without scales, 189–90
evidence-based practice (EBP), 5, 18,
36–41, 62, 126, 132–3; critiques
and limitations of, 37–8, 41, 133;
defined, 37; and diversity, 39–40.
See also professional practice: technical-rational approach
experiential learning theory, 83–6,
88; defined, 85

faculty field liaison. *See* educators
feedback. *See* teaching methods
Feldman, R., 19
field education: in Australia, 12,
    28–9; benefits of, 12, 28–9; chal-
    lenges to quality field education,
    31–4; coordination of classroom
    and field learning (integration of
    theory and practice), 13–14, 16,
    17, 18–21, 22, 23, 40, 42, 54, 57, 68,
    86, 101, 126–7, 132, 135, 136, 141,
    142, 143, 148 (*see also* Integration
    of Theory and Practice (ITP)
    Loop Model); and curriculum
    content, 17, 21–4; definition of,
    12–15, 21; historical research on
    field education in social work, 17;
    identification of most crucial
    issue for, 58; international field
    practicum, 168–70; inter- organi-
    zation models for (studies on),
    24–30; learning opportunities
    provided by, 11; organizational
    context of, 24–30; as professional
    preparation, 15–21; as 'signature
    pedagogy' of social work, 3, 12,
    15, 17, 86, 142, 168, 178, 206;
    structure vs. process of, 21; stu-
    dents' anxiety concerning, 70,
    81–2, 84, 94, 95, 102, 107, 141–2;
    three dimensions of quality field
    education, 148; and role of
    student experience, 84–6; student
    perceptions of field education
    and field instructors, 11, 26–7,
    102–3, 104, 105–6, 110–11, 118–19,
    121, 132, 134–5, 151, 154, 195; in
    the United Kingdom, 12, 32. *See
    also* educators; evaluation;
    formats; principles; students;

student learning; teaching
    methods
Fisher, L., 111
Fleming, D., 70
Fook, J., 47
formats (for field instruction),
    149–72, 208; block arrangements,
    6, 149, 166–8; concurrent model, 6,
    149, 166–8; delayed-entry model,
    6, 149, 166, 167; design studio
    model, 16; and developments in
    technology, 138–9, 170–2; dyadic
    tutorial model/individual field
    instruction, 6, 128, 149–54, 195,
    208; field units, 149, 164–5; group
    instruction, 6, 128, 149, 154–60;
    international field practicum,
    168–70; rotational models, 6, 19,
    20, 149, 162–4; seminars, 13–14,
    19, 20; task instruction, 6, 149,
    161–2; for training field instruc-
    tors, 30–1. *See also* teaching
    methods
Fortune, A.E., 14, 20, 29, 38–9, 104,
    106, 110, 121, 132, 134, 135, 136,
    138, 143, 150, 151, 159, 167, 195
Fox, R., and P.C. Zischka, 150
Fraser, S.W., and T. Greenhalgh, 60,
    62
Freeman, E., 94, 143, 159
Friedman, M., 67
Frumkin, M., 24
Furness, S., and P. Gilligan, 32

Gambrill, E., 37, 139
Geller, C., 154
Gelman, C.R., 142
gender, 39, 78, 89, 93, 98, 116, 170.
    See also social identity
Gergen, K.J., and K.E. Davis, 131

Geriatric Social Work Competency Scales, 64, 72
Geriatric Social Work Education Consortium. *See under* Hartford Practicum Partnership Project
Gibbs, L., 37
Giddings, M.M., R. Vodde, and P. Cleveland, 27, 110, 118–19
Gingerich, W.J., K.M. Kaye, and D. Bailey, 61
Ginsburg, S., 177, 190
Gitterman, A., and N. Gitterman, 193
Gladstein, M., 94
Gladwell, Malcolm, 136–7
Gleeson, F.A., 202
Globerman, J., 12, 24–30, 66, 140, 155, 192, 195
graduate social work programs: competency-based, 57, 64–5; studies concerning master's students, 112, 121, 134, 151, 154; use of seminars in, 14. *See also* undergraduate social work programs; University of Toronto: group supervision study
Graybeal, C., and E. Ruff, 145
Green, R.G., 64
Gross, G.M., 57
Grossman, B., N. Levine-Jordano, and P. Shearer, 92
Gutierrez, L.M., R.J. Parsons, and E.O. Cox, 115, 192

Haber, R., D. Marshall, K. Cowan, A. Vanlandingham, M. Gerson, and J.C. Fitch, 141
Hackett, S., 59
Hall, B.L., 152
Hall, D.T., 70, 102, 118–19

Halston, E.F., 79, 192
Hamilton, G., 91
Hammond, K.R., 53
Hanson, M., 133, 202
Harden, R.M., 67, 70, 71, 202
Hartford Practicum Partnership Projects, 19–20; and development of rotation models, 163; Geriatric Social Work Competency Scales, 64, 72; Geriatric Social Work Education Consortium (GSWEC), 64; Strengthening Aging and Gerontological Education in Social Work (CSWE/SAGE-SW), 63–4
Hartin, J., 111
Hatcher, R.L., and K.D. Lassiter, 71
Haynes, R.B., P.J. Devereaux, and G.H. Guyatt, 37
Hendricks, C.O., J.B. Finch, and C. Franks, 30, 92, 94–5, 97, 150
Hensley, P.H., 92
Ho, D., 78
Hodges, B., 202, 205
Holley, L.C., and C. Steiner, 89
Hollis, F., 131
Holman, S.L., and P. Freed, 82
Hopkins, K.M., 34, 84, 111
Hughes, J., 66, 176, 182, 183, 186, 193
Hundert, E.M., 21, 56, 60, 61, 62
Hyde, C.A., 78
Hyland, T., 60

instructors. *See* educators
Integration of Theory and Practice (ITP) Loop Model (Bogo and Vayda), 45–7, 126–7, 130–2, 146
international field practicum, 168–70
Ivry, J., F.R. Lawrance, J. Damron-Rodriguez, and V.C. Robbins, 163

Jarman-Rohde, L., 28, 33, 164
Johns, C., 44
Jones, E., 168, 169
judgment (professional), 11, 54, 60, 61, 64, 71–2, 124

Kabat-Zinn, J., 48–9, 50, 129
Kadushin, A., 11, 92, 193
Kane, M.T., 60, 61, 177, 206
Kaplan, T., 80
Kaslow, N.J., et al., 56, 60
Kelly, J., and W. Horder, 59, 179
Kenyon, G.L., 185
Kilpatrick, A.C., J. Turner, and T.P. Holland, 33, 176
Knight, C., 105, 106, 132, 135, 146, 195
Knowles, Malcolm, 79, 83, 192. *See also* adult learning theory
Koelewyn, N., 20
Koerin, B., 196
Kolar, P., 33
Kolb, D.A., 43, 84
Koroloff, N.M., and C. Rhyne, 178
Kruger, J., and D. Dunning, 205

Lacerte, J., J. Ray, and L. Irwin, 29
Lager, P.B., and V.C. Robbins, 11, 13, 20, 28
Langer, E.J., 127
Lawrance, F., 61, 163
learning. *See* student learning
Lee, E., 137
Lee, M., 136, 150
Leung, W.C., 60
Levitin, Daniel, 137
Lewin, K., 84
Lindsay, T., 158
Linehan, M.M., 48
Lister, P.G., 175–6

Litvack, A., 26, 102, 103, 119, 152
Lloyd, C.M., 81
Logie, C., 204
Lombardi, J., 201
Lough, B.J., 169, 170
Love, J.P., 93
Lurie, S.J., C.J. Mooney, and J.M. Lyness, 177, 200

MacKeracher, D., 82, 83, 84
Mackey, R., E. Mackey, and B. O'Brien, 91
Maidment, J., 139, 176, 180
Mailick, M., 94
Marshack, E.F., 94
Marsick, V.J., 128
Martin, D., 205
Matorin, S., G. Monaco, and T.S. Kerson, 97
Mauzey, E., M.B. Harris, and J. Trusty, 142
Mayers, F., 154
McCarthy, M., 104, 134, 150, 195
McCollum, E.E., and J.L. Wetchler, 138
McDonald, P.L., 139, 176, 180
McFall, J., 33
McIlroy, J., 190
McKnight, K., 175
McNaughton, N., 202
McNeill, B.W., 111–12
McRoy, R.G., E.M. Freeman, S.L. Logan, and B. Blackmon, 94
medicine: competence in, 56, 60, 67, 70, 177, 179; education of medical students, 4, 15, 17, 25, 56, 60, 139; education of nurses, 4, 25, 43–4; evaluation methods used in medical education, 177, 178, 200–1, 202–5; mindfulness applied

to practice of, 49, 129; observation of practice in medical education, 136, 138, 178; physicians' self-assessment abilities (study), 87
Merriam, S., 79
Mertz, L.K.P., 20, 138
Messinger, L., 95, 116, 118, 152
meta-competencies. *See under* competence
Mezirow, J.M., and Associates, 83
Miller, J., 78, 196
mindfulness, 48–51, 127, 129–30. *See also* reflective practice
Mishna, F., 26, 48–9, 78, 90, 102, 152
Mohr, J., 106
MorBarak, M.E., D.J. Travis, H. Pyun, and B. Xie, 175
Mullen, E.J., A. Shlonsky, S.E. Bledsoe, and J.L. Bellamy, 37, 40
Mumm, A.M., 140
Myers, L.L., 37
Mylopoulos, M., 177

Netting, F.E., K. Hash, and J. Miller, 163
Newman, P., 96–7, 98, 116–17, 118, 152
Norcross, J.C., 133
nursing. *See* medicine: education of nurses

Objective Structured Clinical Examination (OSCE), 202–5
O'Hare, T., P. Collins, and T. Walsh: Practice Skills Inventory, 178
oppression, 45, 46, 48, 55, 65, 78, 90, 116, 117, 130, 131, 208
organizations (health and social service): benefits of field learning for, 12, 28–9; central role in field education, 30; collaboration between universities and, 19–20, 24–30; inter-organization models for field education (studies on), 24–30. *See also* settings

Panos, P.T., 168, 169, 172
Papell, C.P., and L. Skolnik, 43
Parker, J., 32
Peebles-Wilkins,W., and B.W. Shank, 33
Pettys, G.L., 168, 169
Phan, P., H. Vugia, P. Wright, D.R. Woods, M. Chu, and T. Jones, 78
Poe, N.T., and C.A. Hunter, 14
portfolios, 201
Poulin, J., P. Silver, and S. Kauffman, 32, 165
Power, R., 29, 30, 31, 113–14, 122, 192. *See also* University of Toronto: program of research concerning evaluation of competence
Practice-Based Evaluation (PBE) tool, 187–9, 190–1, 236–43; online version, 171, 191
Practice Skills Inventory (O'Hare, Collins, and Welsh), 178
principles (of field education), 5, 6, 54, 98, 101, 104, 105, 123, 124, 125; available and supportive relationships, 105–7, 123; development of reflective and conceptual competence, 105, 126–33; structure and autonomy, 105, 107–11
procedural competence. *See under* competence
Proctor, B., 157
Proctor, E.K., 38
professional education: Carnegie Foundation Preparation for the

Professions Program, 4; education in health and service professions related to social work, 4, 5, 7, 65, 67, 130, 136, 141, 197, 202, 206, 207, 208 (*see also* medicine; psychology); education for professional practice (as field of scholarship), 208; role of field learning in, 15–21. *See also* competence; evaluation; professional practice; social work

professional practice: characteristics of, 35; and the definition of competence, 61; epistemologies of, 5, 36–54; Schon's challenge to prevailing paradigm of, 41; social work as a profession, 35–54; technical-rational approach to, 36–41, 53, 56, 125, 126. *See also* evidence-based practice; reflective practice

psychology: and competence-based education, 56, 60, 70; contributions to social work from psychological theory, 131; supervision of counselling trainees, 141, 149, 157; use of development models in the education of psychology students, 111; use of one-way mirrors as hallmark of training in, 138

race and ethnicity, 39, 78, 89, 90, 93, 94, 97–8, 110, 116, 118. *See also* social identity

Raphael, F.B., and A.F. Rosenblum, 14

Raskin, M., 11, 14, 17, 29, 32, 34, 58, 86, 88, 142, 164, 168, 176

Rasmussen, B., 90

Rawlings, M., 203

Reamer, F.G., 23

reflective practice, 5, 16, 41–51, 127; critiques of, 47; development of reflective and conceptual competence (principle of field education), 105, 126–33; empirical support for, 51–3; and experiential learning theory, 85, 86, 88; knowing-in-action, 41–2; reflection as a teaching method, 102, 109, 124, 125, 127–30; reflection-in-action, 42, 48–50, 71, 127; reflection-on- action, 42–8, 50, 127. *See also* mindfulness; Schon, Donald

Reflective Practitioner, The, 41

Regehr, C., 61, 66–7, 68, 69, 70, 171, 177, 191, 202, 203, 204, 205. *See also* University of Toronto: program of research concerning evaluation of competence

Reid, W.J., 38–9, 181, 184

Reisch, M., 28, 164

Reynolds, M., and R. Snell, 71

Roberts-DeGennaro, M., C. Brown, J.W. Min, and M. Siegel, 171

Robinson, B., 19, 20, 163

Rogers, G., 31, 139, 176, 180

Rogers, R.R., 43, 47, 128

Rolfe, G., 43–5

Rompf, E.L., D. Royse, and S.S. Shooper, 81

Rosen, A., 38, 64

Rosenblatt, A., and J.E. Mayer, 92

Rosenthal Gelman, C., 81

Rossiter, A., 58

Ruch, G., 45, 60

Ruffolo, M.C., and P. Miller, 164

Ruth, B.J., 78

Ruth-Sahd, L.A., 47

Saari, C., 82

safety. *See under* student learning
Saleeby, D., 192
Saks, L.V., 106
Scharlach, A., 19, 20, 163
Schon, Donald, 60, 80, 185; on
  knowing-in-action, 41–2; on
  reflection-in-action, 42, 49, 71; on
  reflection-on-action, 42–3; on
  reflective practice, 5, 16, 36, 41–8,
  51, 68, 86; *The Reflective Practitioner*, 41
Segal, Z., M. Williams, and J. Teasdale, 48, 129
self-awareness: as component of
  reflective practice, 44; concept of,
  78, 93; as professional competency, 71, 72; and social work
  practice, 49, 51, 88–9; and student
  learning, 6, 77–9, 90–3, 97, 98, 101,
  111
self-directed learning, 79, 82–3
settings (field), 13, 19, 24–7; effect on
  student learning, 102, 128–9, 150,
  180–1, 196–7; facilities and equipment for observation in, 138–9;
  ideal, 206; international, 168–70;
  'Key Contact,' 25; 'Lone Ranger,'
  24–5; mezzo and macro, 66, 110,
  137–8, 155, 160; students' perceptions about, 151; 'Teaching
  Centres,' 24, 25–7. *See also* organizations
sexual orientation, 39, 61, 78, 89, 93,
  94–8, 116–18, 123, 152. *See also*
  social identity
Schiller, L.Y., 156
Shapiro, S.L., G.E. Schwartz, and G.
  Bonner, 50
Sheafor, B.W., and L.E. Jenkins, 19
Shulman, Lee, 15, 16–17, 81, 108,

109, 120, 139, 150, 151, 153, 157,
  158, 201, 206; concept of 'signature pedagogy,' 17, 86, 142
Siegel, D.J., 49–50, 88
Siegel, M., 171
signature pedagogy, 17, 86, 142
signature pedagogy in social work,
  3, 12, 15, 17, 86, 142, 168, 178, 206
Silberman, J., 49–50
Simmons, J., 61
Singer, C.B., and L.M. Wells, 164
Siporin, M., 92
Skinner, K., and B. Whyte, 32, 59,
  176–7, 179
Slater, P., 12
social identity: and the practice of
  social work, 39–40, 61, 77–9,
  88–90, 93–8, 131; and student
  learning, 103, 123; theory, 6. *See
  also* class; diversity; gender; race
  and ethnicity; sexual orientation
social work: Canadian study on
  national competencies for, 58; and
  competency-based approaches,
  55–9, 60–1, 62–75, 207 (*see also*
  competence; evaluation); and
  concept of professional use of
  self, 45, 61, 77, 79, 88, 90, 124, 183,
  186, 203; field education as 'signature pedagogy' of, 3, 12, 15, 17,
  86, 142, 168, 178, 206; impact of
  organizational changes on, 35–6;
  practice wisdom of, 11, 12, 34, 38,
  43, 45, 185–6, 187, 189; as a profession, 35–54; as science and art,
  61; use of personal therapy
  among practitioners and students
  of, 90–1. *See also* competence;
  educators; evaluation; evidence-
  based practice; field education;

reflective practice; social work programs; students

social work programs: accreditation of, 3, 12, 13–14, 17, 21, 24, 58, 59, 168, 175, 200 (*see also* Council on Social Work Education); best practice guidelines for, 3, 18, 34, 138, 158–9, 160, 182; collaboration between universities and social service organizations, 19–20, 24–30; components of, 76–7; coordination of classroom and field learning (integration of theory and practice), 13–14, 16, 17, 18–21, 22, 23, 40, 42, 54, 57, 68, 86, 101, 126–7, 132, 135, 136, 141, 142, 143, 148 (*see also* Integration of Theory and Practice (ITP) Loop Model); gatekeeping function of, 55, 175; and licensing requirements, 175; standards for field component of, 3. *See also* curriculum content; graduate social work programs; students; student learning; undergraduate social work programs; University of Toronto

Sousa, D.A., 88

Sowbel, L.R., 190

Sower-Hoag, K., 93

Spitzer, W., G. Holden, L. Cuzzi, S. Rutter, P. Chernack, and G. Rosenberg, 162, 163

Stacey, L., 91

Staudt, M.M., 38

Stephanson, M., J.C. Rondeau, J. Michaud, and S. Fiddler, 58

Stevenson, M., 202

Stoltenberg, C.D., 111–12, 149

Strengthening Aging and Geronto-logical Education in Social Work (CSWE/SAGE-SW), 63–4

Strom, G., 33

Strozier, A.L., 91, 105

student learning (in social work programs), 76–98; as collaborative, 79, 92, 104, 105, 107–8, 121–2, 123, 192; coordination of classroom and field learning (integration of theory and practice), 13–14, 16, 17, 18–21, 22, 23, 40, 42, 54, 57, 68, 86, 101, 126–7, 132, 135, 136, 141, 142, 143, 148 (*see also* Integration of Theory and Practice (ITP) Loop Model); developmental perspective on, 81–2, 111–12; effect of setting or context on, 102, 128–9, 150, 180–1, 196–7; facilitating, 101–23; importance of students' approach to learning, 67–8, 70; and learning contracts, 150; and safety, 90, 95, 96, 97–8, 102, 113, 117, 156; and self-awareness, 6, 77–9, 88–9, 90–3, 97, 98, 101, 111; self-evaluation, 201, 205–6; and students' ability to conceptualize practice, 69–70, 73; students' anxiety concerning field learning, 70, 81–2, 84, 94, 95, 102, 107, 141–2; and students' personal qualities, 66–7, 77, 193; and students' understanding of team context, 68–9. *See also* adult learning theory; competence; educators; students; teaching methods

students (of social work): 5–6; beginning vs. advanced (study differentiating between), 62; challenges confronted by, 77–9, 81–2, 102–3, 110, 112–23; choice to become, 76; instructor- student relationship, 6, 26–7, 92–8, 101–23, 127–9, 149–54, 195–6; instructor-student relationship, power dynamics in, 34, 93, 101–2, 103, 113, 115–23, 124, 192, 193 (*see also* evaluation: interpersonal dynamics in); need for financial aid and flexibility, 33–4; non- traditional, 84; personal and professional issues (interplay between), 6, 92, 97–8, 101, 209; student perceptions of field education and instructors, 11, 26–7, 102–3, 104, 105–6, 110–11, 118–19, 121, 132, 134–5, 151, 154, 195; student views on benefits of personal therapy, 91. *See also* student learning

Sun, A., 81

Sussman, T., 155, 158, 160,

Swanson, R.A., 79, 192

Swick, S., S. Hall, and E. Beresin, 200

Szoc, K.B., 106

Talbot, M., 60, 70, 71

Task-Centered Model for Field Instruction and Staff Development (Caspi and Reid), 149

Teaching centres, 24, 25–7

teaching methods (in field education), 6, 13, 31, 124–48, 208; coaching, 6, 137; 'co-working,' 140, 180; feedback (giving and receiving), 27, 68, 102, 103, 105, 111, 113–14, 119, 120, 123, 124, 125, 135, 136, 138, 139, 143–5, 147, 148, 156, 157, 159–60, 181, 192–5, 195–6, 209; journaling, 95, 128, 139, 141,

143–5, 146; observation, 6, 102, 109, 124, 125, 134, 135, 136–42, 147, 148, 180, 209 (*see also* evaluation: observation as evaluative method); observation-participatory activities vs. conceptual linkage activities, 135–6; reflection, 102, 109, 124, 125, 127–30 (*see also* reflective practice); review of written records and reports, 6, 109, 135, 145–7, 180; role modelling, 6, 127–9, 134, 140; role play, 6; students' assessment of, 134–5; supervision, 6, 15, 105, 135, 138, 141, 149, 155, 161, 175, 177 (for group supervision *see* formats: group instruction). *See also* educators; formats; student learning

Tebb, S., D.W. Manning, and T.K. Klaumann, 154

technology (developments in). *See under* formats

Teigiser, K.S., 20–1

Thyer, B.A., 37, 93

Tolson, E.R., and J. Kopp, 11

Topal, M., 95

Towle, C., 91

Tsang, A.K.T., 137

undergraduate social work programs: competency-based, 56, 57, 64–5; emphasis on knowledge acquisition and analysis in, 40; use of seminars in, 14, 166. *See also* graduate social work programs

United Kingdom: changing the curriculum in, 23; concerns about limited resources allocated to practice teaching in, 32; critiques

of competency approaches in, 59;
use of reflective practice in, 43,
45; views on practice learning in,
12
University of Chicago, 20
University of Toronto (Factor-
Inwentash Faculty of Social
Work): group supervision study,
155–60; program of research concerning evaluation of competence,
6–7, 20, 66–73, 104, 105, 134, 177,
182–5, 186–91, 193, 195, 197, 204,
206; social work competency
model (1970s), 65–6
Urbanowski, M., and M. Dwyer,
106, 110, 145

van der Vleuten, C.P.M., and S.
Swanson, 202
van Manen, J., 45
van Soest, D., B. Garcia, and D.
Graff, 78
Vayda, E., 23, 30, 43, 97, 115, 128,
135, 140, 144, 147, 150, 176, 185.
See also Integration of Theory and
Practice (ITP) Loop Model
Viggiana, P., 181
Vignette Matching Evaluation
(VME) Tool, 190, 216–35
Vonk, M.E., 93
Vourlekis, B., J. Bambry, G. Hall,
and P. Rosenblum: Wilson check-
list, 62, 178

Walker, D., 128
Wallace, G., 141, 146

Walter, C.A., and T.M. Young, 97,
154, 155
Wampold, B.E., 133, 137
Wayne, J., 14, 17, 32, 142, 150, 164,
168
Weinert, F.E., 70, 71
Wenger, E., 22
Westhues, A., 58
Wheeler, B.R., and W.E. Gibbons, 33
Whitcomb, M.E., 178
Wijnberg, M.H., and M.C. Schwartz,
92
Wilson checklist (Vourlekis, B., et al.,
1996), 62, 178
Wilson, G.M., 202
Wilson, S.J., 62, 145
Witkin, S., 37
Wodarski, J.S., M.D. Feit, and K.
Green, 176
Wolfson, G.K., C.W. Magnuson, and
G. Marsom, 171
Woodford, M., 20, 61, 67, 68, 69, 70,
186, 193
Woods, M.E., 131

Yager, J., and J. Kay, 62
Younghusband, E., 91

Zayas, L.H., M.J. Gonzalez, and M.
Hanson, 133
Zeira, A., and M. Schiff, 155
Zendell, A.L., 20, 138
Zlotnik, J.L., 64
Zosky, D.L., J.M. Unger, K. White,
and S.J. Mills, 84, 142
Zucrow, E., 93